COMPETING
THROUGH KNOWLEDGE

About the Author

Madhukar Shukla is Professor of Organisational Behaviour at the Xavier Labour Relations Institute (XLRI), Jamshedpur. A Ph.D. in psychology from the Indian Institute of Technology, Kanpur, he earlier taught at the Administrative Staff College of India (ASCI), Hyderabad.

Dr Shukla has worked as an HRD consultant with the National Productivity Council; was a Visiting Professor at Escuela Superior de Administracion y Direccion de Empresas (ESADE) at Barcelona; and has been associated as a trainer and consultant to several companies, including American Express, Arvind Mills, ECC (L&T), Hindustan Lever Ltd, INDAL, ITC Ltd, Tata Timken Ltd, and TELCO.

A member of the Indian Society of Applied Behavioural Sciences (ISABS), his professional interests include organisation design and strategy, management of creativity and innovation, and organisational change and transformation. He has contributed more than 30 papers to professional journals in these areas and has published two books—*Understanding Organisations* and *Productivity Bargaining* (co-authored with V.K. Goel).

COMPETING THROUGH KNOWLEDGE
Building a Learning Organisation

MADHUKAR SHUKLA

Response Books
A division of Sage Publications
New Delhi/Thousand Oaks/London

First published in 1997 by

Response Books
A division of Sage Publications India Pvt Ltd
M-32, Greater Kailash Market I
New Delhi 110 048

Sage Publications Inc	Sage Publications Ltd
2455 Teller Road	6 Bonhill Street
Thousand Oaks, California 91320	London EC2A 4PU

Second printing 1999

Published by Tejeshwar Singh for Response Books, lasertypeset by Anvi Composers, Delhi, and printed at Chaman Enterprises, Delhi 110 002.

Library of Congress Cataloging-in-Publication Data

Shukla, Madhukar, 1955–

    Competing through knowledge: building a learning organization/ Madhukar Shukla.

        p. cm.   (c : alk. paper)   (p : alk. paper)

    Includes bibliographical references and index.

    1. Organizational learning. 2. Organizational effectiveness. 3. Organizational change—Management. I. Title.
    HD58. 82.S55   658.4'063—dc21   1997   97–18629

ISBN: 0-8039-9388-9 (US-hb)   81-7036-640-2 (India-hb)
        0-8039-9389-7 (US-pb)   81-7036-641-0 (India-pb)

Sage Production Team: Shyama Warner and Santosh Rawat

Contents

Preface   7
Introduction: A New Vocabulary   11

Part I   The Basic Issues

1. The Whirlwind of Change   29
2. The Learning Imperative   55
3. Learning Capabilities   74
4. Leveraging on Knowledge   96

Part II   The Benchmarks

Introduction   129
Case 1 Asea Brown Boveri: The Global Learning Company 135
Case 2 British Airways: Learning as a Means of
        Organisational Turnaround   152
Case 3 Chaparral Steel: The Learning Factory   166
Case 4 Citicorp Inc.: Learning to Innovate   182
Case 5 General Electric: Learning as Cultural
        Transformation   203
Case 6 Xerox Corporation: Learning to Cope with
        Environmental Turbulence   223

Part III   Building A Learning Organisation

5. Architecture of a Learning Organisation   247
6. The Learning Organisation: An Emerging Paradigm 290

References   308
Author Index   325
Subject Index   330
Company Index   333

Preface

The idea of writing this book arose out of contradictions. A few years back, I had started teaching a course on organisational theory at XLRI, Jamshedpur. I was also writing a textbook on the subject. In most ways, these academic pursuits were very satisfactory because they matched well with the nature of the consultancy and training work that I was doing. An understanding of organisational theory helped me immensely to make sense of why and how organisations behaved in particular ways.

But soon I started realising that, in spite of their value, the existing theories also had their limitations. Many of my consultancy experiences and interactions with the business world contradicted the theoretical frameworks. I was also reading about some of the highly successful organisations that challenged the basic tenets of organisation theory. They seemed to represent an anomalous reality in which the practice defied the theory. Using the conventional theories, for example, it was difficult to explain the actions of organisations where seniors reported to juniors, which were market leaders without producing anything, or which produced competing products for their competitors. There were also companies which had no designations, no functional departments, no office timings, no headquarters, or even a permanent place to sit.

Among these organisations, one could sense the emergence of a new paradigm for organising and strategy-making. These organisations marked a qualitative shift from the traditional basis of organising and strategising. My efforts to understand these organisations led to two critical insights, which form the basis of this book. First, these organisations were different because they recognised and *enacted* a competitive environment in which the rules of the game were different. The basis of their competitive strength was not just the products or services which they offered or the market in which they operated; rather, they derived their success from their ability to master the deeper principles which governed the business. This demanded an ability to learn and master new knowledge from these organisations.

The second insight was that the competitive environment was actually, and *qualitatively*, changing—not only around the world, but also in India. The forces of change were so incessant and complex that one could not rely on the past as a guide to the future. Obviously, one needed an altogether different kind of organisation to cope with this emerging environment. So far the criteria of organisational effectiveness had been the efficiency of information–processing and the ability to apply the available knowledge (of market, technology, or regulation, etc.). In the emerging scenario, however, organisations needed to create or learn new knowledge before they could apply it.

These ideas got further refined during my stay in Europe in 1993–94. The one-year visiting assignment at ESADE (Barcelona) gave me an opportunity to study some of the well-known organisations. As I developed cases on these companies, I was struck by the similarity in the ways they mastered knowledge and used it as a competitive weapon.

It was also exciting to find that many Indian companies were discovering a similar path to sharpen their competitive edge. Understanding these companies helped me in building a perspective about knowledge-based competition. It also helped clarify what a knowledge-based or learning organisation would be like. As the future unfolds, mastering this perspective will become essential for understanding and managing the new business realities.

This book is an attempt to share this emerging perspective with management professionals—the practising managers and consultants, and academicians. In many ways, the process of writing this book was also a delightfully inspiring journey. As I learned more about knowledge-based companies, the architecture of an emerging organisational form started becoming clearer. I have tried to retain this excitement of discovery in my writing. I have written this book in an easy-to-read style, sharing the examples as precursers to ideas and concepts. I hope the reader will find it as exciting to read, as I found it to write.

It would be erroneous to say that a book can be the product of one person's individual efforts. As I look back, I realise that there were a number of individuals who personally and professionally encouraged me to put down my ideas on paper. I would like to acknowledge their support and contribution to my efforts.

Two persons whose personal lives got most affected by my writing were my wife, Dr Geeta Saxena, and my daughter, Manasi. It is difficult to think of how this work would have been completed without their constant support and accommodation to my routines. I would like to express my sincere thanks to them for providing the environment in which this book could be completed.

Another person whose support was invaluable during this work was my landlady at Barcelona, Sra. Carmen Figarolla. Even though she did not fully understand the nature of my work, she always treated me and my work as something special. I would like to thank her for her concern and sympathy at a time I needed it most.

There were a number of individuals whose professional comments stimulated me to probe and refine my thoughts further. I would like to acknowledge the support of Professors Jaume Filella, Emil Herbolzeimer, and Max Boisot from ESADE (Barcelona) for those exciting discussions, which were indispensable for the development of my ideas. I would also like to thank my colleagues Professors Mohan Agrawal, V. Venugopal and Sharad Sarin for their support and encouragement.

I would also like to acknowledge the invaluable help which I received from Ms Sandra Rodriguès and Mr S. K. Tiwari in the final preparation of the manuscript.

A substantial amount of this work was done as a part of my visiting assignment to Europe under the Euro-India Cooperation and Exchange Programme. I would like to thank ESADE (Barcelona) for hosting my stay in Europe, and to efmd (Brussels) for sponsoring my trip. I am also grateful to XLRI, Jamshedpur, for providing administrative and infrastructural support for completing this work.

Last but not the least, I owe much to Ranjan Kaul of Response Books, whose patience I have come to admire. Ranjan was both supportive as a friend and persuasive as an editor. I am thankful for his constant support during the preparation of this manuscript.

Madhukar Shukla

Introduction: A New Vocabulary

The world is approaching a turning point. A massive shift in the perception of reality is underway ...

—Fritjof Capra

The business environment across the world is getting swept by a new paradigm. In this emerging paradigm, terms like information, communication, knowledge, learning have acquired a critical relevance to an understanding of the nature of contemporary business. So potent is this new vocabulary that it is subsuming and replacing even the conventional parameters of business effectiveness (e.g., capacity utilisation, cash flow, resource utilisation and profitability). According to Owens (1990): 'Not that profit and product are no longer important, but without continuing learning, they will no longer be possible.'

In other words, the business world is moving from its tangible bases to intangible ones (Sonnenberg, 1994). The nebulous, the abstract, the impalpable appear to have begun to increasingly matter more than do the things one can touch, feel, and move around.

To some extent, this change is not so new. Around the 1970s, there was a growing acknowledgement that we were moving into the 'Information Age'—a term used mainly to acknowledge the growing influence of computers on day-to-day life. Around the same time, another term that became popular was 'knowledge worker'—which was for many, only a sophisticated way of saying that workers now required more skills for doing their jobs (the same jobs, though, which they had been performing for decades—and will continue to perform in the future). Although there were infrequent mentions of competencies, learning, etc., these did not change the definition of business in any fundamental way. Since the mid-1980s, however, there has been a sudden avalanche of a new kind of vocabulary. Corporations, which so far had been economic entities, are being described as 'information-based organisation' (Drucker, 1988), 'educated organisation' (Handy, 1990), 'knowledge-creating company' (Nonaka, 1991; Nonaka and Takeuchi, 1995), 'intelligent enterprises' (Quinn, 1992), and 'learning organisation' (Garratt, 1987, 1990; Pedler, Boydell and Burgoyne, 1989; Senge, 1990), and so on. Instead of product-market strategies, one has started talking about core competencies, intangible assets, knowledge-based capabilities, etc. Tasks are getting replaced by processes; (re-)engineering now has less to do with tinkering with machines and more with reconceptualising the very nature of business. Even the practical, down-to-earth business world has suddenly become obsessed with terms like 'Brain Power', 'Intellectual Property Rights' (IPRs), and 'Intellectual Capital'—and their corollaries in patents, brands, trademarks, etc.

The business world is not the same any more. Knowledge and information are being increasingly described as resources, power-bases, assets, competitive advantage, strategic weapons, and so on. Davidow and Malone (1992) in their book, *The Virtual Corporation*, have even gone to the extent of asserting that: 'In the years to come, incremental differences in companies' ability to acquire, distribute, store, analyze, and invoke actions based on information will determine the winners and losers in the battle for the customers.' Such statements, incidentally, are far from over-dramatic expressions of imaginative academic minds. Rather, they are articulations of an emergent perspective, which has become necessary for interpreting and understanding a new reality. In this reality, knowledge is increasingly being seen as an essential requirement for competitive success. What is more, the new principle applies not only to organisations, but to all spheres of economic activity. The stories of Japanese economic triumph and of how the bar code enlarged retailers' bargaining power over the manufacturers amply demonstrate this principle.

HOW THE WEST WAS WON[1]

During the 1960s and 1970s, Japan did not feature anywhere among the economically powerful nations. The post-War devastation had crippled it, and it had no competitive standing in the world. It was considered a technological appendage to the US (one observer described it as 'that unsinkable US aircraft carrier in the far east'). It had virtually no internal resources, and had a reputation of being a cheap, low-quality imitator. In contrast, the US was the world's largest creditor, and produced roughly 75 per cent of the new technology.

Then how did Japan become a formidable economic superpower? Explanations abound. Initially, Japan's low-cost labour was seen as the backbone of its competitive advantage. But by the mid-1960s, inflation (and the value of the yen) increased, and competitive advantage could no longer be ascribed to low-cost labour; meanwhile, Japan continued to prosper. In the late 1970s, quality replaced low-cost labour as the favoured explanation for its success. While American companies started programmes to match the standard of quality set by Japanese products, Japanese companies continued to invade and grab the world (and American) markets. During the 1980s, there was a profusion of ideas—for example, efficient manufacturing practices, Japanese work ethics, the role of the Ministry of International Trade and Industry (MITI), the institution of *keiretsu*, unique human resources practices, and time-based competition—that aimed at explaining the secret of the phenomenal growth of the Japanese industrial economy.

These explanations, no doubt, were valid, but they neglected a very critical factor which contributed to Japanese success, namely, the investments which Japan made in increasing its knowledge-base and enhancing its learning capabilities. For instance, training and competency development were treated as high-priority activities in most Japanese organisations. Japanese companies sponsored their employees for higher education in established foreign universities. In 1988, of the 100,000 foreign students studying in the US, 13,000 were Japanese. Most of them were employees sponsored by Japanese companies—mostly in engineering and science. In comparison, enrolment of American students in engineering went down in the 1980s. As a result, by the latter part of the 1980s, there were more electrical engineers in Japan than in the US.

The same trend could be seen in Japan's efforts to enhance its technological knowledge. Not only did Japanese companies steal ideas from others (an activity which has now acquired the status of a legitimate managerial activity called benchmarking), they also systematically augmented their efforts to generate and accumulate knowledge-based resources. Between 1950 and 1967 Japan spent a hundred times more money in importing licenses and technology than it did in exporting them. Similarly, between 1965 and 1980, R&D expenditure tripled in Japan (in real-value terms), while it grew by only a third in the US. By the mid-1980s, almost 13 per cent of the budget of the Japanese government was being spent in promoting industrial growth, while only 1 per cent in the US. Also, between 1964 and 1980, the number of researchers in Japan increased 2.6 times, as compared to 1.3 times in the US. In fact, in 1986, the US Patents Office granted 14,000 patents to Japanese nationals, and 38,000 to Americans.

Japan's ability to acquire, create and utilise new knowledge changed the power equation between it and the US. It is not surprising that by the mid-1980s the US had become the world's largest debtor nation, and was importing 80 per cent of its high-tech capital equipment. Its share in the world markets had slipped: from more than 90 per cent to less than 10 per cent in the colour TV market; from about 30 per cent to 18 per cent in cars; from 66 per cent to 4 per cent for floppy discs; from 73 per cent to 17 per cent in Dynamic Random Access Memory (DRAMS), and so on. In contrast, Japan had emerged as an economic superpower, which led the US in seven out of ten high-tech industries. By the mid-1990s, of the world's 20 largest companies in terms of market value, 13 were Japanese, so were the top ten banks of the world.

THE POWER OF BAR CODES

What knowledge did for Japan it did for the retailers in the US as well (Toffler, 1990). During the mid-1960s, supermarkets and departmental stores in the US faced a major problem: how to efficiently service the increasing number of customers. The checkout lines were becoming too long to handle, leading to inordinate delays, and errors in accounting, too, were piling up.

By that time the world, and particularly the US, had started riding the wave of technology. Automation was being increasingly viewed as the key to efficiency. It appeared logical for retailers too to look for the possibilities of a technological solution to their problem. A small committee of retailers, wholesalers and grocery-shop owners approached computer companies like IBM, National Cash Register (NCR), and Sweda for help.

The obvious solution was to let the computer add up customers' bills and keep accounts. This was possible if the products could be coded and the computer made to read these codes. Even though the optical scanning technology was still in its infancy, computer companies sensed a major new market and were eager to help out. The result was the agreement in April 1973 on a 'Universal Product Code'. This code, which became popularly known as the bar code—the array of black lines and numbers which can now be seen on a wide range of items—became the single standard code for the whole industry.

So effective was this system that by the end of the 1980s it was being universally used in developed nations. Almost all products, ranging from soaps to readymade garments to frozen vegetables, were marked with a bar code, and virtually every shop—whether the street-corner grocer or the large supermarkets—was using the electronic scanner.

The reason for its widespread use, of course, was that the bar code helped shopkeepers to efficiently service their customers. But the bar code did more than just speed up the checkout line of customers and reduce accounting errors. It totally altered the structure of the market forces.

Till the advent of the bar code retailers had little power to bargain with the large manufacturers about shelf space utilisation. The sales people from large companies dominated the negotiations regarding shelf space. They would advise (and even browbeat) the retailers about its utilisation. Giant companies like Gillette and Proctor & Gamble (P&G) had not only better access to market information, but also with their major expenditure on advertising, they had better opportunity to mould market forces.

They knew more than any retailer about how, when and to whom a product could be sold. And so the retailers listened to the manufacturers.

But with bar-coded merchandise, customer knowledge moved into the hands of retailers. Now, retailers could not only keep track of the thousands of items sold from their stores, but could also generate additional important information from their database. The bar code and the electronic scanner made it easy for retailers to work out their own profitability on the range of products, the relationship of promotion campaigns to actual sales, customer profiles for various products, the effects of different types of packaging on sales, the combination of products for optimal shelf utilisation, and so on. In effect, retailers now had information about customers and products which was far more accurate than what the manufacturers had. Armed with this knowledge, retailers could negotiate with the sales personnel of manufacturing giants from a position of advantage. In fact, now manufacturers had to pay staggering amounts as 'push money' for getting a desirable positioning on the shelf.

FUEL OF KNOWLEDGE

The rise of the Japanese economy and the increased negotiating power of the retailers well demonstrate the kind of changes that knowledge can create in the business environment. The changing competitive equations are even more visible among corporate sector organisations. Successful and effective organisations have started accepting that knowledge skills (i.e., how to acquire, create and utilise knowledge) are essential prerequisites for growth and success (Shukla, 1995a).

The following cross-section of examples will help in an appreciation of the substance of this perspective:

- According to Andersen Consulting Inc., the knowledge of how manufacturing goods are built and how they work accounts for 70 per cent of their development costs. In service business the knowledge component of development cost may be as high as 90 per cent (Schwartz, 1992).

- IPRs (namely, patents, copyrights, registered · designs, trademarks, etc.) is one way of assessing the value of the knowledge which organisations and individuals have learned and codified in the form of their products, technologies and services. IPRs around the world account for businesses worth billions of dollars. It is estimated that 'intellectual piracy' accounts for losses worth $10–12 billion to software companies, and about $5–7 billion to pharmaceuticals (Rice, 1991).

- In his study of 'postindustrial manufacturing', Jaikumar (1986) concluded that managing flexible manufacturing systems 'calls for intellectual assets, not just pieces of hardware. Thus, the new role of management in manufacturing is to create and nurture the project teams whose intellectual capabilities produce competitive advantage. What gets managed is intellectual capital, not equipment.'

- At American Airlines, three 'knowledge engineers' spent one year studying scheduling of routine aircraft maintenance. The combined knowledge of all aircraft-routing experts was translated into 5,000 rules of their expert-system programme, Moca, which now decides the best schedule for maintenance of the 600-odd aircraft without disrupting the airline's schedule. The estimated annual saving is about $500,000 (Schwartz, 1992).

These examples serve to highlight the new wisdom about the nature of the present competitive environment: namely, while tangible assets (plant, machinery, capital) are necessary for an enterprise to function, it is its knowledge-based resources—its 'invisible assets' (technological know-how, customer information and trust, MIS, corporate culture, etc.)—that provide it with a competitive edge (Itami, 1987). Or, as Quinn (1992) has noted in his book, *Intelligent Enterprise*:

The value of most products and services depends primarily on the development of knowledge-based intangibles, like technological know-how, product design, marketing presentation, understanding of customers, personal creativity and innovation. Generating these effectively in turn depends more on managing the company's intellectual resources than on directing the physical actions of its people or the deployment of its tangible assets.

ORGANISATIONS AS LEARNING SYSTEMS

Since knowledge is the end-product of all learning, any organisation aiming to compete through knowledge must, by necessity,
develop learning capabilities, namely, become a learning
organisation. The concept of a knowledge-based learning organisation has captured the attention of executives and academicians
alike. There is an increasing emphasis on the need to build a
learning organisation 'which facilitates the learning of all its members and continually transforms itself' (Pedler *et al.*, 1989). An
extensive survey (Dodgson, 1993) has concluded that corporate
learning is necessary 'to retain and improve competitiveness,
productivity, and innovativeness in uncertain technological and
market circumstances'. Senge (1990) has described a learning
organisation as a place where 'people continually expand their
capacity to create the results they truly desire, where new patterns of thinking are nurtured, where collective aspiration is set
free, and where people are continually learning how to learn
together'.

Many corporate executives, too, have started recognising business sense in building an organisation in which knowledge and
learning become the axial principles. Consider some examples:

- 'The rate at which individuals and organisations learn may
  become the only sustainable competitive advantage' (Ray
  Stata, Chairman, Analog Devices, USA).

- 'Traditional corporations expend a lot of energy running
  their own internal machinery. It is the learning organisation, with its shared vision and systems thinking, that is
  ideally suited for tomorrow' (Ravi Sanathanam, CEO,
  Hindustan Motors).

- 'In the truly global organisation of the future, knowledge
  networking will be a critical success factor' (K.N. Shenoy,
  CEO, Asea Brown Boveri India).

- 'Learning is not a luxury. It's how companies discover their
  future' (Arie P. De Geus, Planning Chief, Royal Dutch/
  Shell Group of Companies).

- 'To retain and develop managers, we will have to learn to
  build a company that is attractive and less arrogant. Only

the learning organisation can fulfil this need' (Aquil Busrai, Director, Motorola India).

- 'We shall foster a spirit of entrepreneurial leadership and be a vibrant learning organisation' (from Mission Statement of Larsen & Toubro Ltd, India).
- 'We are a learning organisation. The moment someone comes up and says that he has stopped learning, that means there is trouble' (Joseph P. Abraham, Vice President, Tata Consultancy Services).

HISTORY OF THE CONCEPT

Historically, the application of the concept of learning to business can be traced back to as early as the 1960s (Cangelosi and Dill, 1965). This probably was an indication of a growing awareness that an organisation, after all, is not an impersonal mechanical system, as the early forefathers of management had described it to be. An organisation consisted of people whose perceptions, experiences, thinking, and judgements played a critical role in its functioning and determined its effectiveness. Moreover, the rules and systems of the organisation also captured the intellectual and cognitive capabilities of its members. Thus, the early studies on organisational learning aimed at developing an understanding of how the changes in these cognitive frameworks of the organisational members affected organisations.

These works emerged from two streams of management studies: action learning, which focused on the role of learning in facilitating change (Argyris, 1977; Argyris and Schon, 1978); and strategy-formulation processes, which focused on how the thinking and perceptions of the top management led organisations to strategic triumphs or failures (March and Olsen, 1975). By the mid-1980s, the process of organisational change and reorientation had become the defining feature of effective organisations, and researchers had started using the term 'learning organisation' (Garratt, 1987; Hayes, Wheelwright and Clark, 1988).

The boom in the popularity of the term, however, came from Peter Senge's (1990) book, *Fifth Discipline*. Senge arrived at the idea of the learning organisation through his work on systems dynamics. He concluded from his work that all systems (whether an electrical system or an organisation) behave in an integrated manner. No event in the system takes place in isolation—everything affects all other parts within the system. Small, 'insignificant' events of the past can snowball into major catastrophes, forcing the total system to change. Organisations fail because their members, particularly those in the top management team, fail to see these minor, incremental changes and, like the fabled 'boiled frog', remain passive while the environment metamorphoses into an inhospitable and hostile climate.

Learning—and the escape from strategic myopia—according to Senge, occurs only if the organisation develops the discipline of 'systems thinking', namely, the ability to see relationships across time and space, and think holistically (for example, how short-term cost-saving measures in purchase of raw materials can affect the market share in the long run). But, in a marked departure from earlier works on strategic learning and reorientation, Senge pointed out that systems thinking is not the preserve of only the top management team. In fact, in the present context, it is 'no longer sufficient to have one person learning for the organisation. . . . It's just not possible to "figure it out" from the top' (Senge, 1990).

Senge suggested that for effective cultivation of systems thinking at all levels, an organisation must encourage four other complementary disciplines: it must develop a sense of *personal mastery* among its members; it must facilitate the development of a *shared vision*; it must encourage *team learning*; and it must encourage people to question the old and to create new *mental models* of organisational functioning.

The appeal of Senge's work was threefold. First, he translated a complex set of ideas into simple uncomplicated language. Even though some of his ideas challenged the conventional practices of managing organisations, there was no difficulty in understanding and appreciating their wisdom. They were intelligible to the corporate executive, who could relate them to the practical day-to-day realities of the organisation.

Second, Senge actively involved practising executives in this venture, persuading people like Ray Stata, William O'Brien (former CEO of Hanover Insurance Company), and de Geus to contribute to the growing stream of literature on learning organisations. This not only enriched Senge's work, but also created greater credibility for the concept among its practitioners (who are generally wary of esoteric academic ideas).

Lastly, Senge's five disciplines matched the spirit of the time. They provided an intelligent recipe for corporate effectiveness at a time when many companies were experiencing that the previously successful routines and strategies were increasingly becoming ineffectual. Moreover, Senge's ideas were also corroborated by the emergence of many parallel managerial concepts and practices—for example, core competence, self-managed work teams, empowerment, re-engineering, and organisational architecture—which, too, challenged the traditional wisdom about managing.

In the 1990s, the concept of the learning organisation became so popular that many respectable academic institutes—for example, MIT (USA), and Nijenrode University (The Netherlands)—opened centres for Organisational Learning. Academic journals like *Organisation Science, The European Journal of Operations Management, Planning Review, Organisational Dynamics* and *Productivity* devoted complete issues on the topic.

THE MYSTIQUE OF A LEARNING ORGANISATION

Surprisingly, the nature of a learning organisation has continued to remain shrouded in mystery. Studies that have focused on organisational learning from the point of view of deriving application-oriented managerial guidelines have mostly limited the role of learning to specific areas, like technological learning (Dodgson, 1991), developing manufacturing capabilities (Hayes *et al.*, 1988), strategic reorientation (Barr, Stimpert and Huff, 1992), learning from strategic alliances (Hamel, 1991; Hamel, Doz and Prahalad, 1989; Pucik, 1988), organisational development (Garratt, 1990), and developing human resources (Watkins and Marsick, 1993).

There is still no comprehensive theory that integrates these perspectives and describes what a learning organisation is (in the same way as one would describe what a divisionalised, mass-manufacturing, or a transnational organisation would be). Neither is there any framework that explains the competitive dynamics based on a company's knowledge-based capabilities. A few exceptions (for example, Garvin, 1993; McGill, Slocum and Lei, 1992), which have attempted to derive the organising principles for a learning organisation, have focused only on the learning practices, but without defining how the knowledge generated through these practices gives a competitive edge to the firm. Often these studies rely solely on piecemeal examples from different organisations to illustrate how learning takes place in the organisation. While such studies provide useful insights, they fail to communicate the totality, the 'flavour', of a learning organisation—that is, how its structures, processes, systems, and strategies combine to create a radically different competitive advantage. The resultant ambiguity which surrounds the 'how' of a learning organisation can be appreciated through the following two comments:

> The learning organisation is a term currently in vogue. It is, however, less than obvious what it means, except that it is a good thing to strive for'. [Handy, 1990]

> At the end of the Brussels conference we all asked—but how? How do you become a learning organisation? Though the question is often asked I have, so far, not heard a satisfactory answer. So I have come to the conclusion that the question is wrong—or at least incomplete. [Arvedson, 1993]

ABOUT THIS BOOK

One of the purposes of writing this book was to provide a meaningful response to such confusions and to demystify them. The practising executive certainly needs to grasp what is meant by a learning organisation, or why knowledge can be such a potent competitive weapon. But he also needs to understand how a learning organisation can be built, and how knowledge can be used for gaining strategic advantages. This book seeks to clarify the *what, why* and *how* of the learning organisation.

Most of the books on the subject have a Western flavour in terms of cases and examples. This book attempts to discuss the concept of the learning organisation in the context of the Indian business milieu, making it easier for executives to identify with the theme. In the process, it became necessary to accentuate the similarities in the concept of learning and knowledge-based competition as it is being practised across cultural boundaries. Thus, throughout the book there are examples from Indian as well as foreign companies to illustrate the concept.

The book is divided into three parts. Part I consists of four chapters which establish the need for building a learning organisation, and also provide basic theoretical frameworks for understanding learning organisations and knowledge-based competition.

Chapter One gives an overview of the turbulence in the contemporary Indian business environment and a flavour of the pace, complexity and unpredictability of environmental change. It concludes by highlighting how conventional solutions and approaches are becoming obsolete for managing the current business realities.

Chapter Two aims to establish the need for organisations to learn to cope with this turbulence. Effective learning can have varied consequences for the organisation, ranging from passive adaptation to radical transformation. Taking examples of different companies, this chapter describes and discusses the different levels and outcomes of corporate learning.

Chapter Three discusses the theoretical perspective underlying organisational learning. While all organisations learn in one way or the other, a distinction exists between one-time, incremental/adaptive learning and continuous, radical/transformational learning. It is the latter which can help the organisation cope with environmental uncertainty. This chapter also discusses the capability-based view of a learning organisation and identifies the four capabilities necessary for building one.

Chapter Four outlines a comprehensive framework for interpreting knowledge-based competition. Knowledge is the end result of learning. Any viable learning must give the organisation a strategic advantage in its fight for survival and growth. The framework discussed here provides cues for charting out strategies which can help organisations use their knowledge-base as a competitive asset.

Part II consists of detailed case studies of six foreign companies. The choice of making case studies on foreign companies is deliberate. They serve as benchmarks for the nature, processes, systems, and strategies of a learning organisation. While the entire book is interspersed with examples from Indian companies, the cases in this part provide a more integrated appreciation of how organisations create and use knowledge and learning.

In most books, case studies are part of the appendix. Here, they appear in the main body of the text because they fit ideally into the natural sequence of learning. We learn by first developing broad mental models (the theoretical perspectives presented in Part I); we refine these mental models by reviewing information, personal experiences and examples (cases described in Part II); and we generalise these learnings and apply them to broader areas (managerial and theoretical implications given in Part III). As the content of Part II, they provide a natural link to the generalisations which form Part III of the book. Readers are strongly advised to go through the case studies and form their own impressions and generalisations, before going on to the next part.

The last part of the book focuses on theoretical and practical generalisations about the nature of learning organisations—how they operate, and how they can be built. The implementation of learning strategies must be supported by the specific processes and systems characterising the organisation. The two chapters in this part focus on these principles of the learning organisation.

Chapter Five draws generalisations from the cases to identify the structures and processes which would characterise a learning organisation. This chapter describes the distinctive features which facilitate learning and knowledge-based activities in organisations. Also, there are small case studies of some Indian companies to help readers appreciate the applicability of these principles in the Indian context.

The reader will realise that the processes and practices in a learning organisation do not conform to conventional managerial wisdom. Together, they define an entirely new view of an emerging form of organisation. The biggest challenge in building a learning organisation lies in replacing the traditional mental model of the organisation with this new one. The last chapter examines the characteristics of this emerging paradigm of a new organisation.

Notes

1. The emergence of Japan as an economic superpower has been of interest to most observers. The figures and information quoted in this section have been collected from diverse sources. Readers may refer to Badaracco (1991), Hayes, Wheelwright and Clark (1988), Merrifield (1983), and Stalk (1988) for more details.

PART I

The Basic Issues

The Whirlwind of Change

It was the best of times
It was the worst of times . . .
The epoch of belief
The epoch of incredulity . . .
                    —Charles Dickens

THE BATTLE IN THE SKY[1]

1994 was an exciting year for TV viewers in India, with access to more channels, to greater variety, and to programmes of international standards. It was a sea-change from the time when, just four years back, there was only one channel, Doordarshan (DD). Apart from the state-owned DD, which was beaming about ten channels (if one counts the regional channels), there were a host of new satellite channels. In fact, by December 1994, one had lost count of the number of channels being beamed to viewers in India: the estimates ranged from 13 to 30 to more than 100. According to one report, by November 1994, there were 11 satellites in the Indian sky, beaming 42 channels. Television in India had come of age.

For the media-planners in advertising agencies, however, it was a nightmarish year. For the last ten years or so they had been cashing in on the growing popularity of TV and using it as an effective medium for launching, creating and maintaining brands for their clients. Compared to just five or six TV stations in the mid-1970s, during the time of ASIAD 1982, the number had grown to almost 200. Correspondingly, since the mid-1960s when less than a thousand people in India owned a TV set, in 1984 there were 3 million TV owners in India. In the next decade, the number of TV transmitting and relay stations increased another fourfold, with almost 43 million Indian households owning a TV (even at a conservative estimate of five persons per household, this worked out to a captive viewership of about a fifth of the country's population). With such a broad reach, all that media planners had to do was select a prime spot for telecasting an advertisement, and they were assured of a captive viewership of millions of people.

By 1994, however, this advertising utopia started crumbling. Beginning with Star TV (with its four channels—Star Plus, BBC, Prime Sports and Channel V—plus Zee TV), the skies were flooded with new channels (CNN, Jain, ATN, Sun TV, Raj TV, etc.), and more were expected to join the fray (including MTV, Disney, Time Warner, and Sony Columbia) in the coming years. The availability of these channels was fuelled by yet another boom in the cable TV networks, with major global players and Indian companies discovering new opportunities in this enlarging market. Even as early as the end of 1993, India had nearly 73,000 cable networks, servicing about 8.5 million TV sets, with 5,000 cable networks being added every month; by early 1995, the number of subscribers to cable networks had swelled to 14 million.

With this increasing complexity, one was no longer sure of what people would be watching at any given time. The viewer rating of a programme was no longer decided by its quality alone; it was also determined by the quality of the programmes being shown on the other channels. If an advertising agency booked a slot for a popular programme one week, in the very next week, the viewership might shift to another channel offering a better programme. The 'planning' part of media planning started facing rough weather in this age of 'channel competition'.

THE GLOBALISATION OF INDIA[2]

This battle for the attention of viewers was, of course, only a reflection of the greater competitive wars being fought on the ground. Starting mid-1991, India embarked on a large-scale project in socio-economic re-engineering. Faced with an economic crisis and near-nil forex reserves, the country started on the path of liberalisation of the economy. Effectively, it meant an end of the tradition of industrial licenses, a lowering of trade barriers, invitation to MNCs and foreign investors, a gradual divestment of public sector equity, the opening up of core and financial sectors to private and foreign companies, or, in a nutshell, to an explosion of new business opportunities.

The New Industrial Policy of 1991—which suggested changes in the exim policy, encouragement to exports and overseas investments, easy access to foreign capital, and gradual reduction in duties—also made the trade boundaries more permeable. The opportunities opened up by these changes stimulated Indian companies to start aiming at global operations (Box 1.1). They were found experimenting with a variety of choices to move the business beyond national boundaries. For instance, the conglomerate Aditya Birla Group started setting up or acquiring joint ventures abroad; the diversified ITC Ltd stepped up its efforts to establish distribution channels in foreign markets to increase exports; the textile–chemical giant Reliance Ltd started global sourcing of cheap raw material for local production; companies in sectors such as pharmaceuticals (Lupin), textiles (Arvind Mills) and automobile (Maruti Ltd) increased their capacity to achieve global economies of scale; companies such as Chevro Shoes and Hero Cycles, got their brands registered in foreign markets; companies such as Asian Paints, Ceat, and UB Group, started setting up offshore manufacturing facilities, and so on.

The competitive strength of the Indian businesses was being tested at home as well. In a marked departure from its cautious and xenophobic stance, in just one year, 1992, the Government of India approved Rs· 38.87 billion worth of foreign investments, which was twice as much as the total foreign investment approvals granted between 1975 and 1991. In the very next year, 1993, the amount of approved foreign investments skyrocketed to Rs 88.53 billion. The openness of the Indian government was matched by the actual inflow of foreign capital, products and brands. After all, with a 250 million middle-class consumer population, India offered a market which was larger than the total population of many countries, or even of some of the trade blocs such as MERCOSUR

INDIA GOES GLOBAL

The liberalisation of the Indian economy has had a stimulating effect on Indian business. Increased Indian participation in the world's economic activities is evident from the following stray facts:

- Indian exports' growth rate increased from 3.6 per cent in 1992–93 to 22.2 per cent in 1993–94. In fact, between 1990–91 and 1995–96, Indian exports increased more than threefold, from Rs 325,530 million to Rs 1,064,650 million.
- The number of proposals approved for overseas investments increased from 107 in 1992 to 230 in 1994.
- By the end of 1994, Indian companies had more than 500 overseas joint ventures spread across 69 countries, and about 300 wholly owned subsidiaries in various countries, including the US, UK, Germany, and Singapore.
- Once allowed to raise money from foreign capital markets, Indian firms fared exceedingly well: compared to $240 million in 1992, the offerings of Indian companies through Euro-issues in 1994 grossed more than $3.06 billion.

(193 million) and OPEC (100 million). The size of the Indian market was also comparable to two of the largest markets, namely, NAFTA (368 million) and EEC (342 million). What made India an even more attractive proposition for foreign investors was its abundance of natural resources, low-cost labour, the world's third largest technically qualified population, and a relatively large and well-developed industrial infrastructure. The actual foreign direct investments (FDI) in India increased from $68 million in 1990–91 to $1,981 million in 1995–96. Between 1991 and 1993, the combined cumulative investments from the four developed nations, the US, UK, Germany and Japan, increased from a paltry $127 million to $1.7 billion.

When, in September 1992, the Indian stock markets were opened for investments by foreign financial institutions, foreign institutional investors (FIIs) flocked in to play the Indian market. With 23 stock exchanges, listing about 6,500 companies, India offered enormous investment opportunities. By June 1993, 22 FIIs had registered with the Securities and Exchange Board of India (SEBI). In a mere three months, by August 1993, this number had increased to 55, accounting for investments worth $150 million. And in another quantum jump, by April 1994, there were 161 registered FIIs with a cumulative investment totalling $1.76 billion. By March 1996, the number of FIIs had grown to over 350, and their cumulative investment had crossed the $5 billion mark.

It is not surprising that, from just $175 million in mid-1991, the foreign exchange reserves grew to over $20 billion by December 1994.

These statistics, however, reflected only the tip of the iceberg. The underlying reality was much more drastic and turbulent. Not only more money had started flowing into India, the very nature of the business environment was changing in radical ways. The new economic freedom had released forces which were transforming the focus, strategies, and practices of companies in ways unprecedented in Indian business history.

THE NEW PLAYING FIELD

The most visible aspect of liberalisation was that the market suddenly started getting flooded with new products and brands. By 1996, most of the world's top brands (e.g., Coca-Cola, Akai, Kellogg, Sony, Goldstar, Apple, Mercedes Benz, American Express, Nescafe, IBM, Marlboro, McDonald, and Kentucky Fried Chicken [KFC] and major companies (e.g., General Electric [GE], Asea Brown Boveri [ABB], Ericsson, General Motors, BMW, Honda, Matsushita, Samsung, and AT&T) were already a part of the Indian market—either directly or through strategic alliances.

The competitive climate which these entrants created presaged new kinds of perils for most of the Indian companies. The past protection of a closed economy had made a large number of Indian firms complacent and lethargic. Assured of a captive market, most of the firms (particularly large public sectors and companies operating in the core sectors) had not developed any competitive strengths (based on either customer focus, product innovation, or costs) to help them take on the new rivals. Moreover, due to the earlier restrictions imposed by the government, they had not developed adequate financial or technological resources to meet the new demands and challenges thrown on them. In comparison, foreign competitors were better geared in the competitive game; besides having more resources, they were more responsive, innovative, and patient. Consider some examples (Rekhi, 1994):

- Compared to the two Indian companies with the largest advertising budgets, Dabur and Videocon, who spent about Rs 120–130 million each in 1993–94, Hindustan Lever Ltd (HLL) spent Rs 670 million and Procter & Gamble (P&G) spent about Rs 200 million. Moreover, these multinationals were also planning to increase their advertising budget by 50–100 per cent.
- Kellogg launched its breakfast cereals in January 1995, after conducting market research for seven years. Knowing the preferences of the Indian palate, the company was willing to wait 15 years or so for a change in breakfast habits. After all, it had waited 20 years for the Japanese market to get addicted to its products.
- Bausch & Lamb spent almost two years engendering the awareness of its products—contact lenses and Ray-Ban sunglasses. The company invited doctors and opticians for education and training sessions at the various metros. The exercise cost the company Rs 10,000 per person, but only a nominal fee of Rs 500 was charged.

These companies were formidable competitors not merely on account of their financial prowess and large size. In fact, most MNCs operate in India with a very small asset base and with rudimentary infrastructure. Kellogg, for instance, set out to conquer the breakfast cereal market with just 60 people, and in 1994, Coca-Cola had only 100 people to manage its countrywide operations (Vora, 1994). Even HLL, the largest (and one of the oldest) MNCs operating in India, had total assets worth only Rs 2,540 million and ranked a low 49th in the *Business India Super 100* list of 1994. However, in terms of sales and market value, its rank was sixth and fourth, respectively.

The ability to leverage on small resources applied not only to consumer product companies, but also to engineering companies. In 1993–94 (*Business India*, 7 November 1994), Asea Brown Boveri, for instance, generated profits of Rs 305.5 million on an asset base of Rs 528 million, achieving an overwhelming 57 per cent returns on assets. Similarly, Siemens' returns on assets were about 26 per cent. Compared to these, the returns on assets of the Indian engineering giants, Larsen & Toubro (L&T) and Telco, were only 14.8 per cent and 9.4 per cent, respectively. In fact, the combined assets of the top 15 MNCs operating in India were only Rs 20.775 billion—or about 40 per cent of the asset value of the largest Indian company, Tisco, and less than a tenth of the combined assets of the top 15 Indian companies (1994 figures). However, the combined returns on assets of these 'small' MNCs were almost 30 per cent, as compared to 13 per cent of the 15 Indian companies (Table 1.1).

Table 1.1 **Comparison of top 15 MNCs and Indian companies**

	Combined Assets (Rs billion)	Combined Profits (Rs billion)	Return on Assets (%)
Indian Companies	216.603	28.973	13.38
MNCs	20.775	6.202	29.85

* Based on *Business India Super 100* (7 November 1994).

The superior competitive power of these invaders came from the 'intangibles'—brand equity, technology, market experience, etc.—that they brought with them. These intangibles allowed them to manage and mould the market environment in ways previously unknown to Indian companies. By importing their technological know-how, and using their market savvy, they started changing the texture of the market environment— identifying and creating new markets around latent consumer needs, while simultaneously rendering existing established product categories obsolete. For example, within just one year, Philips launched six new models of TV and four of music systems;

between May 1993 and January 1995, its home appliances division unveiled as many as 19 new products. Similarly, within a year from November 1993, HLL launched seven new brands, relaunched a whole range of Pond's and Kissan products, and introduced product extensions of seven existing brands (Chatterjee, 1994).

THE CROWDED MARKET-PLACE

The entry of MNCs was only one part of the changing environment. The economic liberalisation had also stimulated radical changes in the aspirations of Indian companies. Faced with competitive threats, many companies were forced to redefine their business priorities, and their way of doing business. They started restructuring themselves in order to achieve better synergies and focus. Unnecessary and peripheral businesses were hived off and new acquisitions and alliances made. Between 1991 and 1994, the number of mergers and acquisitions increased from 33 to about 150 (*The Telegraph Business*, 20 November 1994). In the process, the structure of the market environment also altered radically.

Along with the trend of refocusing activity was the opposing trend of diversifying into newer areas. The opening up of different sectors and the end of the tradition of industrial licenses was creating new players in almost every industry. Many large and established business houses started diversifying into unrelated areas to cash in on the new opportunities. If they lacked financial resources, technological know-how and market savvy, in the present climate it was easy to find willing foreign collaborators. In fact, between 1990 and 1993, the number of foreign collaboration approvals rose from 666 to 1,476 (CMIE, 1994a). While elsewhere in the world businesses were trying to stay close to their knitting and focus efforts on their 'core competencies' (Prahalad and Hamel, 1990), in India companies were experimenting with the 'anti-core competence' hypothesis. The logic was that sticking to what one can do best might be a good option for an economy growing in an incremental, linear manner; however, if the economic structure of the country itself changes shape, then trying out one's hands at new businesses becomes imperative for growth. After all, in a controlled economy there are not even opportunities to test what one can do best; in the new market-driven economy, success would depend on discovering new core competencies, rather than on relying on the old ones. According to K.R.S. Murthy, Director, IIM, Bangalore (1994): 'The economic context in which the concepts of related diversifications have been developed is different from the context Indian firms face today. ... Today, many Indian firms face a growing economy and expanding markets.'

In India, the Tatas and Birlas in the past, and RPG, ITC, Wipro, L&T, etc., in recent years ventured beyond their defined domains into other businesses and made a fortune. While for these companies the reasons may have been internal, now many Indian companies were diversifying because of the potential of newly opened-up sectors such as aviation, financial services, software exports, telecommunications, automobiles, oil exploration, and so on. Thus, it seemed logical for the textile giant Reliance to venture into areas such as telecom and oil exploration, or the tractor and jeep manufacturers Mahindra & Mahindra (M&M) to diversify into the hotel and real estate businesses.

The large business houses were not alone in seeking fresh pastures. In fact, liberalisation had created larger opportunities for many medium and small businesses as well. In many ways these companies were better placed than their larger brethren, because they could combine the advantage of being small and focused along with greater flexibility and entrepreneurship. Most of them had been in the field long enough—as large volume suppliers, small but dominant regional players, or single niche product companies—to understand the nuances of their own, and related, industry; all they needed was to leverage their existing strengths (often through foreign tie-ups) to create a market for themselves. Many such companies (e.g., NEPC, Mesco, Atul Products, GSL, Kedia Group, Western India Gadgil Group, and Shakthi Group), were quick to capitalise on the emerging opportunities. They diversified into new businesses and surfaced as major players in the market.

One of the major implications of this entrepreneurial surge was that, forced or lured by economic liberalisation, many of the responsive Indian companies started doing business in areas in which they had virtually no previous experience or skills. Moreover, in an increasingly crowded market-place, the market pie was becoming more and more fragmented, and requiring newer competencies to manage businesses. While the war for a market share was most visible in the consumer products (soaps, oil, consumer electronics, etc.), even some of the traditionally protected core sectors were no longer safe (Box 1.2).

BOX 1.2

FRAGMENTATION OF INDIAN MARKETS

In the 1990s, there have been many new entrants in an increasingly fragmented market. This emerging complexity in the market environment is highlighted by the following stray facts:

- In 1993, the refrigerator market belonged to three brands—Godrej, Kelvinator, and Voltas—which among them held more than 95 per cent of the market share. By January 1995, their combined market share had eroded to less than 70 per cent with the advent of the newcomers—Videocon, Allwyn and BPL.

- In the 1980s, the colour TV market was dominated by brands such as Weston, Nelco Blue Diamond, Uptron, and Bush. By 1995, most of these had been replaced by new brands like Videocon, BPL, Onida, and Philips; and other global brands like Sony, Akai, and Goldstar had already started making inroads.

- Between 1989 and 1995, the number of lubricant companies increased from four (the three public sectors and Castrol) to more than 20.

- In the civil aviation sector, the open-sky policy announced in 1991 created routes for eroding the monopoly of Indian Airlines and Vayudoot. By March 1994, the big five private air-taxi operators (East West, Jet, Damania, Modiluft and Sahara) had captured 27 per cent of the market, and on trunk routes, their share accounted for 44 per cent of the traffic.

- Till 1994, the Indian automobile sector was dominated by the big three, Maruti, Hindustan Motors, and Premier

---

Auto, with Telco's indigenous Tata Sierra and Tata Estate starting to carve out a small niche. By 1996, India saw the launch of seven new global brands.

- Even the banking sector found new competitors coming in. In 1994 itself, seven new private and foreign banks were given permission by the Reserve Bank of India to start operating in India, and that too in Bombay which accounts for 60 per cent of the banking transactions in India.

- Traditionally, the state-owned Steel Authority of India (SAIL) and Tata Iron and Steel Company (TISCO) had dominated the steel market. With the decontrol of steel prices, these giants started facing threats from newcomers like Essar Gujarat, Nippon Denro, Jindal, Mukund Iron, and Lloyd, who could provide value-added products at a lower cost. Also, their advantage of having integrated plants was soon to be challenged by the commissioning of Malvika Steel and Kalinga Steel.

It is not surprising that the 1990s saw many old and established companies losing out to new ones, which had started emerging as the new market leaders. The fact that between 1990 and 1994, in the *Super 100* list of business companies compiled by *Business India,* as many as 23 new members had replaced the older members of this illustrious club is representative of this trend. Corporate India was thrown into turbulence.

THE MAKING OF THE SNOWBALL

It would be, of course, naive to assume that the radical transformation of the Indian business environment was initiated overnight through the 1991 budget; or that prior to 1991 India was a stagnant economy. In fact, the issues of privatisation of protected sectors, liberalisation of the economy, promotion of foreign trade, etc., had been part of the political agenda since the mid-1980s; in a limited way during the later part of the 1980s, some measures had been implemented. Thus, what started happening in the 1990s was only a continuation and magnification of the process of change which had started in the previous decade.

Even though popular perception is that the state-controlled, socialist model of economy followed by India had stunted its economic and industrial growth, facts show otherwise. All through the past decades Indian economy had grown. This is apparent from the multifold increases in the various indices of economic growth, as well as from the growth in infrastructure and the performance of the core sectors (Figures 1.1, 1.2, and 1.3). In the three decades since 1960, India's steel production had risen more than three times, coal production almost four times, cement output had multiplied sixfold, and power generation had grown almost 15 times. Similar exponential growth could be seen in natural gas production, in the number of telephone connections, and in the length of paved roads. These achievements had remained imperceptible because they had occurred gradually over the years; their impact was also nullified by the swelling demand created by the increasing population and prosperity.

The outcome of this growth was also visible in the availability of more products to the consumer. Indian industries were not only producing more 'necessities', such as cloth, paper, and fertilisers, but also more 'luxuries', such as cars, scooters, TVs, and refrigerators (Figures 1.3 and 1.4). By the end of 1980s, the Indian economy had matured into one of the largest industrial infrastructures in the world.

Related to these changes were two critical forces which were gradually taking over the control of the country's economy. First, there was a boom in the size of the middle-income group consumer class, which fuelled the growth and direction of the industry. During the latter part of the 1980s, the size of this segment of population grew by nearly 30 per cent. It covered a total of 56.7 million households or 335 million people, and accounted for nearly 40 per cent of the country's population (Rao, 1993). Its demand for conveniences and utility products (e.g., TVs, bicycles, pressure cookers, mixer-grinders, wristwatches, and detergents) not only created the market pull for industries to grow, but also provided the economies of scale for companies to operate. As Box 1.3 shows, at the time of liberalisation, India already had national companies which were producing on globally comparable scales (Abraham, 1994; Parikh, 1994).

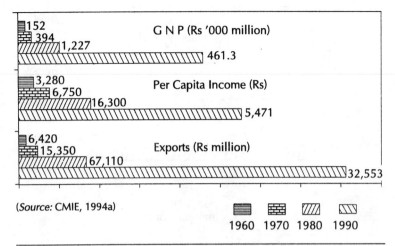

(*Source:* CMIE, 1994a)

| | 1960 | 1970 | 1980 | 1990 |

Figure 1.1   **Growth of Indian economy**

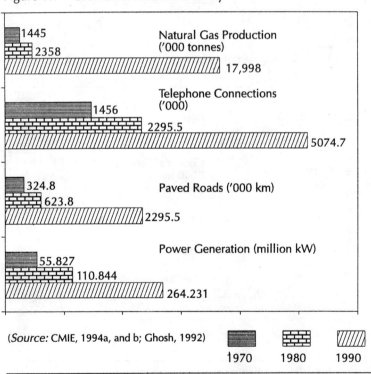

(*Source:* CMIE, 1994a, and b; Ghosh, 1992)

| | 1970 | 1980 | 1990 |

Figure 1.2   **Growth of infrastructure in India**

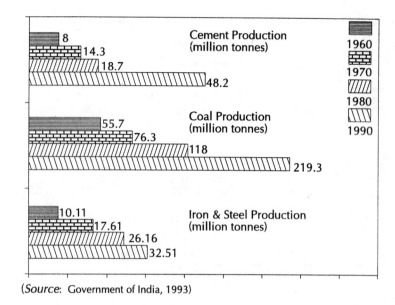

(*Source*: Government of India, 1993)

Figure 1.3 **Growth in core sectors**

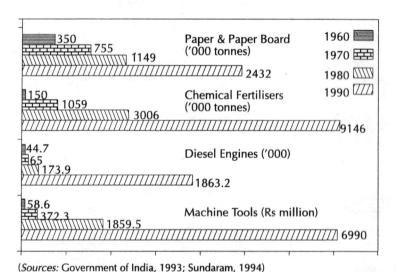

(*Sources:* Government of India, 1993; Sundaram, 1994)

Figure 1.4 **Production growth of 'essential' items**

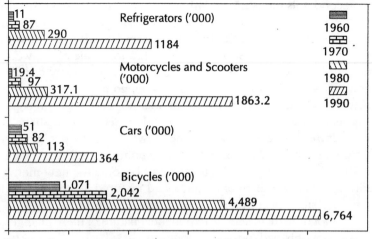

(*Sources*: Government of India, 1993; Ninan and Singh, 1990; Sen,1994; Sundaram, 1995)

Figure 1.5 **Production growth of 'luxury' items**

Box 1.3

GLOBAL CAPACITIES OF SOME INDIAN COMPANIES

- KEC International, an RPG Group company, is the world's second largest producer of transmission towers.
- The Aditya Birla Group is the world's largest producer of rayon fibre, and the second largest producer of palm oil.
- Bajaj Auto is the third largest two-wheeler producer in the world.
- Arvind Mills is the fifth largest producer of denim in the world.
- Lupin Laboratories is the world leader in the anti-TB drug, ethambutol, with 70 per cent share in the world market.
- Hero Cycles is the world's largest producer of bicycles.
- Raymond Mills is the fifth largest manufacturer of worsted suiting.
- Nirma is the world's largest producer of detergents.

Second, this industrial growth was changing the very structure of the Indian economy. India had ceased to be an agrarian economy. Until the 1980s, India's economy had fluctuated with the droughts and monsoons. In contrast, during one of the worst droughts of the twentieth century in 1987, the economy actually grew by 4.3 per cent, and inflation stopped at 7 per cent. The reason was that the primary sector was no longer the principle supplier of raw material to the secondary sector. The share of agriculture in the GDP had gone down from 56 per cent in 1950–51 to about 32 per cent by the beginning of the 1990s (Saran, 1994). The industry and the market had become the new motive forces driving the economy. India had matured as an industrial (and probably, post-industrial) economy (Figure 1.6).

It is not difficult to see the exponential nature of these changes, that is, not only had India's economy grown substantially over the years, but the rate of growth had kept on increasing as well. But all these changes were still shielded by the barriers created by the regulatory controls. Measures such as the Foreign Exchange Regulation Act (FERA) and Monopolies and Restrictive Trade Practices Act (MRTP), import duties and restrictions, protection of core sectors, restrictions on overseas investments, and reservation of certain industries for small-scale manufacturers guarded the economy against market forces, and served to maintain the rate and direction of changes within certain limits.

In removing these barriers, the New Industrial Policy of 1991 marked a departure from the protective era. Though apparently radical, in many ways this shift was an inevitable culmination of the economic and industrial growth of the previous decades. The Indian economy had grown out of adolescence. It now had to seek its place in the global market-place.

LIVING IN A WORLD WITHOUT BOUNDARIES

It is worth considering the terms and phrases that have been used to describe these changes, both by the popular press and in official statements: opening up of the economy, globalisation, lowering of trade barriers, cross-boundary trade, transnational alliances, need for greater transparency, removal of bureaucratic hurdles, and so on. Underlying this terminology is a metaphor—removal of

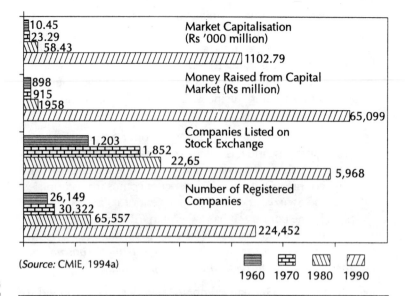

Figure 1.6 **Towards a market-driven economy**

boundaries—which encompasses the gist of the challenge confronting Indian organisations. In the present-day world, the survival and growth of Indian organisations would be determined by their ability to compete in a world which is becoming increasingly borderless.

The most obvious manifestation of the 'world without boundaries' is the growth of MNCs. According to estimates (Sarin, 1995), there are more than 37,000 MNCs with 1,700,000 foreign affiliates operating in the world today. The power of these MNCs can be gauged from the fact that their combined sales exceed global exports by some $1.5 trillion, and that the largest 100 of these control a third of the FDIs worldwide. Greater permeability of trade boundaries, as discussed earlier, has brought Indian companies face to face with these powerful competitors, both on- and off-shore.

But the competitive challenge of the MNCs is not so much about matching their financial power or scales of production. Rather, it is about mastering the new rules of global trade and competition for operating in a borderless world. Operating globally is no longer another form of economic colonialism, as was the case in the past when MNCs used to operate from headquarters, manufacturing and selling standard products around the globe. Increasingly, global companies are coming to represent new centreless organisations—the transnational corporations (TNCs)—which defy the traditional forms of doing business. Consider the following examples and their implications.

- Nestle, the $43 billion Swiss MNC, operates in more than 100 countries, and has 8,000 products in its portfolio. However, less than 10 per cent of these are offered in more than one country. Of its sales, 95 per cent comes from countries outside Switzerland, and 98 per cent of its assets are outside home country. It has a German CEO and five of ten of its GMs are not Swiss (Holstein, 1990; Rapoport, 1994). MORAL: *Operating globally means erasing the boundaries between local markets and global presence.*

- In 1994, the German company Daimler Benz decided to produce the new range of Mercedes Benz MB700 series trucks in Indonesia. The plan is to source components like transmission, axels, brakes and shock absorbers from India, while other crucial components will be exported from Brazil, Argentina, Japan, Spain, and Indonesia. After taking care of the local market demand, more than half of these LCVs will be exported to South-east Asia and the Middle East (*Business India*, 1994a). MORAL: *Operating globally requires mastering skills for operating across multiple boundaries.*

- Corning Inc. describes itself as a 'global network'. It participates in about 40 joint ventures across the world, with organisations in different nations and in different industries. Its partners include Vitro (Mexico) Siemens (Germany), Ciba (Switzerland), Samsung (South Korea), Dow Chemicals and Genentech (USA), Mitsubishi Heavy Industries and Asahi Glass (Japan), among others. This strategy of partnering across industry and national boundaries contributes to 50 per cent of Corning's sales, and allows it to diversify into areas such as fibre optics, computing components, silicone breast implants, environmental technology, enzymes, etc. (Lipnack and Stamps, 1993). MORAL: *Global operations require cutting across industry boundaries to leverage from inter-organisational partnerships.*

- ABB manufactures and sells electrical equipment in 65 businesses in 140 countries through 1,300 companies, which in turn are divided into about 5,000 profit centres with their own profit-and-loss responsibilities. The companies are registered as national companies in the countries of operation; they have the freedom to decide on their products and processes, markets, suppliers, etc., and are managed by local managers. The headquarters in Zurich consist of just 100 people, but the members of the top management team (who are of six different nationalities) are located across the globe. There are just five management levels between the CEO, Percy Barnevik, and the shop-floor of any company (Peters, 1992). MORAL: *Global operations require redefinition of the organisation's internal (i.e., hierarchical and inter-business) boundaries to simultaneously allow extreme levels of decentralisation, with focus and integration of operations.*

- Apple Computers has a joint strategic alliance with Motorola and rival IBM to invest in the Taligent project, and also with AT&T and Sony to invest in General Magic. Sony, on the other hand, has a separate alliance with Apple's rival, Microsoft, while IBM is a supplier of memory tape systems to its own competitor, Digital Equipment. Apple also has a strategic alliance with competitor Toshiba, which has a separate alliance with IBM. All these alliances are to exploit the same emerging market in multimedia (Toffler, 1990; Lipnack and Stamps, 1993). Similar strange bedfellows can be found in other industries as well. In India, for example, Peugeot holds equity stakes in M&M but has tied up with Premier Auto to produce cars which will compete against Ford-M&M cars. MORAL: *In the global markets the competitive boundaries between partners and competitors become obscure; the friends and foes are determined by the market forces.*

These examples highlight the fact that 'going global' is more than just stepping across national boundaries. It means developing abilities to negotiate and operate across several of the boundaries that were traditionally acknowledged as sacrosanct.

THE ALIEN INVADERS

The challenges of operating in a boundaryless world, however, are not limited only to global businesses. The gradually diminishing boundaries cut across various areas of business activities, and create unforeseen sources of threat and competition.

In the traditional business environment, boundaries were the source of stability and predictability. They allowed different business activities to be performed more or less in isolation, fluctuating only within manageable limits. This was not only true of the activities within the organisation, but also in the organisation's relationship with its environment. Every business could plan its activities by taking into consideration only specific segments of its environment and ignoring the rest. Thus, for an automobile company, it was not necessary to worry about changes in the audio cassette markets, just as for the soap manufacturer a fast-food company could not be considered a potential threat.

But these sanctuaries of product–market domains are getting invaded by unusual entrants. Shifts in the bases of product technologies and changes in consumer choices are blurring the traditional market boundaries, making businesses vulnerable to threats from outlandish rivals. A major competitive threat might come not from industry rivals, but from players in totally unrelated industries. Consider, for example, the story of the courier industry in India (Gupta, 1995b).

The growth of the courier industry in India was closely tied to the emergence of a more responsive business environment. During the 1980s, the entrepreneurial initiatives of Skypak virtually built up the industry single-handedly by focusing on the latent corporate need for timely transportation and delivery of important business documents. The only option available to companies was the state-owned Postal Department, which was not only slow, but often not very reliable either. Courier companies capitalised on this gap, and by the latter part of the decade, the market was growing at the rate of more than 30 per cent. The growth of the market also attracted dominant players like DHL, Elbee, and Blue Dart, who grabbed the market from Skypak. By the mid-1990s, the courier business had become a Rs 4,000 million industry.

But very soon, the courier companies started finding their market getting squeezed. Competition came not from the 2,000-odd small and big players spread across the country, but from a totally unrelated, albeit growing product market—the fax. Fax offered a cheaper, faster and more convenient alternative to sending documents by courier. Technological innovations like Faxnet and Broadcast Fax even allowed users to send the same message to different locations simultaneously, instantaneously and economically. The courier market started stagnating, with the growth rate tumbling down to 15 per cent.

Interestingly, around the same time fax too started receiving competition, and from yet another field—the networking of computers through WANs (wide area networks). In their search of new markets, the big courier companies themselves became the alien invaders for yet another industry—the carrying and forwarding (C&F) cargo business. Compared to the traditional C&F agents, courier companies were more agile, gave door-to-door service, and had already invested in information technology to allow them to trace and track parcels. This gave them a better service edge.

Similar instances, of competition from unrelated sources, could be seen repeated in other industries as well. The Indian film industry received competition from the growth of the VCR/VCP market during the 1980s, which in turn received its nemesis from satellite TV and cable networks (Gupta, 1995b). Competition also .comes from 'hybrid' products, which cut across traditional boundaries separating market domains. For example, LCVs ate into the markets of heavy vehicles, the 50–100cc mopeds took away customers from both bicycle manufacturers as well as from the producers of scooters and motorcycles, and banks found that their customers were shifting their money from fixed deposits to the more lucrative real estate, mutual fund and capital markets.

What is also noteworthy is the fact that these cross-industry threats do not only nibble away the market share; very often they strike at the very heart of the business, its core strengths, making it weak in all its activities. In fact, this kind of invasion can be even more perilous than the battles fought in the market-place, because it defies the rules of business logic. For instance, by the rules of conventional logic, a company in the business of vacuum cleaners should hardly be concerned about the growth of credit-card sales or of the holiday-resort business. Yet, precisely these kind of companies hollowed up the one-time direct marketing leader Eureka Forbes (Gupta and Majumdar, 1995). During the 1980s, Eureka Forbes built up its business through a 2,000-odd highly motivated sales force, who would go from door to door persuading people to buy vacuum cleaners. Its salesmen were well trained, and motivated by the hefty commission they could earn from their sales efforts. During the decade, the company grew at a phenomenal annual compound rate of 40 per cent. In 1992, however, the company found itself becoming a favourite poaching ground for the new companies adapting the direct marketing strategy (e.g., Citibank Cards, Sterling Resorts, Real Value). These companies started hiring Eureka Forbes' salespersons. The fact that these companies paid more, that they did not require the salesmen to lug a heavy product around, and that recession had reduced the sales of vacuum cleaners—and, correspondingly, salesman's earnings—further encouraged their exodus. Just at the juncture when Eureka Forbes required greater sales efforts, it found its most valuable resources leaving the company. Probably, Eureka Forbes could have coped with the recession, but in the absence of a committed and experienced sales force, this became almost impossible. By 1994, the company registered losses exceeding Rs 40 million.

CONCLUSION: THE EROSION OF COMPETITIVE LOGIC

What implications do these changes have for Indian businesses? To say the least, they make our conventional understanding of doing business outdated. The new competitive reality is eroding the basic frameworks of strategy-making, which so far were taken for granted. And this is happening in more than one way—and simultaneously!

Let us look at three critical implications of these widespread change:

1. *The past environmental niches are continuously disintegrating and are being replaced by qualitatively new realities.*

The traditional metaphor for strategy was the game of chess. In this game one played against a partner, planned out one's moves according to the rules of the game, and depending on one's own deftness in out manoeuvring the partner emerged a winner or a loser in the end. The rules of the game, however, never changed, and there was implicit agreement on issues such as the strength and behaviour of each piece. One knew, for example, that each player would make only one move at a time, and that the rook would not move diagonally or jump over a piece. The element of surprise was in the moves made by the adversary and oneself, not in the nature of the playing field.

The chess strategy was one of winning by: 'doing more of this and less of that'. The emphasis was on managing changes in the *size* of the environmental niche in which one operated. One planned a strategy—increase market share, decrease costs, improve productivity, make investments, etc.—and implemented it. If one made a sound assessment of the changes in the size of the niche (supplies, costs, competitors' actions, market demand, etc.), and implemented the strategy accurately, success was more or less assured.

Such an analogy, however, hardly applies to the current strategic battles. More and more, the emerging competitive reality is behaving like some sophisticated interactive video game: threats and challenges are manifold and can come from any source; the risks and perils increase, decrease or qualitatively change as the game unfolds; and even the rules undergo transmutation while the game is being played, often as a reaction to one's own moves (e.g., an ally may turn into a threat, or your enemy may change course or shape the moment your weapon hits it).

What one is dealing with here is not the situation of scarcity or oversupply (the size), but with the complexities of a niche which is continuously changing *shape*. The marketers in the earlier, more stable days, for example, could succeed as long as they were able to position their product in a particular market segment. The income groups were good indicators of the customers' desires and purchasing power. This is no longer so. The issue now is to cope with the erosion of segment characteristics: the aspirations of the segment are now influenced by TV ads, and the purchasing power determined by consumer finance schemes. The competitive turbulence and chaos emerges not only from the actions and interactions of the market players, but 'from the field itself. The "ground" is in motion' (Emery and Trist, 1965).

The dynamic complexity comes also from increasingly hazy boundaries among the parts of the environment. It is becoming difficult to distinguish, for example, between suppliers, customers and competitors (your prime supplier or customer may also be your strongest competitor, e.g., SIEL Ltd competes with Amtrex and Voltas in the air-conditioner market but also supplies them compressors for making the product). Similarly, the categories dividing the product from the 'substitutes' are becoming less and less applicable (creation of a new market by leveraging on a latent customer need can attract a host of new technologies and 'substitute' products, which might become standard products in their own right, for example, the overlapping markets among gensets, alternators, and self-charging lighting gadgets).

It appears that planning and implementation play a lesser role in strategic thinking than in learning and making sense of the changes occurring in the environment.

2. *The traditional sources of competitive advantage have become the precondition for corporate survival.*

Companies had always relied on factors like productivity, cost, product positioning, quality, innovation, speed, and service to gain strategic advantage over competitors. In any given market, one of these factors set the standards, and created the basis of winning the competitive game. One could, for example, leverage on the high quality of one's product or service, while compromising on cost and productivity. Or a well-positioned product, with high brand equity, could still command the market in spite of slow customer-response time.

Now, there is hardly any company which is not decreasing its costs, aiming at innovative offerings, trying to provide better service and quality, etc. What used to be strategic initiatives earlier have now become the norm—a precondition for corporate survival, instead of constituting a competitive edge. As Galbraith and

Lawler III (1993) have noted, in the present scenario, these strategic initiatives contribute to:

> survival, rather than to any advantage; productivity, quality, and customer service are competitive necessities, not competitive advantages, because most companies have launched initiatives and made some progress. ... The most effective organisations adopt the newest strategic issue early, perfect it, institutionalise it, and move on to the next. ... This action requires organisational learning and flexibility. ...

3. *Businesses are forced to address demands which are mutually contradictory in nature.*

Lastly, and most importantly, the emerging competitive realities are placing apparently contradictory demands on organisations (Kanter, 1989). Consider, for instance, the following prescriptions:

- to improve efficiency, flatten structures, reduce flab, and become lean; but also value human capital and invest in its development.

- to reduce costs and increase productivity, maintain one's economies; but also customise and provide variety to meet the specific requirements of different niche segments.

- to capitalise on emerging opportunities, innovate, diversify, take risks; but also stay close to one's core competence, and, in any case avoid failures.

- to be responsive and agile, decentralise, empower the front line, encourage self-management; but also maintain control and focus the efforts of people in a given direction.

- to increase one's market presence, acquire, invest, integrate, and grow in size; but also maintain the flexibility of a small entrepreneurial enterprise.

These are no either/or choices of earlier times. It is necessary for survival to do both. What these demands also highlight is the redundancy of traditional strategic logic in dealing with the present-day realities. As Kanter (1989) has observed, the nature and pace of changes are making it 'harder and harder for executives ... to succeed by traditional corporate methods, when technology, customer preferences, employee loyalties, industry regulations and corporate ownerships are constantly changing'.

The answer lies not in past knowledge and learning, but in the ability of organisations to create new knowledge; that is, in their capacity to transform themselves into learning organisations.

Notes

1. The developments mentioned in this section have been traced through a number of articles and newspaper and magazine reports. Readers may refer to Agarwal (1995), Bist (1995), Gupta and Bakaya (1994), Kawatra (1994), Ninan and Singh (1990), and Raman (1993) for more details.

2. The post-1991 metamorphoses of the Indian economy has happened (and is happening) so rapidly that no up-to-date consolidated account is available. The figures and facts given in this section (and in Box 1.1) have been collected from various CMIE reports, newspaper reports, and articles in business publications. For more details, please refer to Abraham (1994), Chakravarti (1994), CMIE (1994a, 1995a, 1995b, 1996a, 1996b), Dass and Jayakar (1993), Jayakar (1993, 1994), Jinshu and Narayan (1995), and Parikh (1994).

The Learning Imperative

*Learning is the new form of labour. . . . The 21st
century company has to promote and nurture
the capacity to improve and innovate. The idea
has radical implications. It means learning
becomes the axial principle of organisations. It
replaces control as the fundamental job of
managers.*

—Shoshanna Zuboff

ABOUT DINOSAURS AND MEN

Millions of years back, the earth was populated with giant powerful creatures, the dinosaurs. On account of their large size and
robust structure, these huge beings could grow and survive in the
inhospitable climate of the time. They ruled the planet for thousands of years. However, when the earth's climate started changing swiftly, these creatures, in spite of their size and strength,
found it increasingly difficult to adjust to the changes. Their
genetic learning had prepared them for harsh weather conditions,
but not for adjusting to rapid environmental change. Over a short
period of time, the species ceased to exist.

In contrast to the dinosaurs was another species of much smaller, and comparatively frail, creatures, the humans, who started
inhabiting the earth a few million years later. Perhaps it was
on account of genetic defect that the members of this species could
violate what was given to them by nature. They showed a

divergence in their behavioural patterns—many of which were often useless for safeguarding their existence—but allowed them to cope with a variety of environmental conditions. While they were naturally endowed to live on the ground, they also learned to climb and live on trees, and to swim in the water. They devised ways of surviving in a variety of weather conditions, ranging from tropical forests to deserts to the polar region; and, above all, they learned to manipulate things, make tools, and create symbols to capture, utilise and transfer the knowledge which they had created and acquired. The climatic conditions on earth kept on changing, but human beings survived. In fact, they even evolved to the level where they could defy the natural laws to suit their aims.

The moral of this evolutionary anecdote can be summed up in a somewhat pedestrian formula:

$$L \geq C$$

that is to say, 'It is a fundamental law of ecology that for any organism to survive, its rate of learning must be equal to, or greater than, the rate of change in its environment' (Garratt, 1987). The example of the dinosaurs and humans is quite instructive for a large number of companies today. In contrast to the dinosaurs, human beings could survive and proliferate through the climatic changes, because they could learn, and because they discovered how to leverage on their learned knowledge. Amidst the present environmental changes, the same principle applies to businesses as well.

COPING WITH TURBULENCE

Indian organisations are in a far more turbulent environment than were the dinosaurs millennia ago. To recall the gist of the discussion in Chapter 1:

1. The *rate of change* is forcing Indian businesses to adapt and reorient themselves at a pace unprecedented in the country's industrial history. The exponential nature of change is creating compulsions to adjust to the fast-changing business realities on a continuous basis. Moreover, the fact that these changes are a continuation of the pre-liberalisation economic growth also counters the chances

that the current transmutations might be only a temporary phase. Learning to adapt to change is, therefore, now becoming a necessity for survival.

2. The pace of change is only one part of the current scenario. The other is the *complexity of change*. In no other era have Indian companies had to cope with so many changes occurring simultaneously, and so swiftly (Box 2.1). Companies must contend with new markets, new products, new technologies, new competitors in the market, new regulations, new rules of the competitive game, and so on. These changes are increasingly making earlier strategies obsolete, and creating new learning requirements.

BOX 2.1

THE COMPLEXITY OF ENVIRONMENTAL CHANGES

- *Global markets* Reduction of trade barriers and the need to enhance economies has made business a transnational, rather than a national, activity.

- *Competition* Not only are there many more competitors in the same industry, but competition is coming from unrelated sectors as well.

- *Technology* The pace and nature of changes in technological innovations are disrupting product life-cycles and traditional investment criteria.

- *Customers* With increasing choices and lower prices, customers are becoming more demanding in terms of value, quality and service.

- *Government* The focus of most national governments is shifting from governance to include business agendas, leading to their greater participation in business activities, formation of economic trade zones, economic warfare, etc.

- *Workforce* Demographic changes in education levels, sex-roles, age distribution, cross-border mobility, etc., are creating workers radically different from those of the past.

---

3. An even greater threat to competitive survival comes from the *unpredictability of change*. Although the figures and data on any parameter of environment might show an upward or downward linear trend, actual business reality is increasingly becoming non-linear and chaotic. The blurring of boundaries among product categories, markets, customer segments, technologies, etc., is creating unforeseen consequences in the competitive environment.

In such a scenario knowledge and competencies remain the most viable (and probably the only) basis for establishing a competitive edge. In the contemporary competitive climate, creation of wealth no longer seems possible unless the company also invests in the creation of knowledge.

In a rapidly changing and turbulent environment, updating of the knowledge-base (about emerging technologies, new trade regulations, opening of new markets, etc.) must lie at the core of corporate strategy. Moreover, this cannot be just a one-time exercise. Competition through knowledge requires continuous updating of one's learning and knowledge-base in order to remain in tune with the changes in the internal and external environments. That is, it requires development of the capabilities to learn on a regular basis, or learning how to learn (Figure 2.1). Or, to use the new management vocabulary, they must become learning organisations (Handy, 1996): 'In an uncertain world, where all we know for sure is that nothing is sure, we are going to need organisations that are continually renewing themselves, reinventing themselves, reinvigorating themselves. These are the learning organisations, the ones with the learning habit.'

But before we discuss what learning can do for companies, it is important to understand why corporate dinosaurs fail to learn, and become extinct.

THE ROOTS OF FAILURE

In the corporate denizens, dinosaurs are not such a rarity as they were in the prehistoric world. One might recall some of the leading organisations (Remington Rand of India, Hyderabad Allwyn) and brands (Rath Vanaspati, Binny Textiles, Vijay Super Scooter,

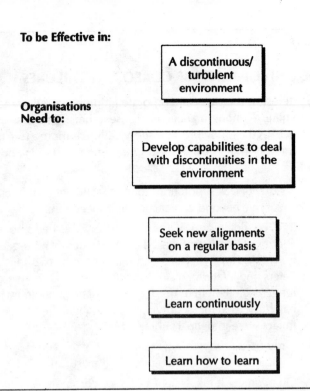

To be Effective in:

A discontinuous/ turbulent environment

Organisations Need to:

Develop capabilities to deal with discontinuities in the environment

Seek new alignments on a regular basis

Learn continuously

Learn how to learn

Figure 2.1 **The relationship of environmental turbulence to the learning imperative**

etc.) of yesteryear which got marginalised or completely vanished amidst the environmental changes. In fact, failure in business is more the norm than are the instances of corporate successes (Box 2.2). Further, that business failures are as frequent in India as anywhere in the world is corroborated by a study, published by the Federation of Indian Chamber of Commerce and Industry (FICCI), according to which there were as many as 300,000 sick units in India in March 1994 (Upadhyay, 1994). The total bank credit locked up in these sick units was 17.6 per cent of total bank credit (of which 72.7 per cent was accounted for by medium and large sick units).

Why do organisations fail? The popular notion about corporate failures is that they are caused by unanticipated sudden changes in the external environment. A closer look, however, often shows

BOX 2.2

THE UNIVERSALITY OF CORPORATE FAILURES

The interest in the study of corporate failures is a rather recent phenomenon among management researchers. This is surprising, since, as the following facts show, failure is more a rule than an exception in the business world (Makridakis, 1991; Shukla, 1994a):

- A study of US corporations found that 90 per cent firms fail to survive beyond 20 years of their inception.

- In 1982, Peters and Waterman (1982) published a book, *In Search of Excellence*, based on their study of 43 organisations. Within five years of their research, two-thirds of Peters and Waterman's 43 'excellent' companies were no longer excellent in terms of the six financial criteria which had been used for identifying them; eight of the companies in fact were in deep trouble.

- A report in *Forbes* found that only 22 of the 100 largest US companies of 1917 still figured in the list in 1987.

- On average, it takes eight years for corporate ventures to become successful, while the majority of new ventures never make a profit.

- For every successful corporate turnaround there are two that fail.

- There were close to half a million business bankruptcies in the world in 1988.

- Between 35 and 85 per cent (depending on the specific study) of new products fail to ever make a profit.

- Over the last 20 years, more than 350 major firms have failed in the computer industry.

- In 1989, there was a loss of more than $7 billion among the top 200 world banks.

- In the automobile industry alone more than 1,500 firms have failed in the past.

that the reasons lie not so much in external factors (e.g., increased competition, changes in government regulations, scarcity of inputs, a long-drawn labour strike, failure of a major product, a bad investment), as in the internal dynamics of the company (Cameron and Zammuto, 1988; Cameron, Sutton and Whetten, 1988). Changes in the external environment merely precipitate the crises and bring to the fore the latent weaknesses (e.g., managerial incompetence, strategic misalignment, lack of leadership of the organisation).

These weaknesses do not become apparent because often a supportive environment hides significant organisational defects. In their study, Hambrick and D'Aveni (1988) found that many shortcomings and deficiencies are apparent in failing companies even a decade before they go bankrupt. They go unnoticed, however, because the environment supports short-term goals (e.g., sales turnover, profitability, and share price). For instance, in the late 1980s, the boom in the colour TV market helped Nelco register a high turnover. The company stepped up its marketing efforts, and more than 50 per cent of its sales were from CTVs. When recession set in the market, the competitors responded by slashing prices. Nelco, however, found itself unable to do so, realising that it had ignored its high operating costs during the peak period (Sharma, 1994). Similarly, the benign protection of the closed economy not only concealed critical shortcomings of many Indian companies, but even confirmed and strengthened their faith in their outmoded products, operations and strategies.

This happens because, just like the dinosaurs, organisations, too, have their own genetic programming. This programming is embedded in the cognitive frameworks and mental models shared by the significant members of the organisation, which determine the managerial response to the change in environment. As Kiesler and Sproull (1982) have noted: 'The crucial component of managerial behaviour in rapidly changing environments is [the] problem of sensing, the cognitive process of noticing and constructing meaning about [the] environment so that the organisation can take action.'

Mental models help executives to make sense of rapid and complex changes. They influence corporate decisions in three crucial ways:

1. They determine the nature of the information that will be considered 'relevant' by the decision-makers.

2. They limit the manner in which this information will be analysed and interpreted.

3. They define what actions are 'possible', 'important' and/or 'necessary' for the organisation to take.

However, mental models can also limit the capacity of organisations to change and learn. They often limit executives' understanding of complex changes, and mislead them in their judgements because they circumscribe perceptions, interpretations, and decisions (Box 2.3).

BOX 2.3

HOW MENTAL MODELS LIMIT OPTIONS

- Till the 1970s, the computer market was defined in terms of mainframes. Even when the possibility of home computers and personal computing started to become a technological reality, market leaders like IBM failed to perceive this new potential. Ken Olsen, President of Digital Equipment Corporation (DEC), said in 1977: 'There is no reason for any individual to have a computer in their home.' As a consequence, by the 1980s, many of the old players had lost their dominance to newcomers like Apple and Compaq (Peters, 1989).

- Atari's success in the video-games market during the late 1970s was built on the mental model that growth comes from marketing and sales promotion. Faced with increasing competition, it recruited more marketing people, and gradually increased its advertising revenue from $6 million in 1977 to $125 million in 1982. In the process, the engineering, software and product development functions were neglected. Its technical talents left the company dejected, and its new product launches lagged behind their competitors'. In 1982, for the first time since its meteoric rise, it registered losses of more than $100 million (Hector, 1983).

- In 1927, a young engineer named DeForest walked into the office of Harry Warner, the co-founder of Warner Brothers. DeForest had worked out a way of synchronising sound and images, which could change a silent movie into a talkie. Harry Warner, after listening to him, remarked: 'Are you crazy? Who wants to hear an actor talk?' (Peters, 1989).
- When the sales of Singer sewing machines dipped, the company's incumbent management found it difficult to believe that the nature of the market had changed. Even when the same trend was repeated in Europe, it was attributed to the communist victory in France and was viewed as a passing phenomenon (Gopinath, 1991).
- DEC is known to have virtually created the minicomputer market. Its spectacular growth was largely on account of the quality of its products, which was emphasised upon and ensured by its entrepreneur CEO Ken Olsen. DEC relied on a market dominated by high-technology buyers. In the late 1970s, when competition started emerging from microcomputers and cheaper mainframes, DEC responded with rigorous quality control and excessive testing of its products. Its 'solidly built' computers became 'the most overengineered and undermarketed products in the world'. In the process, six of its eight products were launched two years behind schedule. It missed out on an emerging new market and, in 1983, for the first time since its inception, its net earnings went down (Kets de Vries and Miller, 1989).

Studies show that reframing old and developing new mental models requires organisations to be receptive to new information and to realign their strategies to the emergent changes in the environment. For instance, a study (Barr, Stimpert and Huff, 1992) found that over a period of 25 years, successful companies showed a more significant and regular renewal of strategy-making cognitive frameworks compared to the unsuccessful ones. The authors concluded: 'Given a substantial change in the environment, firms that successfully renew their strategies will show more rapid succession or change in mental models than firms that experience organisational decline'.

OUTCOMES OF LEARNING

Organisational learning is the collective learning of the organisation. While it does involve learning of individual employees, it is more than just the sum of the learning of its individual members. Like individuals, organisations too have cognitive systems and memories, which are embedded in their rules and procedures, products, norms and values, operating practices, etc. (Hedberg, 1981). In many ways, these 'invisible assets' (Itami, 1987) are independent of the specific individuals, are owned by the whole organisation, and often persist across its history—withstanding changes in its membership, and often even in its leadership. Badaracco (1991) has described an organisation's learning as its 'embedded knowledge':

> A firm is an embodiment of knowledge: it can learn, remember, and know things that none of the individuals and teams within it know . . . complex skills and knowledge are embedded in the minds of its members and in the formal and informal social relationships that orchestrate their efforts. . . . [Organisation learns] through the countless, small, daily endeavors in which sales representatives learn about customers, supervisors learn about suppliers, and through endless adjustments to the routines by which all of them coordinate behavior and judgements with each other.

Empirical studies and the stories of successful organisations show that success and effectiveness come from the ability of firms to scan the environment, to update their knowledge, and to learn from potential threats and opportunities. A study of 107 successful and 54 unsuccessful companies has shown that the successful ones were consistently better in their use of information (scanning, analysis, control, communication, decision-making, etc.) than their counterparts (Miller and Friesen, 1983). Moreover, this difference was apparent across all stages of the organisational lifecycle (birth, growth, maturity, revival and decline).

Dodgson (1991) investigated the biotechnology firms that operate in a rapidly developing field. He found that it was the differential ability of the organisations to learn quickly about technological

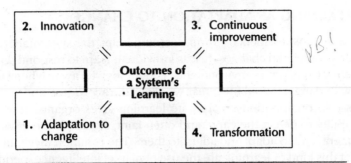

Figure 2.2 **The four outcomes of learning**

opportunities which was responsible for changes in the pattern of competitive relationships among the companies. The study showed that corporate learning was essential for retaining and improving these firms' productivity, competitiveness, and innovativeness amidst the uncertain technological and market circumstances. Similarly, Pavitt (1991) found that the strategies of large innovative firms are determined in part by attempts to learn in highly uncertain environmental conditions. He concluded that: 'the range of possible choices about both product and process technologies open [to] the firm depends on its accumulated competence. ... The improvement of these competencies requires continuous and collective learning.'

There are four ways in which learning helps any system—whether biological or organisational—to survive and grow (Figure 2.2):

1. by helping it to adapt to changing environmental demands;

2. by enabling it to make innovations in its strategies, structures, products/services and practices;

3. by building capabilities to continuously improve itself; and,

4. by creating conditions which facilitate radical transformation of the system.

How effective the new knowledge is for the system, that is, the extent to which it can influence its future direction and growth, would depend primarily on the depth and complexity of learning.

LEARNING AS ADAPTATION TO CHANGE

In its most elementary form, learning helps the system adapt to environmental changes. Just as individuals learn to respond differently to changing environmental conditions (run away when faced with danger, avoid fire, wear woollens during winter, and so on), so do organisations. Corporate learning gives organisations the ability to detect the early, and often faint, signals of the environment, and to adapt and adjust to them. The common mechanisms of this kind of learning are the use of market intelligence, periodic reviews of technology trends, analysis of government policies, etc. In 1994, for instance, Hindustan Lever Ltd (HLL) found that its competitor, Reckitt & Coleman, was planning to launch an anti-bacterial soap through extension of its brand, Dettol. HLL responded by preponing the launch of its Lifebuoy Liquid brand. The early entry helped HLL capture this niche segment, and virtually nullified the competitor's move (Chatterjee, 1995a).

A factor critical to the success in adapting to changing environmental demands is the organisation's ability to recognise and perceive emerging trends. For instance, in the 1980s, when environmental concerns were gaining momentum, many US chemical companies dismissed the anti-litter campaigns as a nuisance and a Left-inspired propaganda. Companies such as Du Pont, on the other hand, perceived an opportunity in the slow but gradual increase in environmental awareness (by the mid-1980s, eight million US homes were already sorting out their refuse into recycling bins). It reoriented its strategy and formed alliance with Waste Management of North America to set up five plastic recycling plants; Du Pont used the recycled plastic as a cheap raw material for moulding into park benches and traffic barricades (Fombrun, 1992).

LEARNING AS INNOVATION

The outcomes of adaptive learning, however, are mostly reactive in nature. They do not create any proactive breakthroughs. Changes in government policies might force organisations to look for new markets, adapt new technologies or new sources of supply; or, a competitor's move may stimulate them to launch a new product or strengthen their distribution channels. But, primarily, learning results in a few minor and incremental changes in the organisation.

At a somewhat deeper level, learning involves creation of knowledge, and enables the organisation to innovate. Learning at this level occurs when organisations develop new business solutions by capturing and combining the demands, opportunities and ideas existing within and outside their boundaries. According to Mohrman and Mohrman (1993):

> Innovations frequently emerge from the blending of multiple perspectives, such as customer's needs and the designer's knowledge base, or a combination of two different disciplines. Consequently, innovation is fostered in organisations that promote integration of multiple perspectives by linking the various organisational parts more closely and by linking the organisation more tightly to its customers.

The innovations achieved through learning might not necessarily be limited to creating a new product; they can include other useful corporate innovations, such as creation of a new service strategy, identification of a new market, and development of a more effective accounting system, personnel policy, or process technology (Box 2.4).

BOX 2.4

LEARNING AS INNOVATION

Mahindra & Mahindra

During the late 1980s, M&M's jeep sales were hit by a number of new competitive factors: increase in excise duties, introduction of competing models (e.g., Maruti's Gypsy), fuel shortage, etc. By the end of 1990, M&M had accumulated a huge pile-up of unsold vehicles. It could, however, turn the trend around by successfully designing and launching the 10-seater diesel-driven Commander within less than a year. This was made possible because M&M capitalised on a critical information from the market—the latent need in the semi-urban areas for a sturdy and spacious vehicle for shared transport (Roy, 1992).

Milton Plastics

For the Rs 1,000 million insulated thermoware market leader, Milton, developing a new product normally costs between Rs 2.5 and 3.5 million. Launching a bad design means not only loss of this money, but also of an opportunity, specially since the thermoware market is seasonal. Milton uses feedback from the market from its 40 distributors, 55 stockists, and 14,000 retailers for getting ideas for new products. Besides analysing the sales trends, the company also holds regular distributor conferences and think-tank meets to facilitate smooth flow of information from market to R&D and manufacturing departments. It is these mechanisms that have helped Milton to innovate new product models like Kool Marvel and Presto (Sharma, 1993).

Mukund Iron & Steel

Mukund Iron's R&D centre is totally aligned to the company's line functions. The annual research plans are developed based on the requirements and feedback from the marketing, production and product development departments (it has no metallurgical lab, because the shop-floor is regarded as the lab). The learning derived from these efforts enabled Mukund to make many innovations: for example, reduce the normal heat treatment time for alloy steel from 32 to 22 hours; design casting for Russian customers which could withstand repeated impact at sub-zero temperature; increase the production of cold heading steel from 450 to 2,500 tonnes per month, produce coloured stainless steel, (the only non-Japanese company to do so) and so on (Kanavi, 1994a).

The competitive advantage of innovations lies in that, if successful, they define the industry standards for quality of products and services. Thus, when British Airways started branding its services, Citibank introduced the automatic teller machines (ATMs), and Maruti launched fuel-efficient cars on Indian roads, they also created new norms for the industry players to follow. A technological innovation might have the added advantage of creating proprietary knowledge. A patented product or technology allows the innovating company to restrict entry of competitors and mould the market structure (through selective licensing of technology) to its own advantage.

Although impressive, innovation is merely a one-time achievement. Not only do patents expire after a time, the advantage of most innovating companies is often surpassed by the swiftness of imitators. Imitators, in fact, often have a greater competitive advantage than the innovators because of the former's low overheads and virtually nil investments in R&D, and because they are constrained neither by traditions nor quality requirements. In spite of the growing emphasis on intellectual property rights (IPRs) and the GATT regime, imitated products and intellectual piracy are a fact of business life. According to a study of 48 innovations in the electronics, drugs, machinery and chemicals industries, 60 per cent of the patented innovations could be imitated—*legally*—within four years of their introduction (Mansfield, 1984). Apparently, imitators are fast learners. They not only learn quickly about the product; they also devise innovative methods to circumvent the regulatory system.

Enduring success, then, lies not only in innovation, but in faster and continuous innovation. In other words, as Arie P. de Geus (1988), the planning chief of the Royal Dutch Shell Group of Companies, has observed: 'The ability to learn faster than your competitors may be the only sustainable competitive advantage.'

LEARNING AS CONTINUOUS IMPROVEMENT

Firms achieve greater sustainable competitive advantage when they learn to make continuous improvements in their already existing products, processes and services. These improvements allow the organisations to stay ahead of others by continuously redefining industry standards, and forcing the competition to meet them. Internally, too, continuous improvements help organisations decrease costs, increase productivity, and improve the bottomline of their operations.

However, this cannot be achieved through the efforts of a single hierarchical level or department. Continuous improvements require tapping the organisation's collective knowledge-base. As Reich (1987) has observed:

Competitive advantage today comes from continuous, incremental innovation and refinement of a variety of ideas that spread throughout the organisation. .... Entrepreneurial efforts are focused on many thousands of ideas rather than just a few big ones. And because valuable information and expertise is dispersed throughout the organisation, top management does not solve problems; it creates an environment in which people can identify and solve problems themselves.

This kind of continuous innovation is possible only when organisations are able to design mechanisms which help them to reflect, review and critique their existing operations and offerings on a regular basis, and to use this learning for developing better business solutions.

Obviously, this is a more complex level of organisational learning because it focuses on controlling not only the outcomes but also the process of learning. This would require devising channels for smooth flow of ideas and information, so that relevant problems can be identified and solutions can be developed on a regular basis. Box 2.5 gives some examples which would help in understanding the nature and advantages of this kind of learning.

BOX 2.5 .

LEARNING AS CONTINUOUS IMPROVEMENT

Eicher Tractor

In the early 1990s, Eicher Tractor decided to tap the experience and knowledge-base of the workers at its Alwar plant. It encouraged its workers to suggest changes in the manufacturing process. Wherever a change was introduced, the area or the particular machine was painted orange, replacing the usual dull green. By the end of one year, the plant looked more orange than green. By the end of three years, the company had increased its production by 45 per cent and productivity by 27.4 per cent and reduced its manpower requirement from 320, to 277 (Bhimal, 1992).

Modi Xerox

In 1990, the photocopier company Modi Xerox was finding it increasingly difficult to compete with low-cost domestic suppli-

---

ers, specially because the depreciation of the rupee significantly increased the company's import costs (Modi Xerox was importing machines from its collaborator, Rank Xerox). On analysing the design of the existing imported models, Modi Xerox found a number of areas of cost reduction. For instance, it was found that the imported version had a built-in heating system, which had little utility in a dry country like India. By redesigning the machine's electronic controls, the cost of the unit could be brought down by Rs 2,500 per piece. Further efforts reduced the need for having three trays for different paper sizes; the company designed a single adjustable tray which could hold all sizes. Not only did this reduce the cost significantly (by Rs 20,000), but it also created a new market: Rank Xerox now wanted to buy these models from the Indian company (Jain, 1992).

Videocon

Videocon regularly tracks 50,000 households to find out what the customers expect from the products. This has helped it improve the design and features of its products and services. For instance, feedback from the market showed that customers often ignore the printed manual for its VCRs. As a result, it makes it difficult to use the gadget, which in turn, increases service problems for the company. So, the company decided to give a demonstration cassette along with the VCR which would explain how to use the machine in a user-friendly way (Chatterjee, 1995b).

LEARNING AS CORPORATE TRANSFORMATION

The process of continuous improvement is often one of learning by specific functions and departments of the organisation (e.g., learning by marketing may help to continuously raise the service standards, or use of learning on the shop-floor may increase productivity levels). Organisations are able to derive greater benefit when the learning process is encouraged at an organisation-wide level. When organisations enhance their knowledge base, and make conscious attempts to alter the mental models across levels and hierarchies they bring about transformations.

There is wide agreement among researchers that corporate transformations involve more than just radical changes in the tangibles of the organisation (for example, in the structure, portfolios, and investments). Rather, they focus on the changes in the mind-set of people—the way they perceive, interpret, think, and feel (Kilmann *et al.*, 1988). Kindler (1979) defines corporate transformation as 'a variation in kind that involves reconceptualization and discontinuity from the initial system'. Even the practitioners are realising that:

> It is not enough to alter the way things are done or the structure under which they are accomplished. To achieve long-term, sustained change, the meaning or belief held within the organisation also must be changed. . . . Organisation-wide transformation requires changing the systems of meaning within a company through an ongoing process of visioning, reframing, and adaptive experimentation . . . [Finney *et al.*, 1988].

The successful implementation of these processes results in outcomes such as corporate turnarounds, strategic reorientation and restructuring, and cultural metamorphosis. What is also important to note is that successful transformations further enhance the learning capabilities of organisations, allowing them to continue to question and reframe their mental models on a regular basis.

Corporate learning as a leverage for organisational transformation requires the designing of processes to ensure regular flow of relevant information across hierarchical, functional and corporate boundaries, and the creation of systems that facilitate constructive use of this information for organisational problem-solving at all levels. For instance, in 1989–90, British Petroleum (BP) initiated a major change initiative, 'Project 1990', which transformed it into a global player. Headed by a team of high-flyer middle managers, the process commenced with an organisational survey to evaluate the company's employee attitudes, review current operations, and generate recommendations for enhancing the effectiveness of] The findings, which were shared across the organisation, painted a candid portrait of BP as an over-controlled organisation with a lack of clarity and sharing of goals and vision even at senior levels. This feedback helped BP to undertake a programme of radical change, which resulted in a change of culture, implementation of a massive communication programme to make people aware of the company's core values, redefinition of corporate structures and systems, and a restructuring of its operations (Butler, 1990).

When organisations are able to use learning as a tool for achieving transformation they become 'learning organisations'.

CONCLUSIONS

The foregoing discussion also highlights a crucial aspect of the process of organisational learning: learning can occur at different levels of complexity, and with correspondingly different outcomes. The kind of learning that helps an organisation to make incremental adaptation to the environment is obviously very different from the one that helps it to transform radically. Organisational learning is not merely a unitary concept.

The plurality of organisational learning also has implications for the understanding and definition of a learning organisation. Defining a learning organisation as one which is an adaptive, responsive or innovative one would be just as meaningful as putting old wine in new bottles. It is my contention that more complex learning processes, which result in continuous improvements and transformations, would be the hallmark of a learning organisation. In the next Chapter, we will discuss a model of organisational learning, which will help develop a more comprehensive understanding of these learning processes and capabilities.

Learning Capabilities

Learning is finding out what you already know.
Doing is demonstrating that you know it.
Teaching is reminding others that they know just
as well as you. You are all learners, doers,
teachers.

—Richard Bach

LEARNING FROM THE PAST

When IBM left India in 1977, DCM Data Products (DCM DP) was in an ideal situation to slide into the vacant slot (Lahiri, 1993c). It was the first Indian company to get into the computer market. It had a reputation for manufacturing reliable, good quality products, and was part of a respectable business house. It had a well-developed designing and manufacturing facility, backed by a strong R&D.

In 1977, the IBM PC had not yet been invented; the industry had not yet moved towards a standard architecture. Computer vendors either sold indigenously designed proprietary machines or sourced them from outside. In India, since government policies were not favourable to sourcing technology from abroad, most companies were forced to design their own machines. The market primarily consisted of large public sector companies and multinationals, which needed large, reliable mainframes, and were willing to pay for the quality. With its strong R&D and established manufacturing base, DCM DP had a clear edge over its rivals (ORG Systems, ECIL, and the fledgling Hindustan Computers Ltd). Its indigenously developed models, like Spectrum, Olympia, and

G32, were perceived as being better designed and of superior quality. DCM DP was clearly slotted to be the market leader, without actually having to do much marketing.

The 1980s saw a change in the scenario for the computer market in India. In August 1981, IBM introduced the IBM PC, which was an open system (unlike Apple's PCs) and could be easily assembled by sourcing the processor chip, operating system and peripherals from suppliers. This not only made IBM the industry standard, but also made computing power cheap and easy to produce. Almost anyone without any R&D and sophisticated manufacturing base could clone IBM-compatible PCs (in fact, by 1986 the worldwide sale of IBM clones exceeded IBM's own sale by more than a million pieces).

Simultaneously, there was a major change in government policy in India in 1984. The new policy allowed Indian companies to bring in CKD and SKD kits from abroad and assemble them in the country. Suddenly, hundreds of small outfits, assembling and selling IBM clones, sprang up. The focus shifted from technology and R&D to wooing of customers. Standardisation of architecture and increased competition gave rise to bitter price wars, and the prices of models tumbled. Keeping costs under control and, at the same time, increasing the market share became imperative to a computer company's survival.

DCM DP, however, continued to make, and attempt to sell, proprietary systems. It remained an R&D-driven organisation, which would first design a product and then try to find customers for it. While some of the old customers, like Unit Trust of India (UTI) and Mahindra & Mahindra (M&M), continued to buy from the company (being stuck with the earlier system), it was becoming increasingly difficult to find new customers.

The company's past experience had also taught it to operate as a functional organisation, in which R&D and manufacturing superseded the marketing function. This structure now became a problem for the company. There was an increasing lack of coordination among the various functions. Often, R&D would come up with products which would not sell; marketing people would book orders, but these could not be delivered; to book larger orders and beat the competition, the sales people would give discounts even when it was unprofitable for the company; the customer support managers would hanker after spare parts and support without considering the cost of support, and so on. For instance, DCM DP had to cancel two major contracts with the Indian Railways for supplying tracking equipment. The marketing department had booked orders and placed them with the purchase department for the components. When the components arrived, R&D was still conceptualising the design. The resultant loss was Rs 35 million.

Similarly, DCM DP lost the market for fast-growing supermini segments. R&D came up with its supermini computer, Cosmos, but found little support from the marketing department, which kept waiting for enquiries; prospecting customers was alien to their past learning. The company got marginalised by the more focused competitors like Wipro, even though its product had a technological edge over others'.

In addition, the company's responsiveness suffered from the tall hierarchy, which it had nurtured; after all, the hierarchical control had helped the company in streamlining its operations in the past. Any message from a trainee sales representative had to pass through the sales representative, the territory manager, the area manager, the branch manager, the regional sales manager, and the sales manager, before reaching the head office. Not only did this delay decisions, but it also cost DCM DP more than Rs 25 million to maintain this network.

It is not surprising that by the latter part of the 1980s DCM DP was completely edged out of the market. It had become a sluggish company, which did not feature in the list of the top 20 Indian computer companies.

SINGLE-LOOP LEARNING

DCM DP provides an excellent example of, what is often described as, single-loop learning and its pitfalls. Just like individuals, organisations also learn from their experiences. Based on the consequences of their actions, they derive an understanding of the actions that lead to successes and those that lead to failures.

To understand this process, let us look at how organisations normally solve problems and take decisions. Faced with problem situation (e.g., a workers' strike, falling sales, competitive threat, and stock-outs) organisations usually rely on their past experience in similar situations (Starbuck, Greve and Hedberg, 1978). The decision is based on the existing rules, systems, or managerial styles, which reflect the earlier experiences and learning of the organisation. A decision which leads to success reinforces past learning, while one which leads to failure often results in some modification in the decision criteria.

Thus, organisations learn to do that which has led to success in the past, and to avoid that which has previously led to failure. This kind of learning has been variously termed as single-loop learning (Argyris and Schon, 1978), lower-level learning (Fiol and Lyles, 1985), adaptive learning (Senge, 1990), and tactical learning Dodgson, 1991). It 'permits the organisation to carry out its present policies or achieve its present objectives (Argyris and Schon, 1978)' without having to make any major qualitative changes, and helps it make successful incremental adaptations to minor environmental fluctuations within a narrow range (Figure 3.1).

This definition of learning views learning as a static product of experience—as lessons derived from successive, but similar, experiences. It provides a focus and consistency to the organisation, and facilitates incremental adaptations to relatively stable and predictable environmental demands. Reiteration of similar patterns of behaviour helps the organisation learn to perform similar tasks in a more efficient manner (e.g., in Boston Consulting Croup's [BCG] 'learning curve'). Obviously, an organisation successfully operating in a market segment or using a particular technology over a long period develops a better system and insight into managing its operations than a newcomer in the field. This is the learning advantage which companies like Hindustan Lever Ltd (HLL) and Procter & Gamble (P&G) would enjoy in the Indian detergent market over newcomers like Henko.

Over time, such learning gets codified in the organisation's strategies, systems, rules and culture. As Hedberg (1981) has noted: 'Organisations do not have brains, but they have cognitive systems and memories. ... Members come and go, and leadership changes, but organisations' memory preserves certain behaviour, mental maps, norms, and values over time.'

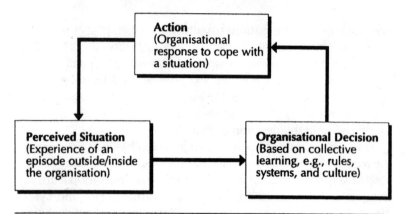

Figure 3.1　**Single-loop learning**

THE TRAP OF SUCCESS

Single-loop learning, however, can help the organisation only in making incremental adjustments but not in developing radical solutions; in fact, more often than not, it hampers the organisation's ability to make 'paradigm-breaking' changes; for example, in envisioning or anticipating new markets and products whose introduction can redefine the very nature of the competitive environment. As with DCM DP, in a changing environment, this form of learning can become more of a liability than an asset for the organisation.

To be fair, DCM DP was not an exception. It merely re-enacted a recurring theme of history (Box 3.1). A number of studies (e.g., Kotter and Haskett, 1992; Marshall, Mobley and Calvert, 1996; Miller, 1990; Shukla, 1994a) support a remarkable cause-and-effect relationship between corporate successes and failures. Miller (1990, 1992) has called this peculiar phenomenon the 'Icarus Complex'—the wax which helped Icarus to make artificial wings and fly was also the cause of his plunge to death in the Aegean Sea. Miller (1992) has noted: 'In fact, it appears that when taken to excess the same things that drive success—focused, tried-and-true strategies, confident leadership, galvanized corporate cultures, and especially the interplay of all these elements—also cause decline.'

BOX 3.1

HOW SUCCESS BREEDS FAILURES

HMT

HMT was once a leader in the watch market. In the 1980s, the watch market started changing from mechanical to quartz technology, and redefined the product as a personal accessory rather than a utility item. HMT, however, continued to focus on its success formula, and produce durable mechanical watches, meant to be utility items. HMT had started producing quartz watches in 1983, but even in 1993, mechanical watches formed 75 per cent of its production (as compared to 15 per cent share of mechanical watches worldwide). It took a newcomer, Titan, to redefine the product and snatch away the market from HMT. By 1994, HMT had a market share of less than 10 per cent as against 70 per cent of Titan-Timex (Krishnamurthy, 1995).

Intercraft

In the early 1980s, Intercraft, the creator of FU's jeans, hit upon the success formula of increasing product range. To provide something for all ages and tastes, it added cotton trousers, shirts, and salwar-kurtas. The number of sales outlets and franchisee were also increased to capture the market in remote cities and towns. However, it was this strategy which became the source of its later troubles; a wide product range diffused brand identity, and a large number of franchisee outlets created logistic problems of control (Lahiri, 1993a).

Nelco

In 1965, Nelco (then known as National Ecko) was one of the leaders in the radio market. When transistors started making an entry, the company ignored it and stuck to its diode sets. Within a few years, the diode was out of the market and by the time the company realised this, its market share was down to 2 per cent (Sharma, 1994).

Remington Rand of India

Till the 1980s, Remington Rand of India was the leader in the manual typewriter market. Its brand was synonymous with the product, and its factories at Howrah, Faridabad and Mysore kept producing at high capacity. In the mid-1980s, the market started shifting to electronic typewriters and word-processing equipment; Remington Rand, however, continued with its manual versions. Things did not change till it started losing to competition, but by then it was too late. After changing ownership twice, and continuing to register losses, in 1993 it was forced to withdraw from the market (Bose and Ghosh, 1991).

Why does success breed failure? The reason is that success reinforces certain behaviours. In his monumental study of the rise and fall of 21 great civilisations, historian Arnold Toynbee noted an identical pattern of failure. He found that the downfall of these civilisations did not occur because of natural disasters or invasions, but because of their own success. Success had made them closed, lethargic, complacent and arrogant. They vanished because their past successes—and the consequent learning—became a stumbling block in the way of adapting and changing with time.

Success creates and reinforces specific mental models discussed in Chapter 2, and teaches firms that certain ways of operating are better than others. It produces strong cultural norms based on the belief that one's past actions were correct—and, worse, that they were the only correct ones. Such strong cultural beliefs, however, also reduce the firm's ability to be flexible and open. New ways of looking at things are discouraged, and past practices are protected with righteous arrogance.

Another consequence of success is that companies tend to 'programme' their past success (Kotter and Heskett, 1992). Once successful, firms try to replicate their achievements and, so, develop clear-cut strategies, structures and processes to be successful on a regular basis. They formalise their effective practices and procedures, start operating around assured markets, standardise their successful products and services, make capital investments in tried and tested technology to achieve economies, and so on.

Inventories, buffers and slack resources are created to insulate the core activities from getting affected by environmental fluctuations. This process of bureaucratisation is further enhanced because success brings growth; and to cope with growth, companies need to bring in people who can retionalise and stabilise activities. Thus, companies hire and select people whose major competence lies in maintaining a status quo, rather than in bringing about change.

Thus, we can see that success (and its 'programming') has an unfortunate consequence; organisations close their options for making a consciously analytical response to the environment; hence, they lose touch with it. They become less sensitive to competitive demands and appear to operate in an imagined environment. Even when they perceive a need to change, their strong culture and rigid routines constrain their choices and actions. Their past learning becomes a hindrance in the way of the necessity of new learning; they must 'unlearn to learn'. As Hedberg (1981) has noted:

> Knowledge grows, and simultaneously it becomes obsolete as reality changes. Understanding involves both learning new knowledge and discarding obsolete and misleading knowledge. The discarding activity—unlearning—is as important a part of understanding as is adding new knowledge. In fact, it seems as if slow unlearning is the crucial weakness of many organisations.

LEARNING HOW TO LEARN

Compare DCM DP's story to that of Richardson Hindustan Ltd (RHL, now Procter & Gamble India Ltd) during the 1980s (Shrikhande, 1985). When Gurucharan Das took over as its President in 1981, the company was in bad shape: profitability was low, labour relations were poor, there was interfunctional rivalry in the top ranks, and the systems and managerial styles were bureaucratic.

RHL managed a turnaround by focusing its efforts on changing the culture and attitudes of people. The process started with an 'unstructured' off-site retreat of the top management team, with the specific aims of reflecting on the culture and ethos of the organisation, setting the goals for change for the company, and of developing a shared perspective at the top. The soul-searching and confrontations during this meeting revealed a startling fact about the company: the top management team had completely divergent perceptions of RHL's problems, goals and objectives. Reflection on these led to major reorganisation (the number of people reporting directly to Gurucharan Das was reduced from 11 to five), and to a decision to change management style (from authoritarian to consultative).

This change cascaded down through a series of workshops and seminars for senior and middle-level managers, sales personnel, supervisory staff, and trade union members. The focus of these efforts was on helping people ponder over their attitudes and behaviour, change their style, and develop better skills for communication and team-building. By the mid-1980s, the effect of the efforts towards change were being felt across the company. As one of RHL's ex-employees has described:

> First of all the way the top management interacted with each other changed considerably and this began filtering down. Senior managers who had been dictatorial and quite unapproachable began to open up and listen to other people's opinions. Tensions between other senior executives began diffusing and they also became approachable. The quality and quantity of information about company plans and strategies given to middle and lower management increased, which gave us all a sense of involvement.

In more tangible terms, by the mid-1980s, RHL had increased its sales by 50 per cent, return on sales from 1.8 to 4.5 per cent, and decreased the earlier high executive turnover to virtually nil. Clearly, the process of organisation-wide introspection had taught RHL new cultural and operating norms, and had freed it from the shackles of its cultural past.

RHL's story makes clear that for any organisation 'learning to unlearn' or 'learning how to learn' is far more important than its past learning. This conceptually contrasting approach views learning as a dynamic process, that is, learning occurs through processes and practices which help the organisation question and change its unconscious assumptions about how it should receive, create, use, evaluate and act on new information (Figure 3.2). In the management literature, this kind of organisational learning has

---

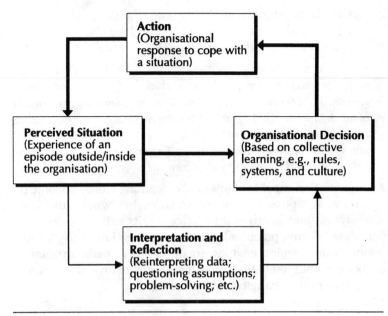

Figure 3.2 **Double-loop learning**

been variously described as double-loop (Argyris and Schon, 1978), higher-level (Fiol and Lyles, 1985), strategic (Dodgson, 1991), generative (Senge, 1990) learning. According to Argyris and Schon (1978):

> Double-loop learning occurs when error is detected and corrected in ways that involve the modification of an organisation's underlying norms, policies and objectives. ... Its members learn about previous contexts for learning. They reflect on and enquire into previous episodes of organisational learning, or failure to learn. They discover what they did that facilitated or inhibited learning, they invent new strategies for learning, they produce these strategies, and they evaluate and generalise what they have produced.

One may liken this process to the operations of an intelligent computer: it does not merely respond to the incoming information according to its existing programming, but is also capable of altering the very nature of its programming in response to qualitatively new information.

As one will notice, the focus of learning is not on *what* the organisation learns, but on *how* this learning occurs. Learning occurs by becoming aware of the nature and quality of one's experiences, rather than by getting bound by them. As Goss, Pascale and Athos (1993) have observed:

> When a company reinvents itself, it must alter the underlying assumptions and invisible premises on which its decisions and actions are based. This context is the sum of all the conclusions that members of the organisation have reached. It is the product of their experience and their interpretations of the past, and it determines the organisation's social behaviour, or culture. ... To reinvent itself, an organisation must first uncover its hidden context.

An organisation capable of this kind of learning would not only be open and receptive to new information, but would also consciously use and interpret it to reflect on its existing operations (strategies, norms, practices), and to create new knowledge. Thus, double-loop learning enables organisations to make qualitative shifts (and not merely incremental and quantitative adjustments) in the face of the changing environment.

LEARNING ORGANISATIONS: A CAPABILITY–BASED VIEW

The capacity of an organisation to reflect on and question its existing operations produces learning. But is the capacity for self-reflection sufficient to create a learning organisation? Actually no. *Self-reflection is a necessary, but not a sufficient, condition for building a learning organisation.*

In fact, some amount of reflection, questioning and/or modification of existing norms and behaviours goes on in organisations all the time. It happens, however, in the unofficial 'unconscious' of the organisation. It happens, for example, when employees privately criticise certain management decisions, when they circumvent official procedure to achieve their targets, when a service engineer improvises a solution to satisfy a customer, or when a shop-floor employee makes a make-shift arrangement to solve a problem, and so on.

Unfortunately, these individual deliberations and improvisations remain largely confined to the individual, or to a small group of people. They are rarely discussed openly in formal forums. Sometimes, even when this knowledge gets disseminated, others

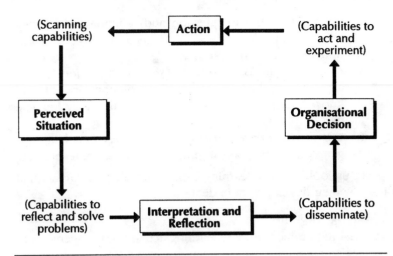

Figure 3.3 **The learning capabilities**

in the organisation lack the procedural sanctions or skills, or courage to try out the new solutions. Thus, even though learning and innovation might take place at the level of the individual or a small group, it has little or no impact on the overall functioning of the organisation.

To build a learning organisation, organisations need to do more than mere self-reflection and problem-solving. Learning organisations require capabilities to link and perform all activities of the learning cycle (Figure 3.3). To do so, they also need to develop other capabilities which facilitate regular acquisition of new information, continuous self-renewal of mental models, dissemination of new learning within the organisation, and experimentation with new responses (DiBella, Nevis and Gould, 1996). The four capabilities critical to completing the learning cycle and, therefore, for building a learning organisation are (Shukla, 1995b):

1. *Scanning capabilities* These are needed to maintain the inflow of relevant and new information, so that the efforts of people are based on valid knowledge of the internal and external business realities.

2. *Capabilities for self-reflection and problem-solving* These enable the organisation to consciously interpret new

information, and to question and redefine the existing business knowledge (e.g., products and markets, procedures, and norms).

3. *Capabilities to disseminate and share information*   These capabilities help distribution of new solutions, insights and knowledge across the organisation, so that they become part of its collective learning.

4. *Capabilities to act and experiment*   These enable the organisation's members to practise newly learnt responses.

Let us look at these learning capabilities and the factors that impede their development in detail.

Scanning Capabilities

The first requirement for any learning activity is the openness to receive and acquire new information. Only if the organisation is open to new, different and challenging information, can it use it for reflection and learning. Astute organisations devise innovative methods for tapping sources, both within and outside the organisation, to stimulate organisational learning. Many organisations conduct customer and employee surveys, do benchmarking, subscribe to patent information, do competitors' analyses, etc., to gain an insight into the changes occurring in their operating environment. Box 3.2 gives examples of the ways in which some Indian companies practise this capability.

While most organisations conduct some kind of internal and/or external audits and surveys, effective organisations fine-tune their scanning mechanisms and information systems to improve the quality of valid and relevant information. The conventional information systems suffer from many shortcomings and are often inadequate for stimulating learning. One can identify three inadequacies which are built into most of the conventional information systems, and the measures organisations need to adopt in order to fine-tune their sensitivity to the internal and external environments.

First, most of the scanning efforts of an organisation focus on *tangible and quantifiable information* and tend to overlook the qualitative and tacit (though significant) details (Starbuck, Greve, and Hedberg, 1978). In contrast, much of the useful information reaches the organisation in intangible and tacit forms. The

BOX 3.2

SCANNING CAPABILITIES

Elbee Courier

Elbee, India's number two courier company, maintains contact with customers on a regular basis. To do so, it has built a huge list of clients—its own as well as those of its rivals. Marketing executives make monthly visits to these clients to check on service levels and problems. These problems are classified under specific heads and assessed on their frequency, and how they can be solved. Often, contact with customers identifies important sources of their satisfaction. For instance, Elbee discovered that next to prompt delivery, customers are concerned about their packages reaching the destination in proper shape (Kelkar, 1994a).

ITC Ltd

ITC uses remote sensing data provided by IRS-1A and IRS-1B satellites. This data provides the company with advanced intelligence on the tobacco harvest in Andhra; hence it can better predict the price of tobacco even before it comes to the market (Kanavi, 1994b).

Modi Xerox

Modi Xerox conducts an annual employee-satisfaction survey of all employees. The survey data is analysed to identify areas for improvements, and to develop improvement plans. The action-planning process directly or indirectly involves almost half the total workforce. Implementation of these action plans is then assessed in the next survey, so that the impact of the action taken can be monitored and evaluated (Parker and Krishnamoorthy, 1993).

Xerox Corporation

Xerox Corporation is known to be the pioneer in benchmarking practices. It has a post of Benchmarking Manager, and a detailed ten-step manual on how benchmarking should be done. During the 1980s, it trained about 200 line managers to continuously keep a tab on changes occurring in pricing, technologies, competition, etc. (Dumaine, 1988; Main, 1992).

members of an organisation acquire a great deal of relevant information when they solve unforeseen problems, deal with customers, tackle breakdowns, read about technological breakthroughs, and so on. The conventional information system formats are not equipped to tap this qualitative database.

Second, an organisation's scanning mechanisms often show a marked *insensitivity to gradual environmental changes*, which extend over a long period of time. As discussed earlier, in reality, most of the significant changes in the environment do not always occur suddenly, but emerge slowly over years or decades (Senge, 1990).

Lastly, and most significantly, the major block to developing scanning capabilities is the *myth of uniqueness*. Organisations often tend to overlook significant information, because it is perceived to be unrelated to their core businesses, products, markets or technologies. For instance, an automobile company may see no reason to study the air-conditioner market, because it is an altogether different industry. In doing so, however, it may also foreclose an opportunity to learn a better system of after-sales service, which some of the air-conditioner manufacturers may be using. Similarly, manufacturing companies can learn a lot from software companies about superior management practices—but they do not do so, because they focus more on the differences than the similarities.

Capabilities for Self-reflection and Problem-solving

The capacity to reflect, reinterpret and solve problems is, of course, the crux of the learning process. It is essential for reviewing existing patterns, establishing more meaningful cause-and-effect linkages, and developing new mental models for understanding problems. Learning depends on encouragement and facilitation of processes which enable employees to question and review existing norms and practices. It is, after all, necessary for people to feel concerned about the shortcomings of the present ways of working before they start exploring other options (Sheldon, 1980).

There are a variety of methods (e.g., building R&D capabilities, training people in problem-solving skills, and forming task forces and project groups to solve specific issues) used by organisations for developing these capabilities (Box 3.3). However, most organisations are based on an unconscious premise that the stability of operations is preferable to change. Hierarchical control, coordination systems, cultural norms and practices, for instance, are rarely questioned because they are considered sacrosanct. Violation of these is discouraged, often penalised, particularly when it is by people lower in the hierarchy. This is a strong deterrent to self-reflective efforts.

BOX 3.3

SELF-REFLECTION AND PROBLEM-SOLVING CAPABILITIES

Jolly Boards

At Jolly Boards each of the 160 employees is given six minutes every month to talk to the entire company about how improvements can be brought about in work systems and practices. He can suggest improvements even in jobs not related to his own. On average, there are 20 suggestions given by each employee every month. The company has found that of the total suggestions given every month, about 600 yield tangible results (Sharma and Gupta, 1994).

Mukund Iron & Steel

Mukund, the 3,700-strong steel-maker, has about 200 Juran Quality Improvement teams and 64 quality circles. These are cross-functional teams, fully empowered to identify and implement process improvements across the organisation. Through regular brainstorming, these groups identify projects, calculate the cost of poor quality, implement solutions, and monitor the savings made through improvements (Dhawan, 1995).

Tandem Computers

The American company Tandem Computers has constituted a formal forum of employees, the 'Critic's SIG'. This is a special interest group with the obligation to criticise all the decisions taken or not taken within the company. By regularly identifying and highlighting shortcomings, this group helps the organisation remain aware of its own functioning (Filipowski, 1991).

The two main factors which discourage self-reflection and problem-solving in organisations are: first, in their efforts to formalise their activities and efforts, most organisations tend to *restrict variety and encourage conformism*. The existing corporate systems of recruitment, training, reward and control (which tend to promote uniformity) can often end up creating a climate in which reflection and questioning is virtually impossible.

Second, corporate introspection is possible only when there is encouragement to think in terms of making changes to meet long-term goals. In most organisations, the *inordinate pressure to meet short-term targets* directs the attention of employees exclusively on measurable tasks, without at all reflecting on how they go about achieving those tasks (Levitt and March, 1988). They get trapped in standard techniques, operating procedures, work norms and rules, and there is no effort to develop new approaches.

Capabilities to Disseminate and Share Information

As discussed earlier, in most organisations the fruits of self-reflection and problem-solving often remain limited only to certain individuals or groups. The capacity to disseminate is necessary for transferring learning to others in the organisation, so that it becomes part of the collective and shared knowledge-base.

The traditional forms of internal corporate communication are mostly formal and low-touch (e.g., house journals, videos, memos, and circulars). These options, however, suffer from one major imperfection: they lack the personal touch and interaction required for stimulating people and creating understanding. Studies (e.g., Nonaka, 1988), on the other hand, show that effective dispersal of learning in the organisation is better achieved through informal and interactive processes. By encouraging collaborative exchange of ideas, organisations allow different viewpoints to be voiced and a common understanding to emerge (Box 3.4).

Unfortunately, conventional organisational set-ups are not suited for free flow of information. They create *functional and hierarchical boundaries* which obstruct ideas and information to move smoothly across the organisation. People at different levels and in different departments learn to follow different goals and priorities; hence, they develop a sensitivity only to specific and

BOX 3.4

INFORMATION DISSEMINATION AND SHARING CAPABILITY

Asian Paints

One of the increasingly popular methods of improving information flow in organisations is through networking computers. Asian Paints Ltd, for example, uses e-mail to instantly communicate production figures, sales targets, etc., across its 14 production plants and distribution centres across the country. Its information system allows it to keep track of the 56 million packs it produces annually (in 40 shades of more than 100 types, sold through thousands of dealers). This helps the company keep the shop-floors completely responsive to market information (Khanna, 1992).

HCL-HP Ltd

In 1992, HCL-HP started using a groupware, which allowed it to tap and pool the knowledge of its service engineers on an on-line basis. Any service engineer could hook into this countrywide data network to find out if a similar problem had been solved earlier by any of his colleagues. Not only did this reduce the solution time from about three days to just four hours, it also gave the company a better service edge over its competitors (Lahiri, 1993b).

Mahindra & Mahindra

At M&M (see also Box 5.1), it is the shop-floor engineers who visit customers across the country twice a month. They videotape their interactions with them, and then play them back to the workmen on the shop-floor. So, a complaint or reaction from a customer that would normally have reached the shop-floor via internal memos from the service engineer, is now heard live by the technical staff (Viswanathan, 1994).

RPG Enterprise

RPG Enterprise uses its diversity and size to create knowledge links among its 35 group companies. The company holds an off-site conference every year, where managers from its 35 companies assemble to compare individual performance on 12 specific parameters (e.g., purchase management, energy saving, and pricing strategy). This exercise helps to identify the best performers in the group, so that these practices can be benchmarked by others. The presentations are followed by site visits (Dhawan, 1996).

limited kinds of information. For instance, the results of a customer-satisfaction survey are unlikely to make much sense to the finance personnel just as cash-flow problems mean little to human resource personnel. So, all information instead of being discussed and shared from the perspective of the total organisation, is interpreted from a parochial viewpoint.

Segmentation of functions and levels also creates groups which often work at cross-purposes (e.g., the production department aims to achieve economies of scale through long production runs, while marketing insists on product variety to cater to the customers' tastes). Such situations encourage *use of information as a political tool.* Information with cross-functional significance is suppressed, distorted, or shared strategically, instead of being used for developing common frameworks for collaboration.

By segmenting work, organisations also force people to *focus on isolated tasks instead of the total work process.* A task-based organisation design segments work, creates artificial boundaries, and separates people whose efforts are naturally interdependent. As a result, the dissemination of new ideas and information gets restricted by narrow task definitions. Recent approaches (e.g., Byrne, 1993; Hammer and Champy, 1994; Ross, 1990; Stewart, 1992) to work design have suggested a more process-based approach to overcome this inadequacy. The aim of these approaches is to make all problem-solving expertise available at the source of the problem. We will discuss the implications of process-based organisation design in a later chapter.

Capabilities to Act and Experiment

There is often a wide gap between what people in an organisation know and believe and its actual practices. Capabilities to act and experiment are essential to bridge this gap because they can translate the available knowledge into relevant actions. This is achieved by developing a focus on core practices, emphasising action orientation, and encouraging employees to act on their convictions (Box 3.5).

BOX 3.5

CAPABILITIES TO ACT AND EXPERIMENT

Citibank India

Staff members deployed for Citibank India's Citiphone service are made to undergo a five-week mandatory training that covers areas like product knowledge and customer interface, and handling customers' problems on the spot. Citibank also empowers its front-line staff to provide full solutions to the customer. Depending on the creditworthiness of the client, Citiphone staff can clear an overdraft of up to Rs 100,000 immediately (Kelkar, 1994a).

HCL Corporation

At HCL Corporation, entrepreneurship is a highly valued quality. Many of the businesses were started by individuals, who recognised new opportunities and got the support from the organisation. For instance, in the early 1980s, Rajendra Pawar spotted a large untapped market in computer education. The company supported him in establishing NIIT, which is the market leader in computer education. Similarly, in the early 1990s, HCL toyed with the idea of diversifying into new businesses—including aircraft manufacturing and aquaculture—and finally decided to go into networking and telecommunications. The plans for the new business, Comnet Systems and Services, were developed by a young management graduate, Vineet Nayar, who became its CEO (Upadhye, 1995).

3M Company

3M is one of the most innovative companies in the world, with a product range of 60,000 items (ranging from Post-it pads to heart-lung machines). Underlying this innovativeness are some of its unique systems which encourage and nurture an entrepreneurial spirit among its members. For instance, the company

---

allows its employees to spend 10–15 per cent of their time and resources on experimenting with ideas, which may not even be a part of 3M's mainstream businesses. If the idea gets translated into a business, the employee becomes the owner of that business (Mitchell, 1989).

What organisational factors discourage employees from taking action and experimenting with new ideas? One major reason is the tendency of organisations to *remain rooted in past success*. People continue practices, that have been successful in the past, even after they have outlived their value and relevance. Familiar and known practices are psychologically secure, whereas a new solution always has a certain amount of risk involved. It is in organisations which value and emphasise short-term results over long-term gains that new solutions are more likely to get sacrificed.

Another reason is the *failure to empower people* who actually perform the work. Organisations encourage powerlessness and inaction (*a*) when they punish failures more than they reward success and, (*b*) when they fail to provide adequate support (information, accountability, resources) to their employees in doing their jobs. Employees lose the motivation to take initiative because they feel that their actions cannot influence the organisational processes.

Lastly, the most critical reason for the gap between the ideas and the action is the *absence of an effective common vision*. An effective organisational vision stimulates the personal aspirations of people and gives larger meaning to their actions. Not only does it motivate employees to take risks, but it also gives a common direction to diverse (and even mutually contradictory) action orientations without stifling one in favour of the other (Nonaka, 1988).

IMPLICATIONS

There are three major implications of the foregoing discussion. First, to really grasp the complexity and potential of organisational learning it is necessary to view it as more than just an exercise in individual capability building. This point is important because many organisations equate the training of their employees with

---

the task of building a learning organisation. To reiterate, organisational learning is more than the cumulative learning of its employees. Besides enhancing the skills and expertise of the employees, learning also moulds the strategies, structure, systems, and work practices of the organisation.

Second, it is necessary to differentiate between the process of organisational learning and the task of building a learning organisation. As discussed, people and groups do learn when they reflect on and question the underlying assumptions of their work. However, organisations need to develop the capabilities of scanning, disseminating, and taking action as well to become learning organisations in the true sense.

Moreover, building a learning organisation is often seen as an exercise in developing (what is often described as) 'a learning culture'. While such a perspective provides useful insights, from the practising manager's point of view, it offers few guidelines for concrete actions. By taking a capability-based view of learning organisations, it is possible to identify specific areas for interventions, and build and implement specific action plans.

Lastly, it is also necessary to appreciate that learning capabilities portray only one aspect of building an organisation that values knowledge as an asset. When organisations develop learning capabilities they learn efficient ways to acquire and process knowledge. However, to effectively leverage on this knowledge organisations must also learn how to use it for building competitive strategy. In the next chapter, we will discuss how organisations can (and do) translate their learning into strategies.

Leveraging on Knowledge

*When I develop my final strategy, I make sure it
is formless and invisible. A formless strategy
cannot be discovered by the best of spies; an
invisible strategy cannot be defeated by the
wisest counsellors. I defeat the enemy by
controlling the situation, but the enemy does not
know how I control it.*

—Sun Tzu

THE KNOWLEDGE WEAVERS[1]

Benetton, the $2 billion Italian fashionwear company, is the
world's biggest knitwear producer (and, naturally, also the world's
largest purchaser of wool). The growth of its complexity can be
assessed from the fact that between 1965 and 1984 its offerings
swelled from 6 models in two colours to 1,200 models in 280
colours. By 1992, it was selling close to a 100 million garments a
year through more than 7,000 franchisee stores, which are spread
across more than 80 countries. Starting with a modest export of 5
per cent of sales in 1970, by the end of the 1980s, exports accounted for more than 70 per cent of its sales.

In spite of such volume and complexity, the company claims: 'If
everyone decided to wear nothing but hats tomorrow, we'd be
ready to produce 50 million hats within a week.'

How does Benetton manage this blend of gigantic operations
and immense complexities with the nimble-footedness and agility
of a small entrepreneurial firm? And that too in an industry which

is one of the most mature, traditional, seasonal, labour-intensive and highly fragmented?

The answer lies in the series of innovations Benetton has introduced in its operations over the years. Here are some examples:

- Though global in its markets, Benetton's manufacturing operations have continued to be concentrated in Italy, accounting for more than 80 per cent of its production. But 95 per cent of its production is done by 700-odd small subcontractors, who receive their raw material or semi-finished goods from Benetton and send the finished products directly to the centralised distribution facility. Benetton, with its manpower of just 1,500 people, focuses mainly on more knowledge-based activities, such as designing, market forecasting, coordination of manufacturing activities, complex chemical processes for creating colours, and CAD–CAM which deliver efficiency and quality in cutting.

- As early as in the mid-1980s, Benetton's designs were being made on video screens, which were linked to computers. Its 15 stylists had a choice of 250 colours to work with, and the designs were converted into data and fed into computerised knitting and cutting machines. A new design could be created and moved into production in a matter of hours. This CAD–CAM system allows the machine to produce 15,000 garments every eight hours, wasting less than 15 per cent of the material.

- Benetton developed a technique, in-house, which allowed it to dye knitted sweaters instead of yarn. The sweaters were knitted in natural colours, and dyed only when the season's preferences had been established by the retailers. Thus, in case market preferences shifted from blue to pink overnight, Benetton could respond quickly and without having to maintain an obsolete inventory.

- Since the early 1980s, Benetton has developed its own private information network which connects retailers to the headquarters in Ponzano. Using advanced telecommunications, Benetton receives data on sales trends around the world on a 'real-time' basis. Production is hooked to market forecasts. If a particular item, colour, size or model is selling specially well or poorly, production can be almost immediately shifted in response to the market information.

- In 1984, Benetton built its fully computerised warehouse, which services all the factories. Staffed with only 7 people, this warehouse can process 36,000 boxes every day. A lorry driver only has to insert a card in a slot at the loading bay; the rest is done by robots, who can read bar codes. The shipment is retrieved from storage and transferred to the lorry on conveyors.

Benetton can be described as a maker of fashion knitwear and garments—which, of course, it is. But if one looks into the heart of the enterprise, it thrives on acquiring, processing and utilising knowledge.

Gordon Moore, the co-founder and chairman of the chip-maker Intel Corporation, once noted (quoted in Quinn, 1992): 'If you look at our semiconductors and melt them down for silicon, that's a tiny fraction of cost. The rest is intellect and mistakes.' Benetton can make an identical statement about itself: more than in manufacturing and marketing, the secret of Benetton's success lies in its ability to efficiently collect, codify, transform, and transfer information and knowledge into products.

THE POWER OF KNOWLEDGE

Benetton, of course, is not the only company (or even one of these few companies) which derives its competitive leverage from knowledge-based activities. The ability to capitalise on knowledge lies behind the success of almost all responsive companies. This is true not only for high-tech companies in the business of computers or biotechnology, but for companies in all industries. Invariably, all smart companies practise knowledge-based activities in some form or the other. For instance, they conduct customer surveys, involve suppliers in designing, invest in R&D, do benchmarking, implement suggestion schemes and quality circles, collaborate and learn from competitors, train their people, or indulge in industrial espionage. The aim of such activities essentially is to maximise the company's knowledge-base and use it as a competitive weapon.

If, for instance, a customer checks in into any of the Welcom Group hotels for the second time, he can expect the services to meet his specific needs (the kind of room and food he prefers, whether he likes tea or coffee in the morning, etc.), without having to ask for them. The organisation is able to offer such customised service because of its investment in a valuable knowledge-based asset; the hotel chain maintains a centralised networked database for each of its guests that records their likes and dislikes, room and food preferences, level of service and entertainment expected, buying patterns, etc., which can be accessed instantly once a guest checks in (Lahiri and Datta, 1993–94).

What such examples (Box 4.1) highlight is the basic premise of knowledge-based competition: that the ability of a company to acquire, generate and utilise its knowledge and information resources is vital for its success. There is also a growing awareness that what is true for organisations is also true for nations. Not only managers and academicians, but politicians and policy-makers, too, are increasingly coming to appreciate the critical role of information and knowledge in a nation's economic growth. There is an emerging consensus that even for a resource-rich country, sustained economic growth is not possible unless it achieves a 60 per cent literacy rate, that is to say, unless it invests in building the knowledge and information-processing capabilities of its citizens.

That is also the reason why building up the 'information infrastructure' has suddenly become a priority for fast-developing nations. The smoother the flow of information in a society, the faster is its economic progress. According to studies conducted by the International Telecommunication Union (cited in Srinivas and Sharma, 1994), for every dollar spent on telecommunications, productivity goes up by $2, and every new telephone line adds $3,700 to GDP. Another UN study, cited in one of the McKinsey reports, found that among the developing countries, a 1 per cent growth in telephone lines leads to economic growth of nearly 3 per cent (*Business Today*, 1995).

BOX 4.1

HOW COMPANIES LEVERAGE ON KNOWLEDGE

AT&T

Since 1986, AT&T has been using an on-line in-house computer service called AAA—Access to AT&T Analysts—to help employees learn from the hundreds of thousands of workers with specialised insight on the competitive arena. Staffers fill out a questionnaire identifying their areas of expertise, among other things. If a user needs specialised information on, say, PBX technology or MCI, he can log in the key words and get a list of in-house experts on the subject, along with their job titles and phone numbers. The network also operates in other directions: If a staffer uncovers a titbit about a subject or a competitor, he can 'broadcast' it on the AAA system to employees on long-distance operations (Teitelbaum, 1992).

Nike and Reebok

Nike and Reebok are world leaders in the sports and footwear market. Nike, however, owns only one small factory that makes some parts of sneakers; Reebok does not own a plant. They have prospered by concentrating on their core strength: their knowledge of designing and marketing high-tech, fashionable sportswear and footwear. Virtually all production is sourced out to suppliers in Taiwan, South Korea, and other Asian countries by the two rivals. It is not surprising that the two companies are listed in the *Fortune Service 500* (Tully, 1993).

Pepsico

Many of Pepsico's major product successes are derived from its knowledge of products of some small regional or local competitor. For instance, its three products, Doritos, Tostitos, and Sabritos, with combined sales of over $1 billion, were copied from the competing chippers in the west coast of California. Similarly, Slice, one of the biggest new brands of soft drinks in history, was an idea borrowed from a Japanese soft drink competitor; and, Pan Pizza, which accounts for a $500 million business for Pizza Hut, was an idea that originated from several local Pizzerias in Chicago (Pearson, 1989).

Procter & Gamble

Procter & Gamble's (P&G) introduction of the calcium-enriched orange juice Citrus Hill was an outcome of the knowledge-networking among its various divisions. Researchers in the Health Care division, in the course of developing drugs for bone diseases, found a worsening of calcium deficiency among American adults. For P&G's Food and Beverages division this was an opportunity for product improvement. But there was a problem: how to add calcium to orange juice and still retain a palatable taste. The solution came from the Laundry and Detergent division, which had long known how to suspend calcium particles in liquid soap products (Labick, 1989).

Whirlpool

Every year the American domestic appliance maker Whirlpool mails its Standardized Appliance Measurement Satisfaction (SAMS) survey to 180,000 households. Customers are asked to rate all their appliances on a dozen attributes. If a competitor's product gets a better ranking, the engineers at Whirlpool rip it apart and reverse engineer it to find out the reason. These features are then built in into their future designs. It is this kind of knowledge which helped Whirlpool come out with its VIP Crisp model, Europe's largest selling micro-oven (Solo, 1991).

The implications of this interest in knowledge can be summarised in terms of the following three principles of knowledge-based competition:

1. Knowledge is important, and is the end point of all learning.

2. A viable learning strategy is one which seeks to create value by investing in the company's knowledge-based assets.

3. A knowledge-based asset is information stored/encoded in the minds of people, or in the company's strategies, systems, or products/technology.

THE ENIGMA OF KNOWLEDGE

Surprisingly, in spite of the focus on intangibles (knowledge, information, and learning), there is no comprehensive framework which tells us how knowledge can be used as a competitive weapon. There is little consensus on the right way to build a strategy around an organisation's knowledge-based assets.

To make the right strategic choice about how to use one's knowledge-based assets, it is important to comprehend the nature of knowledge. One cannot apply the same rules to knowledge, as one applies to the tangible assets (e.g., plant, machinery, money). Consider the following qualities of knowledge:

- Unlike the conventional tangible assets, knowledge is abstract and intangible. Therefore, measuring and assessing a company's knowledge-based assets is a difficult task.

- Unlike other assets, knowledge moves from one place to another. Its migratory characteristic imposes special demands and challenges on the organisation for retaining it.

- Knowledge not only moves, but it can move simultaneously in many directions; also it can be found in many places at the same time.

- Lastly, knowledge is multifaceted. For instance, the knowledge-base of a chemical technologist is very different from that of a chef, a tea-taster, a security analyst. The difference is not merely in the specific disciplines of these experts, but in the very form and texture of the knowledge these experts use. Similarly, the nature of the knowledge which forms the strength of a consultancy firm is qualitatively distinct from that utilised by, say, a mass manufacturer.

Naturally, to use knowledge as a competitive resource, it is essential to look at it in a more differentiated manner, and to understand its various forms and aspects. The story of the development of float glass technology (Quinn, 1988) provides an excellent example of the different forms and stages through which knowledge must grow in order to become useful and relevant.

FLOAT GLASS TECHNOLOGY

For almost two hundred years, till the early part of the twentieth century, the technology for producing float glass (used for making mirrors and windows) had remained largely unchanged. The traditional method was not only cumbersome, but was also becoming cost-ineffective. To produce flat distortion-free glass, molten glass had to be rolled into a plate, then ground and polished. In this process, as much as 15–20 per cent of the material was wasted due to grinding; in addition, rejections at the final stage were very high due to the distortions which would invariably creep in into the end-product. Meanwhile, the advent of cars increased the demand for cheap distortion-free float glass. The invention of the float glass technology by Sir Alastair Pilkington was a major breakthrough in solving this problem.

When he joined Pilkington Brothers, Sir Alastair Pilkington (he was not related to the owners of the company) started dreaming of combining the continuous flow, fire polish, and inexpensiveness of sheet with distortion-free polished plate. As he wrote later: 'A large part of innovation is, in fact, becoming aware of what is desirable. [Then you] are ready in your mind to germinate the seed of a new idea. ... I don't know why, but I have always wanted to invent something.'

Although he had identified what he wanted, his conscious efforts to develop a process to achieve it were disrupted. Being technical director, he had to give his time to routine functions. However, he found regular work boring and uninvolving, and often spent his time thinking about how to create a polished float glass without distortions.

Like many other inventors, the solution to the problem dawned on him when he was not actually attending to it. One day in June 1952, while helping his wife wash dishes in the kitchen, he was struck by what he saw. The idea that a flat, polished finish could be produced by floating molten glass on a liquid surface came to him as he watched the grease solidify on the water in the sink. To pour molten glass onto a bed of molten tin was a direct corollary to that.

Alastair quickly drew the sketches of the new process, got verbal approval for the project from the Pilkington board, and had a pilot plant built to start the experiment in. The project was given 'highest possible priority so that either success or failure would be decided as early as possible'. A small team, consisting of a few engineers, a foreman and a workman, was put together to start working on the project. A remote site was chosen for the pilot plant, and the team was sworn to secrecy. According to Sir Alastair: 'One thing we were good at was security. People easily fail to understand that the greatest secret about a new process is not how to do it, but that it can be done.'

The actual development of the process, however, took seven years and cost $ 7 million. While the team was able to produce the first sample of float glass within six months, the process was neither commercially viable yet nor free from quality defects. In the meanwhile, the board took the decision that float glass would be launched only if it could replace the conventional plate glass, not merely improve upon it.

As the project went ahead, the team experimented and learned more and more about the process (e.g., in molten state tin oxidised quickly and produced a crystalline scale on the glass surface, and impurities in tin could react with glass). Over the years, they were able to refine the process to eradicate most such problems. It was possible to produce large quantities of float glass at reasonable cost. One problem, however, still remained: while they could produce smooth glass plates, it was difficult to remove the bubbles which would often creep in into the glass. Unless the process was further refined, this could make the production cost-ineffective.

The problem got resolved by accident. One day in mid-1958, the spout from which the molten glass was poured broke. Suddenly, the bubbles, which had been a problem for more than a year, disappeared miraculously. The team was able to produce its first sheet of beautifully smooth saleable glass at the rate of about a thousand tonnes a week. Fortunately, Pilkington was able to dispose of even the fruits of this accident. The company sold the float glass sheets to British automotive companies as wind-shields, letting them know that they were produced by 'a new process'. The public announcement of the process was made in January 1959.

Pilkington Brothers patented the technology but chose not to have a monopoly. Instead, they generously licensed their technology to their competitors worldwide. So effective was this strategy that after 1962 every new glass-producing facility built in the world was using the float process. By 1974, float glass virtually replaced polished plate glass worldwide. Hence, the company earned much more than it would have if it had put up its own plants to make float glass.

THE MATURATION OF KNOWLEDGE

As one can see, to become competitively viable, the knowledge of float glass technology had to evolve through a number of stages. Broadly, its maturation process can be traced on two dimensions (Figure 4.1). First, it matured from a hazy implicit thought to a manifest palpable form. It originated from an insight, but became usable only when it could be codified in the form of a tangible technological process. This process embodies the first generalisation about the competitive value of knowledge: *to become useful, knowledge must evolve from a tacit to an explicit form.*

Second, once it lost its elusive and tacit character, it started losing its proprietary nature and started becoming commonly available. By planning and guiding the nature and direction of its dispersal, Pilkington Glass was able to manage its competitive worth. This process defines the second generalisation about the competitive value of knowledge: *to derive value from knowledge, it is necessary to manage the nature and extent of its distribution to others.*

As will be discussed in the subsequent sections, the maturation of knowledge can be comprehended as its movement across these two dimensions. In this growth cycle, knowledge can be understood as evolving through four stages.[2] Each stage is characterised by knowledge in specific forms. These are:

1. *Discovered knowledge* This is the first stage in the life-cycle of knowledge. It is characterised by knowledge created through the discovery of an idea, need or possibility. At this stage, it is largely invisible and confined in the mind of one person.

2. *Codified knowledge* To survive and become useful, the discovered knowledge must get embodied in something physical. The level of codification may vary, depending on whether it is codified in skills, documents or a product.

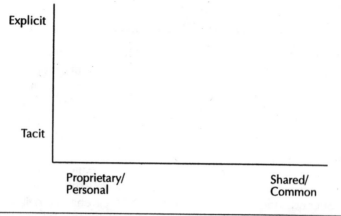

Figure 4.1 **The two dimensions of the knowledge maturation process**

3. *Migratory knowledge* The more codified a knowledge becomes, the greater is its capacity to move. At this stage, knowledge becomes independent of the owner and starts disseminating.

4. *Invisible knowledge* The more the knowledge spreads, the more it loses its special character and is taken for granted. It becomes commonplace; but by becoming the standard, it changes the nature of the social and business reality.

In the following sections, we will look at each of these stages of the evolution of knowledge and the competitive value and nature of the corresponding forms of knowledge.

Discovered Knowledge

Knowledge in its most primal form is personal and tacit. It is concealed, subjective, and often buried in the mind of one person. In this form, often, neither the purpose nor the method of using the knowledge is clear.

Discovered knowledge is mostly acquired through a creative process in which the person (through an insight, accident, experiment or plain effort) extracts a unique idea from a reality which others (and earlier, he himself too) had taken for granted. Sir Alastair's discovery of the need for a more efficient process for making plate glass, and his insight in the kitchen were instances of this tacit form of unformed knowledge.

BOX 4.2

DISCOVERY OF NEW KNOWLEDGE

The process of creative discovery involves a reinterpretation of reality to identify the new potentials and needs latent in it. Consider the following examples:

Just-in-Time System

When Taiichi Ohno, the creator of the Just-in-Time (JIT) system, went on a trip to the US, he was struck by the efficiency of the supermarkets. What appealed to him was that here was a system that made items available in the right quantities and at the right time. He realised that applying this to the factory would yield tremendous benefit in terms of time and low inventories. Ohno studied how the supermarkets operate and, in 1953, for the first time applied this system to the Toyota machine shop in the main plant (Ohno, 1992).

Band-Aid

Band-Aid, one of Johnson & Johnson's leading products, was invented by one of its employees, Dickson, as an efficient first-aid measure for his accident-prone wife, Josephine. Josephine Dickson was an extremely clumsy person, prone to cutting herself with the kitchen knife with unbelievable frequency. One day Dickson sat down with gauze, tapes and a pair of scissors; he cut the tape into small strips and stuck a little square of gauze in the middle of each strip. Now, every time Josephine cut herself it took just 30 seconds to put on this readymade bandage. When some people in the company heard about this bandage, they sensed a new product possibility. After initial trial runs, in 1924 the company installed machines to mass produce bandaging tapes, and started marketing them under the name of Band-Aid (Garrison, 1977).

Assembly Line Technology

In 1912, Henry Ford was fascinated by what he saw during a visit to the Chicago slaughter house. The carcasses were hanging on hooks mounted on a monorail. After each person performed his job, he would push the carcass to the next station. Ford was very impressed by the efficiency of this method of working. He could see that if the same principle was applied in the factory, it would revolutionise manufacturing technology. He implemented this insight in the production of magnetos, thus, started the world's first assembly line in the Ford Highland Park Plant (Bogan and English, 1994).

Traveller's Cheques

In 1890, James Fargo, president of American Express, went on a trip to Europe. He felt very offended because he could not get his cheques encashed in any of the European banks. He reasoned that this must be a problem experienced by the American tourists in Europe. Sensing an opportunity, on his return he asked one of his employees, Marcellus Berry, to develop a method for drawing money in a strange place. Berry's efforts led to the introduction of traveller's cheques by American Express in 1891. Marcellus Berry was awarded four copyrights for his invention (Garrison, 1977).

As the examples in Box 4.2 show, in all these (and such other) cases, new knowledge was created because the person picked up fuzzy signals from the environment and decided to forgo the 'common-sense' interpretation and acceptance of reality in the given form (Figure 4.2). In the initial stage, knowledge is personal and tacit in nature; it is mostly confined to one person, and gets manifested either in intuitive hunches, or through certain 'action-centred skills' (Zuboff, 1988), or in a pattern of behaviour. In organisations, it exists in the form of intangible assets, emergent technologies, skills or insights possessed by a few individuals, and in the sensing of fuzzy opportunities. According to Nonaka (1991):

> Tacit knowledge is highly personal. It is hard to formalise and, therefore, difficult to communicate to others. ... Tacit knowledge is so deeply rooted in action and an individual's commitment to a specific context—a craft or profession, a particular technology or

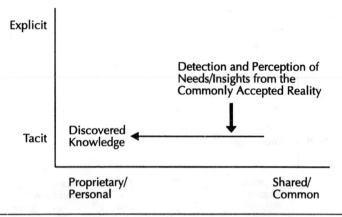

Figure 4.2 **The emergence of discovered knowledge**

product market, or the activities of a workgroup or a team. Tacit knowledge consists partly of technical skills—the kind of informal, hard-to-pin-down skills captured in terms of 'know-how'. A master craftsman after years of experience develops a wealth of expertise 'at his fingertips'. But he is often unable to articulate the scientific or technical principle behind what he knows.

Codified Knowledge

Tacit knowledge is abstract and intangible and can be used only when it gets codified in some tangible form. As long as it remains tacit, it is difficult to share, transfer, or use for economic purposes. To become useful, tacit knowledge must become explicit in its form. Like mind and consciousness, knowledge requires a hardware (the brain) through which it can become discernible. For instance, the expression and use of a graphic designer's knowledge is contingent upon the availability of the required computer and software. After all, Sir Alastair's insight would have been useless if he had not developed it into a technological process, or if he had not had the infrastructure (his team, the pilot plant, the resources) for doing so.

Similarly, consider another interesting story: the genesis of the American textile industry (Anderson, 1992; Williamson, 1985). About two hundred years back, the mass migration of skilled labour from Europe to America was having a devastating effect on European industries. Great Britain went to the extent of

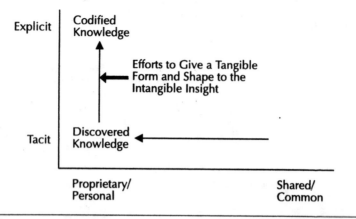

Figure 4.3   The transformation of discovered knowledge into codified knowledge

formulating laws to prohibit migration of skilled textile workers. But in 1790, Samuel Slater, an Englishman, disguised himself as a farmhand and managed to escape. When he arrived in Rhode Island, Slater had a problem. In England, he had worked in mills designed by Richard A. Arkwright. These were the mills he knew and had managed in England as Arkwright's partner. In America, however, since no such mills existed, Slater spent his early years there building cotton textile mills. Thus was founded the American cotton industry. So, to put his knowledge to use Slater had to create the hardware (the mills) that complemented his skills before he could put them to optimal use.

When knowledge becomes explicit it gets codified in objects, rules, systems, methods (Figure 4.3). For instance, this book codifies and embodies the insights, findings and thoughts of many people. Similarly, an accounting system is codified knowledge in an objective form, or a technical manual captures the knowledge required to use a technological process. Even a machine, as economist Kenneth Boulding (1996) has pointed out, is 'frozen knowledge'. Similarly, brand, trademark, patent, technology and service are explicit expressions of the knowledge acquired and generated by organisations or individuals—and of the investments made in doing so.

Codification of knowledge helps in understanding product-based competition. Since a product codifies knowledge, the more knowledge a product embodies, the greater will be its value. For instance, when Lipton introduced the Taaza brand of tea, the product incorporated a crucial bit of knowledge about the Indian tea market: in this country of tea-drinkers, tastes differ widely across regions (e.g., the blend preferred in the western part of India is very different from what a north Indian would like). Lipton built in this knowledge into its product by customising Taaza's polypouches into seven different blends to cater to regional tastes—and captured a large share in a highly fragmented market (Rai, 1993).

By codifying more knowledge in a product, one increases the utility and user-friendliness of that knowledge. A word processor, for instance, is more useful than a manual typewriter because it compresses and codifies more knowledge than the latter. Similarly, compare a textbook on accounting with an accounting application software. The textbook mainly codifies *what* an accounting system is and provides general guidelines for developing and using one. The application software not only codifies the textbook knowledge, but also the heuristics which define *how* this knowledge can be customised for specific use. Naturally, the application software has greater utility than a textbook.

Migratory Knowledge

Codification of knowledge, while increasing its utility, has another consequence: it becomes mobile, capable of migrating and propagating. Whirlpool, Samuel Slater, etc., were instances of this property of knowledge. Once packaged—in a design, manual, formula, machinery, or in the mind of a person—knowledge can move quickly and, often simultaneously, in many directions. Patented knowledge can be stolen (or replicated when the patent expires), products can be reverse-engineered, systems can be copied, and experts can leave or be hired by competitors. As Boisot (1992) has noted: 'Codified knowledge is also inherently more diffusable than uncodified knowledge. That is to say, as it gains in utility, it loses in scarcity. ... Information, especially when codified, is hard to domesticate; it likes to roam'.

There are three far-reaching business implications of the migratory knowledge. First, being mobile, knowledge constitutes a critical challenge in managing knowledge-based resources. Since knowledge can exist in more than one place at one time, loss of these resources may not even be detected for a long time—maybe only when they start reappearing in a tangible form elsewhere. For instance, in the late 1970s, many researchers started leaving the Xerox research facility (see the Xerox case in Part II of this book). For the company it only meant a loss of some disgruntled hi-fi computer scientists. But when these scientists left, they also carried with them the knowledge of many of Xerox's radical innovations in the field of computing (windows, mouse, Microsoft Word, etc.). The company realised what it had lost only when these innovations started appearing in the products of Apple and Microsoft (Uttal, 1983).

Second, knowledge migration also helps to explain why imitators make good innovators and formidable competitors. A company's knowledge moves with its products. It is easy for the competitor to reverse engineer it, copy the knowledge it embodies, and even enhance it by adding more knowledge components. One company invents, others imitate, add more knowledge to the product, and move in to capture the market. According to one report (Sakai, 1990), it was the ability to master the dynamics of knowledge migration that enabled Japanese companies to compete successfully with US companies:

> They [the Japanese companies] seem to have an uncanny ability ... to borrow ideas, rework them, and produce something totally 'new' from a product that originated elsewhere. More often than not, they shrink the new product, add a few gadgets, and find a way to sell it for half what the industry was expecting. ... For records here's what happens behind the scene. Let's say a US company has something to produce—a piece of electronic machinery, for example. It licenses the production to a big Japanese company, which then subcontracts the job to one of the group companies. By the time the original contract is finished, the subcontractor has a clone product ready to go, and the US company will soon discover that it has a new rival.

Imitation (or, if you prefer, *benchmarking* or *innovative adaptation*) allows the company to start at the maximum know-ledge-level of its competitors. For example, in the mid-1980s, when Ford

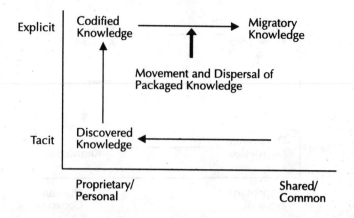

Figure 4.4 **Codified knowledge acquires migratory characteristics**

decided to introduce a new car model it identified 400 features considered desirable by the customers. Then it set about finding the cars with the best of each, matching or improving on each of these features. For instance, it copied the halogen headlamps and tilt wheel from Honda's Accord; door handles, fuel economy system, and front bench for triple-seating from Chevy Lumina; window controls and tail-light bulbs from Nissan Maxima; remote radio controls from Pontiac Grand Prix, and so on. The result of this mass-scale—but systematic—imitation was the launch of Ford's best selling model, Taurus (Main, 1992).

Lastly, when knowledge migrates, it tends to become less scarce (Figure 4.4). In changing its nature from personal to common, it also starts losing its unique competitive value. For instance, while Pilkington Glass made float glass into the industry norm by selectively sharing its technology, by the beginning of the 1980s the company had started facing competition from others (e.g., Asahi Glass of Japan, Guardian of Europe) on its home ground. During 1981–82, due to imports, Pilkington's share in the UK float glass market had come down from 80 to around 68 per cent.

Invisible Knowledge

As knowledge spreads and is widely used, it ceases to be discernible. The more commonly it is used, the more it gets absorbed

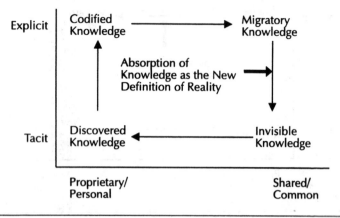

Figure 4.5 **How migratory knowledge gradually becomes invisible knowledge**

and embedded in the habits and life-styles of its users—and the less one is likely to notice it (Figure 4.5). It is surprising how much of the knowledge people interact with and use in their day-to-day life is taken for granted.

Again, for instance, consider this book. It embodies a mind-boggling plethora of streams of knowledge. At the most obvious level, it contains the ideas of many people who view knowledge as something to think about—and have documented and published their thoughts in various journals, periodicals or books. But that is only the tiniest bit of knowledge which went into the making of this book. There are also other kinds of knowledge whose origin and development can be traced back over centuries. The contributions to this book in its present form also come from the knowledge about the various chemical (e.g., bleaching) and mechanical (e.g., rolling) processes necessary for treating wood to make paper. Then, there is the stream of knowledge of printing technology, which made it possible to mass publish books inexpensively and of good quality. Added to these were also those creative individuals (ranging from Charles Babbage and Boole to Steve Jobs, researchers in Xerox PARC, etc.), who created a medium which allowed one to capture one's thoughts on a computer screen (not to forget Pete Petersen's team at WordPerfect Corporation, who developed a user-friendly software for word processing). Thus, a variety of knowledge-disciplines (written language, paper-making, printing, electricity, computers, application software, production and marketing of books, etc.) are invisibly woven into the creation of this book.

As knowledge spreads and becomes ubiquitous, it also becomes invisible and embedded in the unconscious of the user system. But in becoming so, it redefines the nature of ground reality and the rules of the competitive game; it becomes the norm instead of remaining an exception.

Since invisible knowledge creates new norms, it helps in understanding the changes that significantly transform a social system (a society, market environment, or an organisation). Unlike the codified form of knowledge (which *adds* value to a system's activities and outputs), when knowledge becomes invisible, it *creates* new value; consider, for instance, the mutation which IBM PC brought in into the computer market (Badaracco, 1991).

In August 1981, IBM introduced its IBM PC. Since IBM had to invent the PC in a hurry (to make an entry into the PC market opened by Apple), the team assigned to the job broke many IBM conventions. It produced a system which was not proprietary. IBM PC was an easy system to clone for several reasons. First, it was an open system, allowing anyone to write software for it. Second, its operating system, made by Microsoft, was available off-the-shelf. Even the chip, the 8088 processor chip, which lay at the heart of the PC, was manufactured by Intel, and could be bought for $10–15.

Almost overnight, hundreds of companies in the US, Europe and Asia were selling clones—often straightforward copies—of IBM PC. The imitators also copied IBM's PC-XT and PC-AT, which were introduced later. In 1986, the worldwide IBM clone sale was 3.6 million pieces, exceeding IBM's own sale by nearly a million. By default, IBM PC had become the industry standard, and could beat the early pioneer, Apple, on its own turf.

The way in which invisible knowledge is created and used inside an organisation helps explain the difference between transient and durable knowledge. When a company's knowledge is codified in products, documents and individuals, it is likely to be transient and migratory. But, an organisation's invisible knowledge is more durable and establishes new linkages for creating a 'constellation of values' (Normann and Ramirez, 1993). For instance, Honda's knowledge-base of IC engine technology has retained its relevance across the company's range of products (marine engines, motorcycles, cars, power generators, lawnmowers) or, Casio's expertise in semiconductors and digital display has helped it to produce a wide range of products such as calculators, low-cost word processors, pocket televisions, musical instruments and watches.

Similarly, since its inception in the mid-1980s, Titan Industries has acquired two competencies—how to market watches as personal/luxury goods, and how to master micro-precision technology. In 1995, it started planning to leverage on these knowledge-based assets to diversify into new areas of business. The 5000-strong watch retail outlets were to be used for selling items like jewellery, ceramics, leather goods, and crystalware, and the company planned to use its micro-precision engineering skills to make micro items for medical instruments and automobile companies (Urs, 1995).

Prahalad and Hamel (1990) have termed this kind of knowledge as a company's 'core competence', and defined it as the 'collective learning' of the organisation. Such knowledge is less likely to migrate or be stolen, because it is deeply embedded in an organisation's memory—not only in what an organisation does, but also in how it does it. According to Badaracco (1991): 'Some knowledge is not migratory. It moves very slowly ... embedded knowledge resides primarily in specialised relationships among individuals and groups and in the particular norms, attitudes, information flows, and ways to making decisions that shape their dealing with each other.'

COMPETING ON PROPRIETARY KNOWLEDGE

So, how should one compete through knowledge? According to the conventional competitive logic, if one has a valuable and useful knowledge-based asset (knowledge codified in a product, technology, system, etc.) advantage lies in limiting its availability to others, particularly to competitors. Most companies restrict competitors' access to their knowledge-based assets by getting

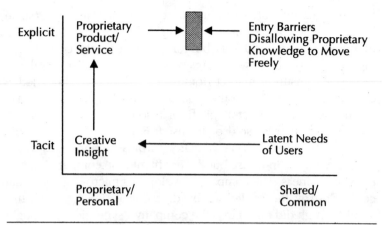

Figure 4.6 **Competitive strategy based on proprietary knowledge**

these patented. This allows them to control the movement of these assets, and to charge rent for use of the knowledge.

There are a number of examples which suggest that the strategic advantage lies in keeping the knowledge proprietary. That is, a knowledge-based strategy must rely on erecting barriers to keep the knowledge from reaching competitors. Companies patent their products and processes, keep their strategies and tactics secret, register their brands and trademarks, and spend billions of dollars on legal battles over issues ranging from the right to use copper rivets in jeans (which the jeans manufacturer Levi claims is its intellectual property) to drug formulations and use of application software with the objective of restricting the migration and dispersal of their codified knowledge (Figure 4.6).

In practice, usually it is difficult for organisations to police the violation of their patents. After all, for a computer company, it is impossible to monitor—and file suits against—India's 500-odd illegal manufacturers of computer systems, who comprise roughly 70 per cent of the market (Abreu, 1994). That is why firms often resort to creating entry barriers by encrypting their knowledge in forms which are difficult to imitate. For instance, in 1993, when VIP Industries found that its soft luggage product, Skybags, was losing out to the innumerable low-cost imitators, it used its technological strength and changed the handles of the bag from fabric to moulded plastic. For VIP Industries it did not add any cost (since these handles were already being used for the company's moulded luggage products), but for the imitators the cost of tooling to replicate the new Skybags was too high (Kelkar, 1994b).

Besides ensuring market dominance, proprietary knowledge derives its value from another source. If the company cannot use it (because of lack of strategic fit or resources), the designs and patent rights can be sold or licensed. For instance, since 1968, General Electric (GE) has sold many 'surplus' technologies which were developed in-house but did not fit into the company's major lines of business. The company developed a micro-organism that could destroy the spilled oil by digesting it. Even though this breakthrough did not fit into the company's synergies, GE fought a patent case to retain the knowledge, but, having won the case, put it up for sale (Ford and Ryan, 1981).

The message is clear: develop the knowledge, patent it, and keep it proprietary. Share it only if you get paid for it, because that is where your profits lie.

THE NEW RULES OF THE GAME

In spite of all such precautions it is not easy (in fact, it seems perhaps impossible) to keep the knowledge privy from and inaccessible· to others—particularly competitors. A small example highlights this fact. In 1983, Hitachi admitted in a US court that its employees had tried to purchase the design workbooks of one of IBM's computers. Though the company was found guilty and had to pay a fine, a few months later IBM lost out on a major contract to equip the Social Security Administration with computers—the winning bid was Hitachi's (Schweizer, 1996).

Hitachi's example is not a rarity. One of the studies commissioned by the American Society of Industrial Security found that theft of proprietary knowledge from US corporations had increased by 260 per cent between 1985 and 1993 (Schweizer, 1996). What makes it difficult to control and contain the incidence of industrial espionage is the fact that often nation-states are as much involved in corporate and economic intelligence as are corporate organisations (during the October 1995 US–Japanese negotiations on car imports, the CIA and the National Security

Agency are said to have assisted US trade negotiators by eavesdropping on the conversations of Japanese officials). Another study quoted by Schweizer (1996) shows that, on average, every month three incidents of theft of proprietary information from US companies involved foreign entities.

Clearly, notwithstanding intellectual property rights (IPRs) and GATT negotiations, once codified, knowledge has a tendency to move, travel and become public.

Smart organisations understand and accept the natural tendency of knowledge to move from private to public domains. Instead of resisting the migration and keeping their knowledge proprietary, organisations support and facilitate its wider dispersal. By accelerating its distribution they gain their competitive edge by making it invisible, that is, ensuring its absorption in the users' repertoire. These organisations leverage on their knowledge-based assets to create new industry norms and standards (Figure 4.7). For example, Microsoft's success has primarily relied on its ability to create new industry standards (Ichbish and Knepper, 1992; see Box 4.3). Similarly, consider the story of the HP LaserJet Printer (Huey, 1991): In 1983, Hewlett-Packard assigned a team of seven engineers to Boise, Idaho, to develop a desktop laser printer for the office market. The only other laser printer available at the time was for mainframes, costing minimum $100,000.

In developing this product, the Boise team threw all HP norms to the winds—to develop all required technology itself, keep it proprietary, and design in a way that it can be used only with other HP equipment. In contrast, the team licensed Canon's technology for the printer's engines, used Motorola chips for designing the electronic formatting components, had Microsoft and others write the software, and got Canon to assemble some of the final product in Japan. This was not real engineering, only architecting, but it saved time and money.

What also got flouted were the norms of proprietary standards, which kept one brand of machine from working with another brand. The printer was designed to work not only with HP150 PCs, but also with other non-HP PCs. It took a major battle within the company before the HP LaserJet printer could be unveiled connected to an IBM PC in the HP booth at the Comdex show in

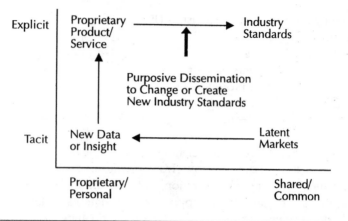

Figure 4.7 **Competitive strategy based on industry standards**

1984. The first LaserJet printer was priced at only $3,495. By 1990, the company had sold more than four million units, and acquired 70 per cent of the US and 55 per cent of the world printer market share. HP LaserJet did to the printer market what IBM PC had done to the PC market.

KNOWLEDGE-BASED COMPETITION: THE INVISIBLE STRATEGY

While creating new industry standards (establishing new product/ service standards, redefining the market, etc.) gives an edge to an organisation, by itself it is not sufficient for sustained competitive advantage. As discussed earlier, to establish new standards, knowledge must be made freely available to others. The obvious danger in following such a strategy is that one can lose out to a competitor who is quick to replicate (and even improve upon) the offering of the innovator.

That is why the ultimate knowledge-based strategy relies not on leveraging on one or a few innovations, but on the ability to innovate continuously and rapidly (Box 4.4). Having set new industry norms, the company must continuously revise them— often making the earlier ones obsolete—in order to stay ahead of the competition (Figure 4.8). Sony, for instance, operates in a market where competition from imitators is rampant. To offset this,

BOX 4.3

HOW MICROSOFT MADE MS-DOS THE INDUSTRY STANDARD

When Microsoft launched its operating system, MS-DOS, in 1981, nine of ten software programs were being written for the older competing operating system, CP/M. Microsoft followed three strategies to establish DOS as the new industry standard (Ichbiah and Knepper, 1992). First, it did not completely differentiate its product from the competing one. There were a number of similarities between MS-DOS and CP/M; any software which could run on CP/M could also run on DOS. Thus, CP/M users would not have any difficulty in switching over to DOS.

Second, Microsoft established DOS as the interface that made applications and languages independent of the hardware. All programs written according to DOS conventions could function on any machine supporting DOS. This enabled Microsoft to offer its operating system to several hundred different computer manufacturers.

Third, Microsoft priced DOS at a fourth of the price of CP/M ($60 against $240) making it well within the reach of the lower end of the market (which is invariably the largest in any market).

Very soon, major application software (e.g., Lotus 1-2-3, dBase, Wordstar) were being written for DOS, which further enhanced the 'constellation of values' DOS could deliver. Even though CP/M's new version, CP/M-86, was technically better than DOS (it allowed multi-tasking—one could simultaneously receive electronic messages, print a document, and work on a spreadsheet), by the end of 1983, 99 per cent of the installed bases of PCs were using MS-DOS. By the end of the 1980s, there were 30 million MS-DOS machines in the market.

80 per cent of Sony's nearly 1,000 product launches every year offer improved versions of the existing products to make the earlier models obsolete. When it introduced Walkman in 1979, thousands of companies around the world started making and selling pocket-size audio cassette players. Sony managed to maintain its

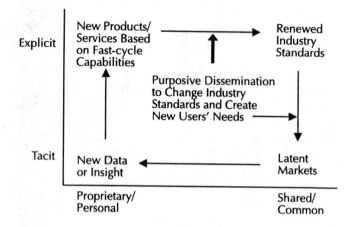

Explicit	New Products/ Services Based on Fast-cycle Capabilities	Renewed Industry Standards
	Purposive Dissemination to Change Industry Standards and Create New Users' Needs	
Tacit	New Data or Insight	Latent Markets
	Proprietary/ Personal	Shared/ Common

Figure 4.8 **How organisations use invisible knowledge for competitive leverage**

leadership by continuously introducing upgraded models of Walkman at a phenomenal rate—between 1979 and 1992, it had introduced 227 new models of Walkman, that is, about one new model every three weeks! (Peters, 1992; Schlender, 1992).

BOX 4.4

SUPER CASSETTES INDUSTRIES: CREATING NEW STANDARDS

During the late 1980s, the definition of the market for music was limited to the urban elites, who bought LP records (at that time, considered superior to audio cassettes) for their classical value. People bought music of enduring value. The market leaders, HMV and Polydor, focused mainly on producing LPs for the upper end of the market.

In this scenario, Super Cassettes Industries (of T-Series fame) built its business by identifying a latent niche in the market, which had been largely neglected by the established music companies (Sheikh, 1992; Shekhar and Vijay, 1990). Super Cassettes' strategy was based on a simple insight: namely, music—

---

particularly film music and folk songs—has an appeal for the majority of people, who are not much concerned about quality, and have a low purchasing power.

Super Cassettes started in 1978 by recording and selling Bhojpuri songs, and then shifted to selling pre-recorded cassettes of Hindi film songs. At that time, T-Series was known for its low-quality and cheap cassettes. It sold a cassette for Rs 16–17 (with a margin of Re 1), as against Rs 40–45 of the major companies. Focusing its product for 'the man on the street', T-Series sold its cassettes through roadside kiosks and grocery stores. It was a low-price–high-volume strategy. Between 1978 and 1985, the turnover of Super Cassettes had increased from Rs 60,000 to about Rs 200 million.

Having created a market, the company soon found others flooding the market. To keep ahead of the competition, Super Cassettes kept on changing the market with one innovation after the other. When competition started emerging from other 'low-cost me-too' producers, the company identified loopholes in the Copyright Act, and came out with 'version recorded' cassettes (old popular songs recorded by new up-and-coming voices). When others started version recording, Super Cassettes started bidding for music rights for films, even before the music was composed. When that became common, Super Cassettes again changed the rules of the game by innovating the concept of 'Music Bank'. This bank contained recorded songs composed and sung by new artists. Any film producer could buy and retrofit the songs in their films for a price. From being a buyer of music rights, Super Cassettes became a seller of music rights.

Simultaneously, it ploughed back its profits into improving its manufacturing facilities and the quality of its products. It also diversified its portfolio to include regional songs. In the 1990s, it also made a foray into film production. By 1992, Super Cassettes had grown into a Rs 2,150 million company, employing 7,000 people, churning out 150,000 cassettes every day. It had nearly 6,800 titles in audio cassettes, and more than two-thirds of the share of the audio cassettes market.

The capability to continuously innovate and transform industry standards is dependent on more than just the quality of an organisation's accumulated knowledge-base. Rather, it hinges on the ability of the organisation to effectively generate, acquire and utilise this knowledge. When, for instance, in 1981, Honda decided to snatch back its position as the world's largest producer of motorcycles from Yamaha (Stalk, 1988), it unleashed a blitz of new models. In just 18 months, Honda introduced or replaced 113 models (as compared to 37 models by Yamaha), effectively turning its product line twice. In the process Honda not only set new standards of technological sophistication (by introducing four-valve engines, composite, direct drive, and other features), but also transformed the motorcycle from a utility item into a fashion product. The competition between Honda and Yamaha was based not on the quality of the product, but on the superiority of capabilities. Honda won because it proved superior in its capability to create and leverage on invisible knowledge.

To leverage on invisible knowledge in the market an organisation requires another kind of invisible knowledge as well. This is the knowledge which is deeply embedded in its social architecture (Spender, 1996). It resides in those specialised relationships among groups and individuals that frame an organisation's operating practices—in its particular norms and attitudes; in its information flow; in its ways of performing tasks, making decisions, and formulating goals; and in the way in which its people and teams have learned to behave and interact with each other.

The replication of social architecture by competitors is far from easy. These practices are mostly rooted in certain group-based skills, which are difficult to capture by tangible description. Rosenberg and Frischtak (1985) in their study of technology transfer have noted this characteristic of an organisation's invisible knowledge:

> Technology might be more carefully conceptualised as a quantum of knowledge retained by individual teams of specialised personnel. This knowledge, resulting from their accumulated experience in design, production, and investment activities. . . . It is acquired in problem-solving and trouble-shooting activities within the firm, remaining there in a substantially unmodified state.

This very nature of invisible knowledge also explains the confidence of Gordon Forward, the CEO of Chaparral Steel (see case in Part II of this book) in allowing competitors to freely visit the plant and talk to people: 'We will be giving away nothing because they can't take it home with them.'

Notes

1. By all standards, Benetton is an ideal target organisation for strategic benchmarking, specially because it achieved success in a highly traditional and fragmented industry. Reader may like to refer to Belusi (1987), Bruce (1987), Heskett and Signorelli (1989), Ketelhohn (1993a, 1993b), and Signorelli and Heskett (1989) for more details.

2. I have borrowed generously from the works of Max Boisot (1983, 1987, 1991, 1992, 1993) and Ikujiro Nonaka (1988, 1990, 1991; Nonaka and Takeuchi, 1995) in formulating the framework for the knowledge-based competition described in this chapter. While Boisot's work deals primarily with cultural learning and technology strategy, his insights were very useful in understanding the nature of knowledge. Also, Nonaka's ideas on tapping the tacit knowledge-base of organisations were very valuable for comprehending the development of knowledge.

PART II

The Benchmarks

Introduction

Based on the discussion so far, learning organisations would be specifically characterised by processes and mechanisms which:

(*a*) expose the organisations to new information, whether created internally (through R&D, employee surveys, etc.) or acquired from the external environment (from customer feedback, competitive benchmarking, etc.);

(*b*) create receptivity in the organisation, so that it can consciously interpret and codify this information into business-relevant knowledge (new products and markets, procedures, work norms, etc.);

(*c*) enable the organisation to disseminate this knowledge across the organisation, so that it becomes its collective learning; and,

(*d*) institutionalise the above knowledge-based activities, so that they can be carried out on a conscious and continuing basis.

This theoretical understanding, however, does not help much in defining and describing what a learning organisation would be like, as a living system. The case studies in this part of the book were developed with the aim of providing precisely this 'feel' or 'flavour' of the learning organisation. The aim was also to benchmark the processes and mechanisms that enable an organisation to learn smarter and faster.

WHY THESE ORGANISATIONS?

Given the fact that 'learning organisation' is still a term in search of a definition, the search for a learning organisation was a difficult task. Even though (in the previous chapters) We have dealt with the nature and value of corporate learning, there are a number of unanswered questions, for example:

- What is a learning organisation?
- What are its defining features?
- How does a company become a learning organisation?
- How would one recognise a learning organisation if one comes across one?

There was one simple assumption in selecting the organisations in this part of the book as benchmarks of learning organisations. Namely, any organisation making quantum (discontinuous) changes in itself, or showing consistent growth in a discontinuous environment, would be doing so through some kind of learning.

Thus, the selection of an organisation for studying as a prototype of a learning organisation was based on the following criteria:

1. the company had grown through showing a qualitative change in its strategic paradigm (e.g., changes in product/market strategy, creation of a new market, strategic turn-around, acquisition/innovation of new technology; and/or
2. the company had successfully transformed itself in a highly competitive and fast-changing industrial/service sector; and/or
3. the company had been successful in carving out a niche for itself in a fast-changing technological environment (e.g., companies operating in the information, communication, and biotechnology sectors); and/or
4. the company had successfully managed through environ-mental discontinuities effected due to politico-economic changes.

The implicit aim of selecting these organisations was also to establish the universal relevance of the learning processes; that is, organisations, irrespective of their size, nature, products, technology, etc., will show similarity in their learning processes. Correspondingly, the six companies studied are quite varied in nature and context. The aim was also to explore and establish the similarities in the ways in which these organisations managed their knowledge-based activities.

BRIEF DESCRIPTIONS OF THE COMPANIES[1]

The variety and diversity of these companies can be assessed from the following briefs:

Asea Brown Boveri

Asea Brown Boveri (ABB) was formed in 1987 through the transnational merger of Asea of Sweden and Brown Boveri & Company (BBC) of Switzerland, thus creating a truly transnational company with operations spread over 140 countries. It had a turnover of $17 billion and a staggering portfolio of businesses which included generators, powerlines, toxic-waste treatment plants, diesel locomotives, telecommunications, oil pipelines, robots, leasing, and insurance.

Within two years of its formation, ABB had increased its profits by 53 per cent and sales by 54 per cent and emerged as the largest electrical engineering company in Europe. By 1990, it had gained one-third market share of the European power equipment market, and captured over 20 per cent of the world's business. It had also become the largest producer of railway vehicles. In the US, its product range in the power equipment market was broader than was offered by either Westinghouse or General Electric (GE) (GE described ABB as 'the most formidable adversary it has ever faced').

ABB grew at an astonishing pace in a very short time through a series of mergers and acquisitions. By 1993, the ABB empire comprised nearly 1,300 companies, structured as 5,000 profit centres, with a combined turnover of $32 billion. More than its size and complexity, ABB had also emerged as a model for the new kind of organisations in a global economy.

This case focuses on the mechanisms and processes used by ABB to achieve fast-paced global growth in the face of established industry leaders (e.g., GE, Siemens, Hitachi, Mitsubishi).

British Airways

Till the late 1970s, British Airways (BA) was a typical bureaucratic, public sector organisation, known for its inefficiency and increasing losses. Its lack of service orientation was well known to the extent that its acronym, BA, was often referred to stand for 'Bloody Awful'.

The transformation of BA started when it was privatised in the 1980s and made a dramatic turnaround to become the world's most profitable international carrier. In 1992 it was the only European airline to make profits ($500 million, on a sales revenue of $9 billion). Its market value stood at $3.85 billion.

Between 1991 and 1992 it moved up 397 places on the *Business Week Global 1000* list, to emerge as the world's largest airline. It had an enviable fleet size of 230 aircraft, which reached over 150 destinations in over 70 countries. It was considered the 'airline of the future', and even won the *Business Traveller* magazine's Best Airline Overall for its customer orientation.

This case analyses the learning strategies used by BA to achieve this turnaround.

Chaparral Steel

Chaparral Steel is a mini steel plant near Texas, which was established in 1975. By 1990, it had emerged as the world's least cost steel producer, with a productivity rate of 1,100 tonnes per worker, which is the highest in the world. With an annual production of 1.5 million tonnes, it had also become America's tenth largest steel producer.

Over the years, Chaparral Steel has become a benchmark for many companies worldwide for its numerous achievements. Since its inception, it has maintained an annual productivity growth rate of 25–40 per cent. It is also the only US company, and the second company outside Japan, which has the right to use the Japan's Industrial Standard certification on its products.

This case explores the learning mechanisms and processes which make continuous improvements possible at Chaparral Steel.

Citicorp

Changes in Citicorp's performance and reputation started during the 1970s. By the 1990s, it had changed its image from that of a traditional conservative bank to that of an innovative, competitive, and customer-oriented organisation. Between 1970 and 1984, it became the largest American bank, and the fifteenth largest in the world. Its assets exceeded $210 billion and it had a growth rate of profit of 258 per cent. Its operations accounted for 35 million outstanding charge and credits around the world. It had also become a truly global financial company; in 1990, 40 per cent of its revenue came from its operations in more than 90 countries outside the US.

During the past decade, it has consistently featured among the top ten banks in terms of profits, ability to arrange loans and note facilities, developing new financial solutions, providing information service, and pricing sophisticated transactions. In 1993, for the fifteenth consecutive year, it was polled the best bank for arranging foreign exchange by *Euromoney*; it has access to 140 currencies. In 1993, it was also voted as the second-best bank for trading and arranging syndicate loans.

This case focuses on the organisational mechanisms used by the bank to maintain its lead as an innovative organisation.

General Electric

General Electric (GE) is one of the world's leading producers of items ranging from light bulbs and refrigerators to locomotives and power plants. It manages more credit cards than American Express, and owns more commercial aircraft than American Airlines. Since the early 1980s GE has undergone a successful cultural transformation. During this period, its real earning per share shot up to an average of 7.6 per cent, as compared to 4.9 per cent and 1.6 per cent during the 1970s and 1960s, respectively. Between 1983 and 1993, its sales rose from $26.5 billion to $62 billion; in 1993, it ranked as the world's largest company in terms of assets, and the fourth most profitable one; and, its market value went up from $12 billion to $65 billion.

This case analyses the practices and processes innovated by GE to achieve this strategic and cultural transformation.

Xerox

Xerox is a unique organisation with the history of being a market leader, losing its position to the point of becoming extinct, and then rebounding back to success. During the 1970s and mid-1980s, Xerox lost its market to competitors, with its market share dipping from more than 90 per cent to about 13 per cent, and its profits plummeting from $1.15 billion in 1980 to $290 million in 1984. During the mid-1980s, it achieved a turnaround; it regained its market, doubled its turnover from $8.98 billion in 1986 to $18.3 billion in 1993, and increased its assets from less than $10 billion to about $34 billion. Between 1982 and 1993 its rank in the *Fortune 500* list went up from 42 to 21.

This case traces Xerox's history to focus on the role of the learning processes in its turnaround.

Notes

1. These cases were developed by me while in Europe as a Visiting Professor under the Euro-India Cooperation and Exchange Programme. The assistance extended by the European Federation of Management Development (Brussels) and Escuela Superior de Administracion y Direccion de Empresas (ESADE, Barcelona) is gratefully acknowledged.

Asea Brown Boveri: The Global Learning Company[1]

ABB . . . an entirely new breed of corporation, breaking ground for the postmultinational company of the 1990s.

—Business Week
23 July 1990

I'm anxious to set an example. ABB will be a success story. We have no choice. There is no way back.

—Percy Barnevik
CEO, Asea Brown Boveri

THE BEGINNING

Asea Brown Boveri (ABB) was formed in 1987 through the transnational merger of two well-established 'national' companies, Asea of Sweden (established in 1890) and Brown Boveri & Company (BBC, established in 1891) of Switzerland. It was a marriage of two equal and opposite, but complementary, competitors in the electrical equipment market: ABB was a fast-growing market-oriented company and had achieved an unbelievable turnaround since 1980; BBC was Switzerland's largest, but barely profitable, manufacturing company in the business of making heavy-duty transformers and generators with major assets in West Germany. Merged together as ABB, they created Europe's largest electrical engineering company, capitalising on the strengths gained from both the parent companies—the superior profit performance of Asea, and the relatively strong order book and technological strength of BBC. Further, the merger created an organisation phenomenal in its business diversity and global in its reach. ABB's businesses include generators, powerlines, toxic-waste treatment plants, systems for steel-making, oil pipelines, diesel locomotives and coaches, telecommunications, robots, leasing, and insurance. At the time of its formation, its operations were spread over 140 countries, with a workforce comprising 240,000 people, and its annual turnover was over $17 billion.

Even though the merger took place in the background of a history of failures of transnational mergers in Europe (e.g., Pirelli–Dunlop, Citroen–Fiat, and VFW–Fokker), ABB defied the dismal forecasts. Over the years, it has become the world's leading supplier in the electric power equipment industry—its sales in the power equipment sector far outstrip those of the well-known names such as Mitsubishi, General Electric (GE), Hitachi, and Siemens. By 1990, it had captured as much as a third of the European market and over 20 per cent of the world's business. In the US, it offers a broader line of power equipment than either Westinghouse or GE. It also emerged as the largest maker of railway vehicles.

The most remarkable feature of ABB's growth is the speed with which it consolidated its position. Within a couple of years of its formation, ABB had acquired or taken minority stakes in about 60 companies worldwide, and invested about $3.6 billion. Between 1988 and 1991, its score on acquisitions and divestments figured 126 and 55, respectively. The acquisitions and minority stakes included companies such as Norway's Elektrisk Bureau AS, Stromberg in Finland, Marelli, Adda, Sadelmi and Franco Tosi Group in Italy, Cadermesa, Cenemesa, and Conelec in Spain; railway equipment manufacturers such as BREL (UK) and Thyssen (Germany), to name a few. There were also prize catches, such as the acquisitions of Westinghouse's transmission and distribution operations involving 25 factories (bringing up its profits by 38 per cent in two years), and the $1.6 billion Combustion Engineering (outsmarting negotiations of Alsthom of France). These two acquisitions also established ABB as one of the major competitors in the US, prompting one of GE's senior executives to describe it as 'the most formidable adversary it has ever faced'. In making these acquisitions, ABB's strategy was directed on building up a long-term advantage of market share rather than focusing on short-term profits. Nevertheless, by 1989, ABB's sales had risen by 54 per cent, and profits had gone up by 53 per cent.

In 1990, ABB started expanding in Eastern Europe, investing in companies such as the turbine manufacturer Zamech in Poland, and in Bergman-Borsig and Automated Plant Assembly in East Germany. It also has plans to spend $1 billion over the next five years to expand its activities in Asia (where it hopes to achieve a third of its sales by the year 2000). In fact, in August 1993, ABB restructured itself into three regions, Asia, America, and Europe, By 1993, the ABB empire comprised about 1,300 companies, structured as 5,000 profit centres, with 218,000 employees, and a combined turnover of $32 billion across 140 countries.

A NEW ORGANISATIONAL PARADIGM

The financial victories, however, are only one part of ABB's success. Of greater importance is the fact that ABB has emerged as the metaphor of a new kind of organisation—a stateless, borderless organisation in an increasingly deregulated, borderless world. It is the prototype of the successful corporation of the future, when trade barriers would be down, and large transnational operations would be the economically most viable option. However, ABB is different from the traditional multinational organisations, lacking what has often been described as the 'headquarters mentality'—in its Zurich headquarters, there are barely 100 professionals, most of the eight (earlier 12) members of the top executive committee are based in different parts of the world, and its 1,300 companies are registered as national companies in the countries in which they operate. According to ABB's CEO, Percy Barnevik: 'We are a federation of national companies with a global coordination center. ... We are not homeless. We are a company with many homes.'

Yet, ABB successfully manages to integrate and coordinate the extreme diversity of its products, operating regions and national markets. Following the dictum of 'think global, act local', its organising principle aims to combine a global perspective for product and performance strategies, with freedom to its companies to focus on and serve their home market effectively. Building on this premise, it has innovated a unique set of organisational structures, systems and practices. These allow it, on the one hand, to leverage on its core technologies and achieve global economies of scales, and on the other, they give it the competitive edge to maintain local market presence and responsiveness to specific customer requirements. The ability to be simultaneously global and local has created a new form of post-multinational organisation, the 'multi-domestic organisation'.

Related to this aspect of ABB's functioning is the way in which it contends with, and is able to incorporate in itself, strategies, systems, and processes traditionally considered mutually incompatible. According to Barnevik: 'ABB is an organisation with three internal contradictions. We want to be global and local, big and small, radically decentralised with centralised reporting and control. If we resolve these contradictions, we create real organisational advantage.'

ABB has been able to achieve more than that. It has created an organisational model that transcends these contradictions and incompatibilities, and represents a new paradigm for organising. In many ways, ABB exemplifies a transformational leap in the very concept of organisation and management.

ORGANISING FOR CONTINUOUS TRANSFORMATION

To appreciate the significance of ABB's organising principle, it is necessary to understand how its size, diversity, and global reach simultaneously create opportunities for phenomenal growth and generate enormous pressures in order to remain strategically and financially viable. Its vast size and global operations, for instance, not only allow it to achieve global economies, thus giving it a competitive advantage, but also give it certain clout to manage its relationship with its environment (e.g., with annual purchases of millions of dollars worth of raw material, ABB can, and does, insist with suppliers on zero-defect and just-in-time deliveries, and on highly competitive rates). Its size, however, presents the danger of the company becoming atrophied and rigid, making it difficult to effectively respond to environmental shifts and local market demands.

Similarly, ABB's product market and regional diversity enables it to have access to a larger variety of resources, talents and solutions than many of its competitors. It can select, transfer, and utilise expertise and technology from around the world to meet specific local requirements. On the other hand, this diversity also strains the organisation's integrating mechanisms. It creates enormous pressure on the organisation to effectively control and coordinate its operations.

ABB's way of dealing with these challenges has been to evolve an organising principle, which is as simple (and as cryptic), as described by Barnevik: 'The only way to structure complex global organisation is to make it as simple and local as possible.' In the following sections, we will discuss some of the salient processes and mechanisms ABB uses to implement this oxymoronic principle.

'Shocking' Systemic Changes

In spite of its size and complexity, ABB is a leader-led company. Like many highly entrepreneurial organisations, its policies and practices bear a distinct mark of its tough and action-oriented visionary CEO, Percy Barnevik. He has been described as a disbeliever of incremental growth, as hard-driven but informal and easily accessible, a stickler for detail, with sharp and swift analytical skills, and a self-confessed workaholic who is willing to gamble on a vision. His own words describe the working philosophy behind ABB's functioning:

> I would say that in any business decision, 90 per cent of success is execution, 10 per cent is strategy. And of that 10 per cent, only 2 per cent is real analysis. Eight per cent is the guts to take uncomfortable decisions, to say we will close the plant anyway; it is the vision to see beyond analysis, to ask whether one really believes. ... Vision and guts—this is what strategic analysis is all about.

Barnevik's vision is to create an organisation, that can grow in a fast-changing world, even if it means demolishing accepted barriers and norms. Throughout his career, Barnevik has used this vision and gut-based maverick approach consistently, and successfully, in building success. Much before becoming the CEO of ABB, Barnevik, an MBA from Gothenburg School of Economics and a computer scientist from Standford, showed the skills for achieving quantum growth. Between 1975 and 1979, he managed to turnaround and triple Swedish steel-maker Sandvik's US sales. In 1980, this earned him an offer from Swedish industrialist Marcus Wallenberg to run Asea. As the chief of Asea, Barnevik again achieved a stunning turnaround (fourfold increase in revenues, tenfold in profits, and twentyfold in market value), which made him something of an industrial folk-hero in Sweden. His approach was always similar to the one he has used in turning around ABB's new acquisitions: get over hard decisions quickly, swiftly implement a new structure, mobilise and empower latent talents within the organisation, and demand high targets.

Even the consolidation of the Asea–BBC merger followed the same pattern. It was architectured by the strategic vision of Barnevik, who 'saw [the] writing on the wall' when, in 1986, the concept of 'a united Europe' began to seem an imminent reality. It meant not merely greater opportunity for transnational operations; rather, to him, it amounted to transnational operations becoming a necessity for corporate survival. To avoid political obstacles, the merger was planned secretly and swiftly. In Barnevik's words:

> We had no choice but to do it secretly and to do it quickly. . . . There were no lawyers, no auditors, no environmental investigations, and no due diligence. Sure, we tried to value assets as best as we could. But then we had to make the move, with an extremely thin legal document, because we were absolutely convinced of the strategic merit.

Once the merger was announced Barnevik created an internal task force of five top managers, each from the former companies—the Manhattan Project—and gave them just six weeks to design the new structure. In two months the main features of the new structure—breaking down ABB into four business segments with 40 different business areas, setting up of the matrix, closing down of certain plants, designating new regional and national geographical alignments—were broadly agreed upon. The top team, including Barnevik and Thomas Gasser (ABB's deputy CEO and the chief of the erstwhile BBC), personally interviewed hundreds of managers from the ranks to head the operations. The new organisational leaders (described by Barnevik as 'tough-skinned individuals, who were fast on their feet, had good technical and commercial background and had demonstrated ability to lead others') were identified and given new responsibilities, and, within the next three months, the restructuring of the merger was complete—a remarkable feat, given the size and complexity of ABB. According to Barnevik, to make real changes:

> You have to be factual, quick and neutral. And you have to move boldly. You must avoid the 'investigation trap'—you can't postpone tough decisions by studying them to death. You can't permit a 'honeymoon' of small changes over a year or two. A long series of small changes just prolongs the pain.

ABB's leadership has repeated this swift, bold and revolutionary approach to implement change in most of its plants. For instance, the German operations of BBC were curtailed and drastically reorganised in a single phase. Similarly, in its Polish joint venture, ABB Zamech, reorganisation of the plant into discrete profit centres was completed in just four weeks. For one, quick decisions and implementation, of course, preclude a long period of uncertainty for people, and do not allow time for opposition to form. The other reason is the underlying belief held by organisational leaders that for change to take place, it is necessary to give just the right amount of shock to the system. As Eberhard von Kroeber; ABB's European regional director, explains: 'You need a big chemical reaction to change a company operating with an outdated view of the world. ... The important thing is to judge how much you can rock the boat without sinking it.'

Along with this tough-minded (and to many, reckless) decisiveness is an attitude of experimentation and acceptance of failures as a part of the process. While managers are expected to make fast and good decisions, the risk of making a mistake, is also not ignored. This organisational attitude is neatly summed up in, what is known within ABB as, the 'Barnevik 7-3 formula': it is better to make swift decisions and be right seven out of ten times than to waste time trying to achieve perfection. Barnevik says: 'I'd rather be roughly right and fast than exactly right and slow. We apply these principles everywhere we go. ... Why emphasise speed at the expense of precision? Because the costs of delay are vastly greater than the costs of occasional mistakes.'

The tolerance of failures, however, has another outcome as well. It encourages individuals to take legitimate risks, and learn from their mistakes without feeling defensive about them, and it creates a climate where individual enterprise and an innovative spirit can flourish.

Empowering the Bottomline

A unique aspect of ABB's functioning is that, for a leader- and vision-driven organisation, it is remarkably decentralised, and relies heavily on pushing initiative down to the grassroots level. In 1993, Barnevik initiated a new experiment in Sweden—decentralising to the level of the factory-floor worker in an attempt to break down the traditional hierarchy and promote continuous learning and teamwork without formal supervision. More autonomy was given to small work groups, and job rotation was introduced to increase versatility. While it is too early to judge the results of the experiment, the change did bring down instances of sick leave in the workforce from 25 per cent to 42 per cent.

The empowerment strategy is most obvious in the way in which ABB manages to turn around its acquisitions. Once the restructuring has been done and the structures of the profit centres, with budgets, performance and control mechanisms, have been worked out, the company is virtually handed over to the local management. While ABB's expertise from around the world is available to support the change process, it is never used for running operations directly. Rather, the attempt is to bring decision-making down to the shop-floor level.

For instance, when ABB took over Zamech (Poland's leading manufacturer of steam turbines, transmission gears, marine equipment, and steal casting), it was made clear that there will be no 'rescue team' from Western Europe or from headquarters; all managerial positions from CEO down will be managed by the local managers of Zamech. Moreover, the selection was made without consideration for seniority or rank; the premium was on identifying a team of young, ambitious and innovative leadership talent and handing over the responsibilities of managing to them. Once this pack of Zamech's 'hungry wolves' was assembled, the members were given the task of identifying the priority issues for consolidating the company's health (e.g., reorganising and retraining the sales force, streamlining operations, slashing down cycle-time, redesigning factory layout, planning and taking up responsibilities for championing these projects, and creating a steering committee to monitor progress. Barbara Kux, president of ABB's Power Venture, and one of the chief negotiators of Polish acquisitions, described the group thus: 'We put in place a management team that lacked the standard business tools. They didn't know what cash flow was, they didn't understand much about marketing. But their ambition was incredible. You could feel their hunger to excel.'

To overcome this 'minor' shortcoming (of managers not knowing the basic management tools and techniques!), ABB created a 'mini MBA program' to introduce managers to the basic business concepts of strategy, marketing, finance, manufacturing, and human resources. The course was conducted over weekends by the faculty of the French business school INSEAD. The structure of the course was similar to that of other MBA courses. In addition, ABB placed a team of its functional and technological experts from around the world at the disposal of the local management to provide support, if solicited. The members of this expert panel did not live in Poland but visited the plant frequently, and offered advice when needed. In less than a year, ABB Zamech was reporting significant progress—financial reporting systems had taken root, cycle time for production of steam turbines was reduced by half, and as part of streamlining the operations, a 20 per cent reduction in factory layout was achieved.

ABB has applied the empowerment strategy time and again to its different companies, and has reaped its numerous advantages: it creates conditions for leveraging on the existing expertise, skills, and knowledge of organisational members, which often lies untapped below layers of hierarchy and control systems; it stimulates people to feel motivated to excel in their performance and to achieve organisational goals; and, perhaps most importantly, it pushes the responsibility for change to the lowest levels of actual control.

The key to this empowerment lies also in the structural autonomy given to the units and operating centres. This is ensured in many ways. First, ABB's structure does not allow any bureaucratic hurdles to develop at the headquarters' level. For an organisation of ABB's size and expanse, the staff at its headquarters in Zurich is infinitesimally small, consisting of barely a hundred professionals. In fact, reducing the number of headquarters staff is the first part of all ABB's restructuring: in its Finnish subsidiary Stromberg, it was reduced from 880 to 25, in the Mannheim operations, from 1,600 to 100, and at Cumbustion Engineering, based in Stamford, Connecticut, from 600 to 100. According to Barnevik:

> You can go into any traditionally centralised corporation and cut its headquarters staff by 90% in one year. You spin off 30% of the staff into freestanding service centers that perform real work—treasury functions, legal services—and charge for it. You decentralise 30% of the staff—human resources, for example—by pushing them into line organisation. The 30% disappear through head count reductions.

Second, the 1,300 ABB companies around the world are not mere extensions of the parent company. Each company is a separate legal entity, with separate balance sheets and responsibility for cash flow and dividends. While this places greater pressure on the local management to perform, it also gives them freedom to take their own decisions, such as for launching products, making design changes, altering production methods, without seeking permission from headquarters. Likewise, the business operations handled by these companies constitute, in all, about 5,000 profit centres (some with as few as ten people), each an autonomous business unit, responsible for its own profitability and accountable for its own failure. This small-business atmosphere, which combines a complete operational autonomy with finite, but challenging, responsibilities, gives managers sufficient self-motivation and sense of ownership to take initiative and innovative risks. In many cases, feeling empowered to manage their profit centres in their own way, many managers delegate responsibility even further down, creating mini profit centres in their own plant.

Lastly, ABB is a 'razor-thin organisation': it is one of the flattest organisational structures in relation to its size and complexity. Between the top management team, consisting of Barnevik and the executive committee members, and about 200,000 shop-floor employees, there are never more than five hierarchical levels. This not only makes communication smoother, it also decreases the power distance between levels.

Patterning the Internal Diversities

The description of ABB so far broadly paints a picture of a highly differentiated and somewhat 'disorganised' organisation. Consider some of its salient features: it is an extremely large multi-unit, multi-product organisation, operating globally across different nations and cultures; it operates through its commitment to local management and domestic markets; it is growing and diversifying at a phenomenal rate; the top leadership believes in, and practices, 'rocking the boat' to achieve major changes; and delegation and decentralisation are practised in extreme by giving the operating units complete autonomy. The obvious question, then is: *What holds ABB together in this flux and diversity?*

Paradoxically, what binds ABB together and integrates it into a coherent form is its implicit acknowledgement and acceptance of its highly diverse and differentiated nature. ABB does not attempt to control and reduce its diversity; rather, it encourages it, and weaves it into a pattern. This pattern is most apparent in its unique structure, which translates the organisation's acceptance of variety into its actual day-to-day business practices.

The conscious concern for nurturing variety emanates from the top. The executive committee of ABB, for instance, reflects the globally diverse nature of the company. It consists of Swedes, Swiss, Germans, and Americans. Although the headquarters are in Zurich, many of the members stay in other countries, and the committee meets every three weeks in different parts of the world. Similarly, ABB's 200-odd business area (BA) leaders and CEOs of national companies (described later) represent a diverse mix of nationalities, and operate from different global locations. The diversity is not merely legal and demographic; it is also one of minds. As Barnevik says:

> We do need a core group of global managers at the top: on our executive committee, on the teams running our business areas, in other key positions. How are they different? Global managers have exceptionally open minds. They respect how different countries do things, and they have the imagination to appreciate why they do them that way. ... Global managers are generous and patient.

It is perhaps out of this respect for other cultures that, although Swedish Asea was a larger partner in the Asea–BBC merger (and

Barnevik was the CEO of Asea), after the merger, the ABB head-quarters were shifted to Zurich, in BBC's home country Switzerland. Moreover, ABB's official language is English and its accounting is done in US dollars, even though there are no British in the executive committee and, at the time of merger, ABB had no major interests in the US.

The most obvious and tangible example of this patterning of diversity is ABB's global matrix structure. ABB's matrix is a unique mechanism for blending the company's global and local operations in such a way that they complement, rather than encroach upon, each other. It allows the local national companies to maintain their unique identity and market focus and, at the same time, function as a part of ABB's global network as well. Let us look at how the network functions.

ABB is organised along two dimensions. On one, ABB's country-wise operations are organised as national enterprises. The national company functions like any other local company, with a CEO in charge of the operations of ABB units operating in that country. It has its own hierarchies and career levels, balance sheets, income statements, and a board of directors with representatives from local government and financial institutions, trade unions, etc. The task of the national enterprise is to coordinate ABB's various local operations (e.g., power generation, switchgears, process automation). For instance, among the responsibilities of the national CEO would be those of building an efficient distribution and service network across different product lines; optimising use of material, financial, and human resources across companies; managing environmental boundaries with government and major customers and suppliers; and negotiating with labour. The country structure gives ABB the advantage of being a national company and working on synergies across different product lines at the national level.

On the second dimension is its structure along BAs, which divides the company's activities in terms of its different products and services. ABB has some 65 BAs (e.g., transformers, power systems, locomotives, robotics, instrumentation), which are clustered in eight business segments. The BA leader, along with his mixed-nationality team, is responsible for globally optimising that particular business. The responsibilities of a BA leader include devising and implementing a global strategy for the product/ service, maintaining cost and quality standards in companies around the world, allocating export markets to each factory, encouraging sharing of expertise across borders by facilitating communication, and rotating people and creating mixed-nationality teams.

The country and BA structures intersect at the level of ABB's member companies. The presidents of ABB's 1,300 companies, in effect, report to two superiors: the national CEO and the BA leader. The gains of such an arrangement are enormous, the most important being that it enables ABB to capitalise on the strengths of its diversity (across countries and businesses). At the global level, each company benefits from its access to superior expertise, technology, and markets from around the world. Simultaneously, at the national level, it has the opportunity to gain from cross-product synergies. For instance, ABB's power transformer plant in Norway being part of the $1 billion power transformer BA, can avail itself of the best technology and expertise from 25 ABB power transformer factories located in 16 countries. According to Sune Karlsson, the power transformer BA leader, the strength lies in:

> having factories around the world, each with its own president, design manager, marketing manager, and production manager. These people are working on the same problems and opportunities day after day, year after year, and learning a tremendous amount. We want to create a process of continuous expertise transfer. If we do, that's a source of advantage none of our rivals can match.

Moreover, being part of the global network gives a company easy access to larger export market and distribution channels. These allow it to better utilise its capacity and optimise its costs, and become more competitive in the domestic market. At the same time, it is also part of the country structure, and can gain from coordinating with ABB's other local operations (the Norway power transformer plant would benefit by working with ABB's Norwegian operations in power generation, switchgear, and process automation). Hence, local cross-product coordination would enable synergies to be built through common distribution and service networks, sharing resources, offering a more complete and integrated 'package' to customers, and so on.

Since ABB's global matrix builds upon diversities instead of streamlining and channelising them into some narrow, rigid framework, the individual unit is able to focus better on its specific local market, and to specialise and to build around its core competence—not by segregating itself from the whole, but by remaining a part of it. In this way the matrix provides a basic pattern in which diversities not only coexist, but even support and complement each other.

Enhancing the Synergies

Obviously, formulating and installing a structure, however perfect, does not necessarily mean that it will be practised in the spirit intended. The matrix only provides the broad framework, an overall map, within which the organisation can function. Its effective functioning, however, rests in large part on the ability of individuals to deal with its complexities and ambiguities: on their skills to deal with conflicts and ambiguities, on a problem-centred (as opposed to power-centred) approach, on the mutual trust necessary for information sharing, and so on.

The success of the matrix in ABB has resulted largely from the use of processes and practices that encourage and develop people to think and operate meaningfully and constructively within its structure. It is these underlying processes and practices that actually give life to the matrix framework and make it work. As will be noted in this section, these mechanisms focus predominantly on creating a change in mind-set, developing new competencies and skills, and helping people to learn from each other.

The most important success factor underlying ABB's matrix structure is the way in which the company manages the flow of information and communication. For the whole organisation to move in the same direction, it is essential to communicate with tens of thousands of people around the world. There are, for example, 25,000 managers in ABB, scattered all over the world. If their efforts are to be aligned, it is a huge communications exercise. Barnevik's dictum, therefore, is: 'You don't inform, you overinform.'

Correspondingly, the ABB management lays a great deal of emphasis on communicating quickly and clearly to its managers and employees. Barnevik himself interacts with 5,000 people a year in small and big groups. Describing one such series of meetings, he says:

> These are active, working sessions. We talk about how we work in the matrix, how we develop people, about our programs around the world to cut cycle times and raise quality ... we'll focus on problems. ... [Some manager] may be unhappy about our research priorities. Someone may think we're paying too much attention to Poland. There are lots of tough questions, and my job is to answer them on the spot. We'll have 14 such sessions during the course of the year ... [with] top managers from all over the world living in close quarters, really communicating about business and their problems, and meeting with the CEO in an open, honest dialogue.

Similarly, the executive committee members have hundreds of meetings annually with people around the world. The pattern is repeated at lower levels. For instance, members of the BA staff (who consist of some of the veteran managers with worldwide responsibilities for critical areas such as purchasing, R&D, etc.) constantly travel and have meetings with presidents and managers of the local companies. Similarly, all chiefs of profit centres hold regular meetings with hundreds of middle managers to share their financial and operating performance. The middle managers are, in turn, responsible for sharing that data—both good and bad—with thousands of ABB workers.

The vertical information-sharing and clarification meetings held by the management, however, are only one aspect of ABB's communication practices. Meetings are held to also facilitate horizontal communication among colleagues from different parts of the world. In all BAs, every six months or so, functional coordination teams, consisting of functional managers from local companies worldwide, come together to discuss and exchange information, ideas and solutions. The emphasis is not so much on creating a formal system as on developing informal relationship among colleagues. As Sune Karlsson explains:

> Sharing expertise does not happen automatically. It takes trust, it takes familiarity. People need to spend time together, to get to know and understand each other. People must also see a payoff for themselves. I never expect our operations to coordinate unless all sides get real benefits. We have to demonstrate that sharing pays—that contributing one idea gets you 24 in return.

Another unique system adapted by ABB is that of 'internal benchmarking' of performance. ABB's centralised information system, Abacus, collects performance data from all 5,000 profit centres every month and translates it in terms of the US dollar. The performance rankings (on failure rates, throughput time, financial indices, etc.) of different companies in each business area are made public every month. While on the one hand, it boosts internal competition (and, therefore, productivity), on the other it paves the path for the units to know where to look for superior solutions and practices within the organisation. To further capitalise on internal variety, ABB shuttles managers across units. The successful managers are often rotated to the less profitable ones, so that they can transfer their expertise, while managers from less profitable units are sent on tours to the more successful ones, so that they can learn and pick up the best available ideas. For instance, when ABB acquired its US ventures, it sent a European production team there, while the US managers travelled across the high-performing ABB units. According to Barnevik:

> You have to exploit your success stories to break resistance. We human beings are driven by habits, history, and rear-view mirror. If you want to break direction, you have to shake people up, not by threatening them, not by offering a bonus, but by illustrating in a similar situation what can be accomplished.

Lastly, one of the working philosophies of ABB is to erase the conventional boundaries that segment the functions and the stakeholders from each other. To generate better synergy, ABB often pushes the support/service functions nearer line functions. For instance, after the merger, a large number of researchers from the modern and spacious R&D labs, near Baden, were transferred to the business units. This was not done because ABB does not value research (in fact, it spends $1.3 billion on R&D every year, which is about 7 per cent of its sales, and the highest in the industry). Rather, it was consistent with its policy of bringing the knowledge-generating function nearer where that knowledge would be used, hence making it more need based. Similarly, in the ABB roter factory at Birr, Switzerland, the entire administrative staff was relocated from separate office buildings to the factory premises. Again, the underlying reason for this was to bring the service people near to where that service would be needed. Such 'mergers' create settings for different functions to interact with each other and to build up synergy.

Notes

1. Material for developing this case has been drawn from various sources. Details given in the case can be found in the reports published in *Business Week* (Kapstein and Reed, 1990; Schares, 1993), *Fortune* (20 September 1993), and *International Management* (Arbose, 1988; September 1992), and in the articles and books by Horovitz and Panak (1992), Kennedy (1992), Lipnack and Stamps (1993), Peters (1992), and Taylor (1991).

Case 2

British Airways: Learning as a Means of Organisational Turnaround[1]

*The real problem ... was quite easy to identify.
The airline had forgotten that it was a service
industry.*

—Colin Marshall
CEO, British Airways

*The award for being the Best Airline Overall in
the world is given to British Airways for the
enormous and continuing progress the airline
has made in listening and responding to its
customers, as well as its rapid expansion in
terms of routes, frequency and new products.*

—Business Traveller, 1989

THE RESURRECTION

Learning, by traditional definition, is 'to become able to respond to
task-demand or an environmental pressure in a different way'
(English and English, 1958). The development of this ability to
respond differently to situations is nowhere more apparent than in
the recent history of British Airways (BA).

In the late 1970s, BA was a loss-making, inefficient state-owned
enterprise. It was slow and lethargic in its operations, and insensi-
tive to its customers. For most travellers BA stood for 'Bloody

Awful'. By 1983, however, the carrier had cleaned itself up and was making profits. Its image had gained such a face-lift that when it was privatised in 1987, its initial stock offering of $1.36 billion was heavily oversubscribed. Since then, it has acquired the status of being the largest, and one of the most profitable international carriers, with a fleet of 230 aircraft, reaching over 150 destinations in 70 countries. In 1992, the airline generated about $500 million as profit on a sales turnover of $9 billion.

In a short time span, of less than a decade, the airline has successfully expanded its sphere of operations through a series of grand acquisitions and alliances: in 1987, it acquired a 20 per cent stake in the new European computerised reservation system, Galileo; in 1988, it acquired Britain's second largest airline, British Caledonian; in 1990, it formed Air Russia with Aeroflot, slated to fly worldwide in the mid-1990s; in 1992, it acquired a regional German carrier and renamed it BA Deutsche, initiating a move to build the first European hub-and-spoke system; in 1992 it also initiated forging of the world's largest airline alliance with USAir, which would give it entry into the highly competitive, but lucrative, US market. In addition, it has made a bid for the Australian government-owned Quantas Airways Ltd, has shown keenness to buy stakes in Air New Zealand, has plans to build its own hub at Singapore airport, and so on. Between 1991 and 1992, BA moved up 397 places (from 908 to 511) on the *Business Week Global 1000* list, with a market value of $3.85 billion. These changes have made it a fearsome competitor in the global skies, changing its image from 'Bloody Awful' to 'Bloody Awesome'.

BA's turnaround was guided by a vision to provide the best customer-oriented service in the industry. And, in less than a decade, it achieved this status: not only did it grow into a formidably competitive organisation, but it also built an international reputation for the quality of its service and customer-responsiveness. For most service-conscious travellers, in fact, BA became the acronym for the Best Airline to travel with. In 1989, the *Business Traveller* magazine judged it the Best Airline Overall in the world The award was given to acknowledge 'the enormous and continuing progress the airline has made in listening and responding to its customers, as well as its rapid expansion in terms of routes, frequency and new products'. A poll by the International Foundation for Airline Passengers Associations ranked it with Singapore Airlines, Cathay Pacific, Swissair, and American Airlines.

This is a long way to come for an airline, in which, according to John Bray, CEO of Forum Europe Ltd, a consulting firm hired by BA in 1984, 'The attitude was, "This would be a nice place to work if it wasn't for these bloody customers"'.

What is remarkable is that BA has gained and maintained leadership in an environment characterised by discontinuity and turbulence (the gradual, but bumpy, deregulation of the EC market, opening up of the skies, increasing competition, changes in customer preferences and profiles, increasing costs of operations, etc.). In a way, not only is the airline responding in new ways to familiar problems, but it has also learned to forge solutions to meet the expediencies of an entirely unfamiliar set of environmental challenges. In a period of just about 12 years, BA is, in the words of its chief executive, Sir Colin Marshall, 'all set for fulfilling our ambitions to be the airline of the future'.

THE CHANGE-MAKERS

BA was formed in 1974, as a result of the merger of British Overseas Airways Corporation (BOAC) and British European Airways (BEA). In 1981, the outspoken confidante of Prime Minister Thatcher, industrialist Lord King (at that time Sir John King) was appointed chairman of BA. King was chairman of the engineering company, Babcock International. His brief was to spruce up the state-owned company, make it profitable, and prepare it for privatisation. At that time, the company was heavily overstaffed, had insufficient capitalisation, and was managed by civil servants, who ran the business without any vision or strategy. King's first action was to reduce staff from 58,000 to 38,000, and to replace the board of directors with people with experience in running industries, which included a former chairman of Barclay Bank, a director from Cadbury Schweppes, and a chairman of Unilever. He also got rid of the ageing aircraft, instituted new work systems, and withdrew the company from some of the unprofitable routes. The costs of these changes were charged off in the same fiscal year, thus avoiding the burden being carried over to the following years. With this, the company was ready to implement more fundamental changes in the managerial systems.

When King recruited Colin Marshall as CEO of BA in 1983, the airline was already making profits. It was Marshall, however, who, with his experience of managing service industries, crafted the winning strategy of quality-based service for BA. Marshall had started his career as a deputy purser on an ocean liner, Orient Steam Navigation Co., when at the age of 17 he ran away from home to see the world (it is there, he claims, that he 'learned the importance of making travellers feel more comfortable'). Later, as head of Avis's European division, he transformed the company into first position by almost reinventing the European business travel market. This won him a top job in Avis's New York headquarters, where he spent six years before leaving it to join Sears Holdings PLC as deputy chief executive for two years in 1981.

The reason for recruiting Marshall was that he knew a great deal about serving customers—without knowing much about the airline business. As King commented: 'We were looking for someone who understood service. But there seemed to be an advantage in not knowing too much about the business. In my ignorance, I could do things I might not have done if I had been better informed.'

Marshall brought with him a work ethics and style entirely new to the company. He is a workaholic who regularly clocks in 12-hour workdays. Unlike the slow and laissez-faire style of the earlier days, he was much more directive, and believed in making and implementing decisions fast. His philosophy of keeping the 'shine' on the product on a daily basis had made him a stickler for detail, sometimes even testing passenger seats before they were installed. Every day, he goes through the press clippings from around the world and sometimes even monitors such tasks as the upgrading of inflight menu.

There were many others who were recruited around that time—for instance, Alastair Cumming, now BA's director of engineering, Michael Batt, a consumer-marketing expert from candy-maker Mars Inc., who developed BA's marketing research function, Eva Lauermann, a research chemist from ICI, who now heads the human resource division—who were new to the airline industry. Their entry marked the beginning of change in BA. The airline became more externally focused. Customer focus became the cornerstone of BA's turnaround. 'The real problem ... was basically quite easy to identify,' recalls Marshall. 'The airline had forgotten that it was a service industry.' Accordingly, this team started tackling issues that had never been touched previously (e.g., customer service, punctuality, cleanliness, material maintenance, support service). Change was also visible in its new visual identity, evident in the new colour scheme, a new polished logo ('To Fly, To Serve'), new uniforms, new seat covers, even a new advertising campaign ('The World's Favourite Airline').

In 1986, the airline developed a corporate mission statement to guide its activities, with the main goal being: 'To be the best and most successful company in the airline industry.' To a large extent, BA has been able to translate this mission into near reality. The following sections will explore the mechanisms and strategies BA devised to achieve this transformation.

THE MECHANISMS OF TRANSFORMATION

It is obvious that leadership played quite a dominant role in BA's transformation. The King–Marshall combine and the new team which managed the key performance areas were the major players in the creation of a new architecture for BA. It is important, however, to recognise the premise on which BA built its winning competence: To succeed in a service industry, it is essential to align company activities with customers' expectations. To do so, the organisation must know what the customers want, must develop mechanisms and competencies to do so on a continuing basis, and must learn to organise its actions around these expectations.

Focusing on Customers

Interestingly, BA's customer-oriented strategy was designed through a customer-oriented process. In 1983, soon after Marshall took over, BA conducted a survey of customers, asking them what they wanted. The results showed that a friendly and responsive staff was twice as important for generating goodwill than operational factors such as food service and speedier check-in. This decided that focus on service excellence will be the key to running the business; operational efficiencies will support customer-service activities, not dictate them.

Over the years, the airline has developed comprehensive and innovative methods to serve customers. Many of these were made possible by better organisation of activities, and through use of sophisticated technology to add to customers' comforts. For instance, many UK international airports have touch-screen multi-lingual information points; stewardesses are equipped with portable computers which make on-board duty-free purchases easier and quicker; installation of personalised video system allows passengers to select from 50 or so movies during the flight; the self-service 'Turn-up and Check-in' Super Shuttle system on key UK domestic routes enables passengers to purchase tickets and get the boarding pass within 40 seconds.

However, more important than these are the more humane and personalised efforts to make customers feel cared for. BA has evolved a service-oriented culture, which guides the behaviour of each of its staff members. A report described such instance of BA's hospitality:

It was our first transatlantic trip with our infant daughter, and my wife and I arrived at London's Heathrow Airport laden with luggage and baby gear. To our dismay, a computer failure had left check-in lines 40-deep. We were just about to settle in for an ordeal, when a British Airways staffer pulled us aside. 'You don't want to wait in those queues with a baby,' he said. Grabbing our cart, he ushered us to a special desk and stood by until we checked in.

Such an attitude of helpfulness, however, can neither come automatically nor can it be ensured by creating formal procedures. People can be helpful only when they are sensitive to others' needs and problems, and perceive them as a part of their legitimate responsibilities. According to Shaune Shaw, who heads Ground Operations at Heathrow Airport: 'We started with people who liked aircraft. We were an operationally driven culture and that meant "we are the professionals and we know best"'. For BA, to become customer oriented meant changing this culture to one which values people and is receptive and sensitive to others. If people must learn about and respond to customers' needs, they must develop psycho-social capabilities, and learn to overcome their own defences in interpersonal contacts.

To achieve this, BA put its 35,000 employees through a two-day training course: 'Putting People First'. The course was designed to make them sensitive not only to the needs of others (customers and colleagues), but also to their own needs and beliefs. It aimed at making people realise how their own attitudes towards customers, and towards co-workers, influenced the way in which customers saw them. Managers, too, from all levels were sent out from their sheltered offices to spend time in airport terminals, on the ramps, in the catering kitchen to acquire a better understanding of customers. People were also trained in helping and problem-solving skills so that they could provide better service to customers. Many of these skills have been institutionalised in the regular activities of the airline. According to a description in an article:

> The airline employs 60 trained problem-solvers, called 'hunters', who roam BA's Heathrow terminals. Recently, a hunter spotted two women who had come off a delayed Lufthansa flight and had 20 minutes to catch a BA plane. After radioing ahead to preserve their seats, he snatched their hand baggage and ran with them to the gate.

Upgrading the service skills of the employees and using service quality as a strategic weapon are now part of BA's routine activities. For instance, during 1990–91, when the airline was planning its entry into the US market (through a tie-up with USAir), it spent £6 million to upgrade the training of its transatlantic staff (and another £10 million for making new lounges, improving check-in facilities, and increasing ground staff). Even competitors grudgingly accept BA's superiority in quality customer service. After all, which other airline can boast that its staff can recognise 60 per cent of its passengers by name (and is trying to improve upon it), or that the maximum number of passengers on each flight are personally escorted from check-in desk to departure gate.

Building a 'Transparent Organisation'

BA realised that the aim of building a customer-oriented company cannot be achieved without making corresponding transformations in the internal organisational processes. The staff who deal with customers are usually at the lower end of the hierarchy, and, if they are expected to volunteer in helping customers, they must also feel empowered and free to take initiative. Customer-responsiveness is more than a matter of training and policy; it is an expression of the organisation's culture. As Brian Robson, the head of corporate development, expressed it: 'We use the phrase "transparent organisation"; that is customers can actually see into BA. If they see a cold, authoritarian style of management, they know not to expect a warm, caring type of service.'

Correspondingly, the 'Putting People First' initiative was followed by 'Managing People First', a course designed for BA's 2,000 managers to help them learn how to motivate, to involve people in decision-making, to delegate responsibility, and to plan and create a vision. These were the essential skills for an organisation attempting to change from an hierarchical, operationally driven way of managing to one which nurtures customer-focused initiatives and entrepreneurship. To achieve this, managers were specifically trained in group decision-making techniques, so that they could involve workers in solving problems related to efficiency and service.

Initially, BA started with the cabin crew; then, in 1987, it followed up these efforts with the support staff at terminals. It also trained a cadre of 100 internal change agents, who coached managers and workers in sharing ideas on improving services such as baggage handling and ticketing. These efforts also proved useful and showed tangible results. Customer-service initiatives started coming from those in direct contact with customers instead of being transmitted down the hierarchy. For instance, one of the Customer First Teams (created from staff volunteers for proposing ways of improving service to customers) proposed special facilities for children under twelve. As a result, special lounges for children with toys and appropriate refreshments have been set up in some of the BA airports.

The efforts to change the culture were not limited only to departments interfacing with customers. Changes in manager–worker interactions were apparent in other departments as well. In the engineering division, for example, every Friday afternoon managers would actually take off their coats and spend time with workers at the workplace. There was a strict code governing these interactions: do not argue or get involved in arguments; focus more on listening than on speaking; do not merely socialise (e.g., ask about wife and kids), but try to understand workers' problems, and follow-up on whatever has been discussed. In effect, the aim was to build a collegial, but task-focused, relationship between the managers and the workers. Workers and technicians too, were trained and encouraged to take part in problem-solving activities. These efforts translated into greater motivation and productivity, with many ingenious technical solutions coming from workers. According to a report, the achievements were remarkable:

> 'The numbers are magical,' says Alastair Cumming, BA's director of engineering. In 1991, a very hard year, he achieved a reduction in engineering costs that went 'beyond my wildest dreams. . . .' after budgeting for 2 to 3% reduction (and absorbing an 11.5 to 13.5 % pay raise for 1990, plus higher costs for aeronautical materials), the results came to 9% below 1990. The total underspend was £38 million, and the process is continuing. The engineering budget is on a 5% reduction path, and 10% gains in labour productivity combined with 2% on raw materials.

Fact-based Problem-solving Approach

Underlying BA's turnaround has also been a remarkable process of developing mechanisms for identifying, focusing on, and solving relevant business problems.

This was apparent even in its earliest initiatives when, in 1983, it started its market research activities. To better understand customers' needs, the newly recruited marketer, Michael Batt, assembled a team of brand managers for each of the passenger classes. Their task was to oversee research and identify what the customers wanted. This was a systematic effort to understand the nature of the market, customer profiles and preferences, and to build up a database to enable the company to give a more discerning and focused response to varied customer groups. The result was 'branding' of services—a unique concept in the airline industry. BA now offers a wide range of 'brands', such as Club World (for intercontinental travellers), Club European, Super Shuttle, Euro Traveller, Skyflyers (for children), and so on. Moreover, based on its market research findings, BA also offers a choice of services to its passengers, within the same segment or brand. For instance, first-class passengers have a choice of a light meal soon after boarding (many of them are business travellers who, after a long day's work, would like to have something quickly, and then catch up on their sleep or work) or wait for a more wholesome course.

Services are also. regularly reviewed through customer feedback, and research is conducted on an ongoing basis to identify customer segments and their needs. Customer satisfaction and feedback on key indicators are monitored on a monthly basis. As part of the regular service audit, customers are sampled and interviewed every day. BA conducts some 150,000 interviews in a year, in addition to the use of focus groups and the ongoing dialogues with its regular passengers. Even complaints and suggestion letters are systematically analysed to identify trends and ideas. These organisational systems, and the information which they generate, contribute much to BA's ability to learn about its customers, and about itself, on a continuing basis.

Once again, receptivity to new ideas and information is not limited only to the functions related to customer service but gets translated into other operational activities as well. For instance, the marketing people work along with other operational functions. The information generated from customers is used even in decisions such as which aircraft to purchase, internal layout of the aircraft, the scheduling of flights, and so on. Other departments and functions have also developed their own mechanisms for learning how to improve their performance. For instance, in the engineering division, about 20 managers visited different engineering locations around the world to learn about new methods and practices. They picked up and applied many of these ideas in their own facility.

To build an organisation-wide problem-solving orientation, the airline disseminates relevant information across the organisation. Customer feedback is regularly shared with the staff. So is the information about the airline's performance in different areas. BA works with over 200 separate performance/business targets, which are both qualitative and quantitative in nature. These are published and circulated among managers, so as to provide a direction to their efforts. The progress on some of the critical indicators is published monthly in the internal journal, explaining the activities and achievements in different service and operational areas.

The airline has developed methods to tap the internal problem-solving potential and skills of its staff. It uses small group-based initiatives such as customer-focus teams and TQM to encourage and use employees' solutions and insights for improving performance. Employees are also trained in systematic problem-solving methods (e.g., the Krepner–Tregoe method), which they can apply to their work problems to generate new and more effective solutions. To encourage problem-solving efforts, BA has implemented awards for innovative and useful solutions under its suggestion schemes 'Brainwaves' (suggestions for improving efficiency) and 'Greenwaves' (for environmentally conscious solutions).

Building Up Synergies/Aligning the Diversities

Probably the biggest challenge that BA had to overcome in the process of transforming itself was to achieve and communicate to its employees a sense of a single corporate identity. To understand the complexity of this task, one needs to appreciate the historical and politico-cultural context in which BA operated (and still operates).

First, BA, as mentioned earlier, was formed out of the merger of BOAC and BEA. However, till 1981, when Lord King took over as chairman, there had been little rationalisation over the issue of the creation of a single corporate identity. Also, there had been hardly any effort made to bring the cultures of the two organisations together. Thus, in a way, at that time BA was actually two organisations working together under an enforced common name. While the merger did make greater assets and resources available to the organisation, their effective utilisation depended largely on integrating them into a unified whole.

Second, in an increasingly expanding and deregulated market, BA's growth strategy was to acquire a pan-global (and definitely pan-European) character. This meant more than merely routing flights to more international destinations. Rather, it involved establishing an acceptance of having a geographically and culturally diverse workforce, and developing the organisational capabilities to value and use the potentials of this diversity. A diagnosis of training and development needs also showed that an understanding of cultural differences was a significant requirement for realising the business strategy.

Third, in the airline industry, a large proportion of the work-force, particularly in the cabin-crew and customer-service arenas (e.g., ticketing, check-in) consists of women. Due to their family commitments, the turnover is high, which becomes a source of constant loss of trained skills and resources. The continuous flux of a new and untrained workforce meant extra organisational efforts to socialise the newcomers into the airline's norms and methods of working.

Lastly, the functional division of the professional activities in BA (e.g., engineering, maintenance, flying operations, marketing) had, as often happens with many bureaucratically managed organisations, fractured it into segments. The departments would often function in an independent and unrelated manner, some-times even countering each others' efforts. One of the challenges for the new management was to align these efforts in a way that they complement, rather than contradict, each other.

Thus, while BA had the advantage of having a diversity of resources, it had to simultaneously bear the cost of managing this diversity and directing it towards a common goal. Only by gaining employees' commitment to the total organisation, and enabling and encouraging them to work beyond their narrow functional and cultural boundaries could this diversity be converted into a synergistic advantage. The organisation devised a number of unique and innovative measures to achieve this goal.

One of such solutions was to train and enable (often force) employees to work as a team (King had even gone to the extent of combining BA's marketing and operations departments—an extraordinary move that allowed marketers to drive such key decisions as aircraft purchases and flight schedules). As part of its 'Putting People First' initiative, BA conducted a number of team-building workshops. It put most of its employees through group-training courses, which would often include surprising team-building activities, such as tiddlywinks, jigsaw puzzles and logo-building. These programmes were quite useful in creating an awareness of group processes, and helped in building inter-personal skills relevant to working in groups.

BA also has an extensive portfolio of management develop-ment programmes. These include an in-house MBA, a scheme to sponsor executives to programmes conducted by Harvard,

INSEAD, IMD, MIT, etc., and even a development programme for secretaries, which uses skill-assessment workshops to help them identify the areas they need to improve upon for higher posts. Besides improving personal competence, the educational efforts also provide a means of developing a critical mass of employees who think and talk in a common managerial vocabulary.

However, in the course of creating inter-cultural sensitivity, BA also realised that training alone may not be the most effective way of building inter functional and inter cultural understanding. Eva Lauermann, General Manager, Human Resources, describes that these efforts

> consisted of putting all senior managers through a training programme a major component of which was an explanation of the Hofstede model for understanding the cultures of different nationalities. ... [The model] makes it possible to understand which nationalities get on with which and why. It also can highlight potential problems. ... However, 18 months later, it is quite hard to find people whose thinking was affected by it.

A major reason for the ineffectiveness of training appeared to be the lack of personal and immediate stakes in learning among the participants. BA's efforts have been to increase these stakes by creating a greater sense of participation among employees, and by incorporating the learning processes in the normal daily routines and practices. Some of these initiatives to increase commitment are quite elementary, for example, when BA was privatised, shares were issued to 74 per cent of its employees.

Other solutions are more innovative. One such is that system of 'monitoring' which contributes much to the creation of a common corporate identity. It is a learning experience for the mentors as well in that they have to develop skills for relating, communicating, appreciating and guiding people of different backgrounds and cultures. According to Eva Lauermann:

> We have recognised that work needs to be done to prepare the receiving department just as much as the selection of the right person. Mentors can help with the initial adaptation phase. BA has a number of formal mentoring schemes especially for new graduates and cadet pilots. The value of having a more senior person to help ease the transition into a very different culture has been proven to be very high. In the case of entrants with a different national identity, the

need is even greater—especially at senior levels. *There is, incidentally, usually great benefit for the mentor as well.* [emphasis added]

In addition, BA has evolved systems to make better use of internal skills and resources. From the point of view of managing a diverse and fluctuating flow of manpower, these systems also create a cultural continuity (as in the case of mentoring). For instance, the airline offers a variety of atypical choices for employment contracts: people can work on a part-time basis; split and share their jobs; work in a 'twilight shift' (which is short so that the husband can look after the children); have career breaks to raise a family. There are also nurseries on the site for working mothers. Such measures ensure that trained and capable talent is not lost to the organisation. In addition, BA takes care of the seasonally fluctuating workload, without overstaffing on a permanent basis.

Notes

1. Material used for developing this case has been drawn from various articles published in *Business Week* (9 October 1989; 24 August 1992; *Moremont*, 1990), *European Management Journal* (Lauermann, 1992), *Fortune* (Labick, 1988; Stewart, 1990b), and *Management Today* (Barrell, 1989; Heller, 1992; Lynn, 1991). Horovitz and Panak's case study (1992) of British Airways' customer-satisfaction strategy also provided useful details for the case.

Chaparral Steel:
The Learning Factory[1]

*One of our core competencies is the rapid
realisation of new technology into products. We
are a learning organisation.*

—Gordon E. Forward
President and CEO
Chaparral Steel

*In other companies, the word is—don't rock the
boat. Here we rock the hell out of the boat. We
don't know the factory's limits. We want it to
change, to evolve.*

—Paul Wilson
Production Manager
Chaparral Steel

THE ACHIEVEMENTS

In 1975, Texas Industries Inc. wanted to put up a new mini-steel plant, and invited Gordon E. Forward, a Ph.D. from MIT working with a Canadian steel company, to become the founder and CEO of the new venture. Located in South of Dallas, Texas, this small factory now attracts executives from far-flung places as curious visitors. They come because Chaparral Steel has achieved the unique distinction of being the world's lowest-cost, and America's tenth largest, steel producer. With a total manpower of just 950, it churns out 1.5 million tonnes of steel annually, and is the largest supplier of steel rods to the oil industry and of rods for mobile homeframes in the US. It is also the only US company, and the second company outside Japan, which was awarded the right to use the Japanese Industrial Standard certification on its general structural steel products.

Ever since its inception in 1975, Chaparral Steel has been creating new records. In October 1982, it created a new world record of producing 67,666 tonnes in one month from a single electric furnace–continuous casting combination. In 1984, it was rated by *Fortune* as one of the ten best-managed US companies. It has been improving its productivity at the rate of about 25–40 per cent annually. In comparison to the Japanese average of 600 tonnes per worker, and the US average of about 350 tonnes per worker, Chaparral's output is about 1,100 tonnes of steel per worker. In 1990, it produced a record low of 1.5 hours of labour per rolled tonne of steel, as compared to 2.4 hours of other mini-mills, the US average of 4.9 hours, Japanese average of 5.6 hours, and German average of 5.7 hours.

Of course, Chaparral uses lean manufacturing methods, and employs the latest electronic technology of achieving productivity gains—its labour costs are about 10 per cent of sales, as compared to about 40 per cent of the industry average. But this alone does not explain its enviable success. Its success is built on a clearly defined vision of how a company should remain flexible in order to incorporate continuous improvements. It is a vision of an ever-changing organisation in a state of continuous flux. As Gordon E. Forward now Chaparral's president and chief executive, puts it:

> We simply can't wait until we've been forced into a corner and have to fight back like alley cats. . . . We can't treat our business as if it were a large, mature operation that needs to be popped up and pampered. We can't relax and build monuments to ourselves.

To achieve this vision, Chaparral has created a new paradigm for the factory. In normal businesses, the factory is the most conservative place to experiment in/with. It is, after all, the core of all business activities. Thus, while the rest of the organisation may try out new changes, only the tried and tested improvements are implemented in the factory organisation. This is more so in a traditional industry like steel.

What is noteworthy about Chaparral is that it has designed a factory which is capable of experimenting, evolving and changing continuously. One researcher has described the Chaparral factory as a 'learning lab'. In fact, it would be wrong to say that Chaparral has a factory which can learn; rather, Chaparral is the learning factory which contains all other functions and processes.

ORGANISATION AS A HOLOGRAM

A holographic plate is a unique thing. It is like any photographic plate which contains a picture. The uniqueness of a hologram is that if you break it into a hundred pieces, the picture does not get broken into a hundred pieces; instead, each of the hundred pieces retains the image of the whole. It is as if, in a hologram, not only does each part belong to the whole, but it contains the whole in itself. The part has access to the information contained in the whole.

The metaphor of a hologram accurately describes Chaparral. It is like a live, internally integrated organism, in which each subpart pulsates and is in communication with the rest. It is this interdependence and integration of each part with the rest of the system that makes it difficult to describe and capture it in discrete piecemeal terms. Nevertheless, in the following sections, we will review this unique inter-relatedness of the parts, which characterises Chaparral Steel, and its impact on the company's learning capabilities.

Creating a Learning Community

Perhaps the most unique aspect of Chaparral is that it has been created primarily as a community of learners, not steel-makers. In fact, the organisation's recruitment policies operationalise this conscious choice in its hiring activities. While some of the senior managers and specialists have experience of working in steel industries, most of the employees have no prior steel-making experience. When Chaparral was set up in 1975, the management deliberately did not take workers with industry experience. They wanted people who had no exposure to traditional steel-making practices, and, therefore, would not resist new learning. They hired (and continue to do so) ranchers and farmers with basic technical abilities. These were people who were open to learning new things, and could enjoy novelty in work; they were selected for their potential for learning and their attitude towards it. Dennis Beach, Vice President Administration explained this choice: 'We were looking for bright, enthusiastic, articulate people, and we preferred people who had not been exposed to other company's bad habits ... basically conscientious people who can put in a strong day's work and enjoy what they were doing.'

The effort to create a community of learners is also apparent in the rigour and selectivity of the recruitment procedure. The new entrant must not only be a good learner, but should also be capable of getting integrated into Chaparral's existing culture. For this, he can be assessed only by the people with whom he is going to work. While the two personnel people at Chaparral do some initial screening, the actual decision to hire is taken by the five employees, including two supervisors, who interview the applicant for almost a whole day. The procedure also ensures that at least one supervisor is committed to ensuring the entrant's learning and growth, and all members of the existing team feel they have some stake in his success.

Once recruited, each person undergoes comprehensive training. Chaparral has developed a rigorous apprenticeship programme to provide a thorough grounding in the use of the equipment and operating processes of the factory. The three-and-half-year programme, which requires completion of 7,280 hours of on-the-job training, helps apprentices reach the level of senior operator/craftsman. In addition, the apprentices are expected to complete study programmes in a wide variety of areas such as safety, programming, operating processes of the entire company, metallurgy, basic mechanical maintenance, the behavioural and interpersonal skills necessary for working with others, and so on.

Although Chaparral has such a detailed training programme, it has no formal training staff, except for a couple of trainers in highly specialised areas. All training is the responsibility of the line. Selected foremen rotate and conduct training on the shop-floor. Forward is emphatic about it: 'We don't delegate that kind of thing.' This procedure has other advantages too, which are often missed out in conventional apprenticeship programmees. Being trained on the shop-floor by line functionaries has greater credibility than being trained by a separate training staff in a technical workshop. It also ensures that the organisation's best practices get transmitted to the new entrants.

Besides the formalised apprenticeship training, Chaparral also encourages people to acquire new skills in other ways. It sponsors people to develop in the areas of their choice, and in those which might prove to be important to the organisation. Forward narrates an incident:

> One fellow who came in had a BA in biology. He joined our metallurgy department and thought he'd like to learn more about the field by taking part-time course. That got us thinking about it, and we told him instead we'd send him back to school. We've paid his whole tuition and salary while he's been in a school. It was a risk we took— he might graduate and say, 'I'm not coming back there.' But he came back, and now he's our general foreman.

Learning never ceases at Chaparral. The company makes sure that at any point of time, at least 85 per cent of its employees are enrolled in courses and cross-functional training in such varied disciplines as electronics, metallurgy, finance, and computers. To keep its knowledge-base up to date, the company regularly sends people outside to attend courses of all types. If the organisation requires competence in vibration analysis, recycling or the latest human resource practices, it deputes one of the line personnel to attend a seminar or conference on the subject. The aim is to equip existing personnel with new skills and competence rather than hire new skilled employees.

It is also important to understand why people continue to learn and contribute. One reason is, of course, that people are rewarded for learning. If a worker learns a new skill, say, how to run a new equipment, he might get a 5 per cent raise. Perhaps, greater in importance than incentive is the organisationally created urgency to learn and improve.

Chaparral management keeps the organisation humming with tension by articulating goals which are ambitious and involve a continuous outpacing of oneself. Learning and improving on past performance are seen as necessities for survival rather than as mere luxuries to achieve better rates. For instance, when Pohang, the Korean steel-maker, became the benchmark for landed cost in the US, the company articulated its goal thus: 'To get our labour costs below the per ton of the ocean voyage from Korea. That way, they can pay their people zero and we can still meet them at the unloading docks with a cost advantage.'

Similarly, in late 1988, the management embarked upon the 'near net-shape project'. The company set for itself the ambitious goal of producing 18- and 24- inch wide structural steel at the same cost as that of its first product, the simple round reinforcing bars. The existing technology for producing structural steel of such dimensions in highly capital- and labour-intensive. By committing itself to this low-cost target, Chaparral aimed at producing a product at half its existing cost in the industry. In operational terms, this meant finding ways of reducing energy costs by as much as 25 per cent, designing new kinds of moulds, discovering new processes of casting steel into as near the final shape as possible (so that less rolling is required), and so on. Not only did the company achieve this target in a record time of 27 months but also, in the process, designed and patented a mould for doing so. The process of achieving a challenging goal forced the organisation to learn, generate, and codify new knowledge.

Articulation of ambitious goals, and the sense of urgency it generates, however, is not merely a management tactic for spurring learning and innovation. It is based on a genuine understanding of the company's competitive environment. In spite of its success, Chaparral management perceives, and communicates to its employees, an environment in which complacency would be fatal. According to Forward:

> If we succeed in making our business less capital-intensive, we would be naive not to expect a lot of others will want to get into it. If we succeed at what we are trying to do as a minimill, we'll also lower the price of entry ... if we start making too much money ... all of a sudden lots of folks will be jumping in. ... This makes us our own worst enemy. We constantly chip away the ground we stand on.

Learning is, thus, viewed as its survival strategy by the organisation.

'Management by Adultery'

While the creation of conditions for continuous learning depends on management initiative, the implementation of learning requires commitment on the part of the workers. To achieve this,

Chaparral practises, what it jocularly describes as, 'management by adultery'. This actually means that in managing its people, the company recognises that they are adults. That is, people do not need to be controlled and commanded, as is done in most companies, but that they are capable of initiative and creativity and of managing themselves. According to Dennis Beach:

> From the very beginning, we designed this organisation with Maslow's hierarchies of needs in mind [which proposes that once the lower-order needs of survival, security and belonging are satisfied, people aspire to satisfy their self-esteem and self-actualisation needs]. I know it's not stylish, but we really believe in that hierarchy, so we constantly look at what will help people become self-actualised, at their ego needs. . . . People like a challenge and a well-defined goal out there.

Chaparral implements this organising principle in many ways. One of these is the concept of ownership. In its most concrete form, in 1988, the company allotted one share per year of service to each employee. Thus, the majority of Chaparral employees are also its stockholders: 93 per cent of the employees collectively hold 3 per cent of Chaparral shares, and about 62 per cent buy additional shares every month through payroll deductions. While this might not give them much operational ownership, symbolically it does create a sense of working for one's own enterprise. In addition, the bonus scheme of the company is linked to its profits—and it applies to everyone, from shop-floor workers to the secretary and janitors. Further, this increases their sense of identification with the company's overall objectives and performance.

More important than the financial stakes is the equality and freedom that the company gives to its employees. Forward believes that real 'motivation comes from within. People have to be given freedom to succeed or fail.' Correspondingly, Chaparral is a classless organisation. There are only three levels between the CEO and the shop-floor workers. Employees park their vehicles next to the CEO's, walk through the executive offices to their locker rooms, and eat in the same local diner with everyone.

The organisation empowers people to manage their respective jobs without interference from superiors or the staff. There are no clocks to punch, and employees decide their own lunch hours and breaks. The managers coordinate and facilitate; they do not control and command. Similarly, most of the staff jobs, for example, safety, research, quality, recruitment, training, do not exist as separate functions. They are part of the line responsibilities; supervisors and their groups decide on whom to hire, how to improve quality, how to operate a machine in the most efficient way, how to upgrade a process, and so on. Gordon Forward describes this extreme delegation of responsibility and authority:

> Our people in the plants are responsible for their own products and its quality. We expect them to act like owners. We do have a quality control department that removes the red tags that the people in the plant put on, but the people who put on the tags are the ones who made the products. They are their own toughest critics.

In addition, Chaparral has some unique practices, aimed at giving people freedom to perform, and challenging and enabling them to put in their best. For instance, Chaparral realised that 70 per cent of its employees report to front-line supervisors. Thus, if Chaparral was to be an innovative and path-breaking organisation to work in, then supervisors must also feel excited about what they are doing. In most industries, after the initial two or three years of excitement, the job loses its novelty and becomes routine. People stop thinking and start looking for excitement outside the job.

To counteract this inertia, Chaparral devised a system of 'sabbatical' for front-line supervisors. Every now and then, Chaparral sends its supervisors on a sabbatical, and puts them on 'special projects'. The project might be travelling, being assigned to some customer, visiting other steel mills, looking into a new kind of furnace, or anything which is different from the regular duties. The supervisors come back rejuvenated. They bring in new ideas and try to implement them.

The sabbatical plan also works in another way. When the supervisor is absent from regular duty, his work is not looked after by another supervisor from the previous shift. Instead, responsibility is assigned to one of the operators from the group itself, who works as the vice-foreman. If the previous shift supervisor is there, he takes up a subordinate position. Forward described the interesting dynamics which takes place in this situation:

> While they are gone, we move some people around and choose substitute foremen. Usually, the substitutes manage to break

production record while the first person is away—just to show what they can do. When the people on sabbatical come back, they have their adrenalin pumping again. Our challenge is to keep cycling our people in and out, keep them doing exciting things, so they don't go stale.

Experimentation and Continuous Improvement

The freedom to act is most visible in the technological capabilities and the variety of innovations which Chaparral can boast of. It has designed an automobile-shredder which turns 300,000 second-hand cars into scrap every year (i.e., one every 20 seconds), and provides the factory with about 30 per cent of its raw material; it has some of the most advanced digital furnaces; it innovated a horizontal caster, to replace the conventional vertical ones; in the 'near net-shape project' (mentioned earlier), it developed a technology that makes production of structural steel possible with just eight to 12 passes through the system, as compared to the traditional method which requires up to 50 passes. When one of the New York bankers suggested that there is an international market in small developing countries for really micromills, which can be cost-effective by producing just 25,000 tonnes annually, Chaparral designed one which could be run by just 40 people (they studied McDonald's to learn how the giant manages its franchise!).

Chaparral's innovative efforts also focus on improving the performance of the purchased equipment—sometimes to the extent that the new design can be patented. For instance, when Chaparral bought its rolling mill equipment, it was supposed to be turning out 8-inch slabs. Chaparral's employees upgraded its capability to producing 12-inch slabs, and the company patented the new design. Similarly, it increased the capacity of its two electrical arc furnaces from 250,000 and 500,000 tonnes of scrap metal to 600,000 and one million tonnes, respectively.

The emphasis in all these efforts is on designing equipment and processes in-house, so that the knowledge remains proprietary. Of course, very often Chaparral does not leave itself much choice in the matter, since its design and cost requirements do not exist anywhere else. For instance, in its 'near net-shape project' there was only one other steel mill in the world which could hot-cast steel and send it directly into the rolling mill; but the technology used by it required heavy capital and labour investment. Chaparral decided to design its own moulds and asked German and Italian firms to fabricate them.

For all its innovative credentials, Chaparral is surprisingly short of many systemic and procedural trappings, which would conventionally characterise an innovative organisation. For instance, the company does not have any research departments, barring the three on-site labs which help production with chemical and metallurgical analysis. Research is supposed to be a line function. 'The whole plant', according to Forward, 'really is a laboratory.' New projects and ideas evolve and are developed right on the shop-floor. Experimentation takes place on the shop-floor, while working, and the line managers have authority to allocate tens of thousands of dollars for such experiments without having to seek permission from the top. (One would suppose that such an approach will stifle ground-breaking ideas and confine developmental activities to only incremental improvements—an accurate as-, sumption, provided one looks at the 30 per cent increase in production, reducing costs to a tenth, or energy consumption by 25 per cent, etc. as 'incremental' improvements.)

Chaparral has neither suggestion boxes nor incentives for accepted suggestions. Unlike some Japanese companies, the company also does not emphasise any target of suggestions per person. The underlying philosophy of the company is that improving and innovating is a routine activity in which everyone is involved and everybody interacts. Ideas emerge from the total process by which work is performed in the factory and not from individuals. Dave Fournie, Vice President, Operations, explains this organisational insight into the innovative process:

> You don't have to have credit for particular ideas to be thought good at your job. Lots of innovations take more than one good idea. They go through a gestation period, and lots of people figure out how to make sense of it. The point is to focus on the good of the whole. That's why we don't have suggestion boxes, where you hide ideas so someone else won't steal them.

Innovations and improvements are fuelled not by incentives and targets, but by a freedom to perform and fail. By refusing to personalise ideas, Chaparral creates a climate in which blames and successes alike are shared. The attitude is that even if one commits a mistake one does not have to cover it up, 'You just fix it and keep on going'. For instance, when Dave Fournie was a medium-section mill superintendent, he made the company invest $1.5 million on an arc saw for cutting finished beam. The whole project was a failure. The magnetic field created by the arc attracted all small metal pieces, including pens and watches, from yards around. Far from being penalised for his blunder, Fournie continued and eventually became vice president of operations.

This openness and acceptance of the common wisdom that everybody commits mistakes, and that growth lies in learning from the mistakes, is thus articulated by Forward:

> When you're operating in a technical field, when you're trying to go one step beyond in research, one of the things you learn fast is that you can't fool yourself. You can't try to hoodwink Mother Nature. You've got to be open in your questioning. You can't play games. And you can't succeed by pretending that you know things that you don't. You have to go find them out. You have to try an experiment here, an experiment there, make your mistakes, and learn from it all.

KNOWLEDGE ACQUISITION

For a steel-making company of its size, Chaparral spends a considerable amount on employee travel. In a year, as many as 8–10 per cent of its employees, from operators to vice presidents visit the sites of the company's competitors, suppliers and customers to look for ideas and practices that can be exploited back home. For the company, their travel expenses are just an investment into their and the organisation's learning. Most of these visits are part of the employee 'sabbaticals' discussed earlier.

Right from its inception, Chaparral had set out its target: to be the best in the industry. It started identifying and benchmarking the practices of the best makers, rollers and finishers of steel in the world. It established contacts with leading steel-makers in Europe and Japan, and started visiting them. It typically sends a small heterogeneous team (an operator, a supervisor, an engineer, and a maintenance technician) to leading steel-makers and equipment manufacturers in the US and abroad. These employees spend considerable time interacting with their counterparts at the target site. They collect data not only on specific parameters like cycle times, yields, and inventory levels, but also observe and examine the practices and methods that underlie their superior performance. Their observations and findings then become the basis of comparison with the practices existing at Chaparral, and for defining new and higher operating targets and practices. Since the operators themselves have seen the implementation of these practices and targets, and are aware of the competitor's strengths, it is no longer required for the management to trickle down the information from the top. The process of benchmarking itself establishes the credibility and necessity of the new targets and practices.

Just like learning from competitors, it is also a priority at Chaparral that people inside the organisation receive regular feedback from the customers. What is unique is that this feedback is considered important not only for the production and engineering operators, but for everyone in the company. Forward describes this practice:

> If we have bent bars coming off our production line that are causing problems for our customers, we might send a superintendent over with the salesperson or the person who did the bundling or somebody from production or metallurgy. It's everyone's job: We mix crews. We send off maintenance people along with some people from the melt shop and from the rolling mill. We want them to see Chaparral the way our customers do, and we want them to be able to talk to each other. We want them to exchange information and come back with new ideas about how to make improvements or new ways to understand the problem.

In addition, while Chaparral does not have its own research department, it collaborates with universities and centres for higher learning to create a networked research organisation (this is also probably due to Forward's own background as a researcher). For instance, it co-sponsors researches in new leading-edge technologies with universities, and seeks out experts in places like MIT and Colorado School of Mines to help solve its problems. Similarly, for testing out its near net-shape caster, Chaparral sent out its people to a Mexican production laboratory for overseeing and trying out the simulation of the future mill design. These collaborations help in two ways; to the university researchers they offer a chance to work directly in a field setting, while for the Chaparral employees they are venues to acquire and get acquainted with knowledge of new technologies.

These learnings from the environment also find their way into improving the company's performance. In the early 1980s, Chaparral sent out a team of four employees (a team leader and three factory workers) to Europe, Asia and South America. Their task was to visit other factories and evaluate the mill stands used by them. Mill stands are large and expensive equipment (something like old washing machine rollers for wringing clothes), which flatten and shape hot steel as it passes through the mill. When the team returned it discussed the advantages and disadvantages of different mill stands with other workers and the top management. Having narrowed down the choices through discussion, the team eventually decided to buy a West German model. The top management merely endorsed the choice. The benefit was that not only was the whole process completed in less than a year, but since everyone was either directly or indirectly involved in the choice, they knew everything about the equipment by the time it arrived. It took no time to commission it and start working on it.

Networking the Organisation

The previous sections hint at how Chaparral tries to incorporate the concept of the organisation as one large team in its methods of working. This too, is essential, since freedom to act and to take individual initiative, by itself, can have undesirable consequences; the organisation might lose its cohesiveness of action and identity and become a cluster of disjointed, and individualistic efforts. Thus, one of the major challenges for Chaparral is to create an organisation in which individual efforts are in tandem with each other, and have a common direction.

Chaparral goes about achieving this in a variety of ways. One aspect of these activities is to promote a sense of being part of one totality. For instance, its educational course, the 'Chaparral Process', which all employees undergo, describes not only what happens to a piece of steel as it moves through the company, but also covers the roles of finance, accounting, and sales in the whole process. Having gone through the course, the worker fully understands the relevance, and inter-relatedness, of his job and others' jobs in the company. Similarly, the flat structure of the company, group incentive for profits, making the employees shareholders, etc., ensure that people and activities integrate around a common theme.

There are other practices which ensure that each of these parts also contains the totality itself. One of these is ensuring regular face-to-face communication among people. In Chaparral, memos and written notes are considered anathema. People discuss problems and take decisions, but many decisions are not seen as necessary to record (which, in turn, makes it more essential for people to meet). On the other hand, meetings are a regular feature of working. Each working day starts with groups meeting to plan and decide on activities. Even the plant layout is designed to facilitate workers to go through the offices at least once a day, which brings them in contact with many others; even Forward's own office is just a few steps away from the furnaces and mills. In such a place it is almost impossible for pockets of information to develop. Any new knowledge, from a visit, or a conference, or an experiment, quickly gets disseminated across the organisation.

In planned activities too, knowledge transmission is an important consideration. The main operators for a new project are selected for both their innovative potential and ability to communicate their learning to others. For instance, in the commissioning of the new mills for the near net-shape caster, only two teams of operators were trained. Once the project was over they were dispersed across the plant to diffuse their newly acquired knowledge about the new process to others.

Of course, Chaparral's small size can be viewed as an advantage in these efforts. Chaparral's success in being able to create a spontaneously inter-related community, however, is due more to how it designs its processes and activities than to its being small. Forward is quite emphatic about this: 'The issue isn't size; it's breaking things down into smaller size. ... If we had to expand our capacity significantly, we wouldn't build onto our facility here. We'd create another unit of manageable size elsewhere.'

The other significant aspect of Chaparral's functioning, which endorses Forward's views, is the way in which it has redefined the traditional hierarchical and horizontal boundaries to allow for greater permeability of information across them. Almost all employees are multi-skilled. There are very few functional jobs in the company in the traditional sense. In a way, everybody does every job. Production workers, for instance, do about 40 per cent of maintenance tasks. Similarly, security guards do not just keep watch; they also enter data into the computer, fill up fire extinguishers, and work as paramedics and drive ambulances. In the early 1980s, Chaparral made everyone, from secretary to factory worker, a member of the marketing department. If the customer had a problem, they could directly contact the employee on the shop-floor.

Such intermingling of jobs and erasing of boundaries also yields results. In one instance, for example, the company eliminated the field sales force for high-tech forging steel—they were retrained and assigned to other jobs. The responsibility for sales and service of the product was assigned to the quality and reliability group. Since these people were already doing much of the sales development work, they could serve better through close customer contact. Not only did this use of existing skills improve productivity, the sales for the product also tripled in just a few months.

Perhaps the ability of the company to function as a holistic organism can be best seen in the following example of its functioning. Leonard-Barton describes an incident during the commissioning of a project, when the group working on the project faced a problem:

> An incident during the first few weeks of operating the near net-shape caster, when cooling hoses were bursting, provides some insight. 'When something like that comes up, and there seems no immediate solution,' explains a senior operator, 'you go see what the problem is. You don't say, "that's not my area," or "I don't know that much about it." You just show up.' In this case a group of operators, a welder, some foremen, and a buyer spontaneously gathered to discuss the problem and just spontaneously scattered to seek solutions. 'Everybody telephoned some person they thought might know how to fix the problem—vendors, experts—and within three to four hours we were getting calls back,' says the operator. 'Service people were showing up, and we worked the problem out. If it had been just one guy, probably a foreman, and everyone walked out ... it would have taken him ten times longer to find a solution.'

It is this living quality of the system that the metaphor of the hologram describes accurately. An organisation such as Chaparral cannot be re-created by putting the pieces of a jigsaw together; it needs to be evolved and designed holistically. Being fully aware of this advantage, Forward claims that even if the competitors see everything that Chaparral does, 'We will be giving away nothing because they can't take it home with them.'

Notes

1. Material for this case has been drawn from a number of sources. Readers may refer to Dumaine (1990, 1991), Hayes, Wheelwright and Clark (1988), Kantrow (1986), and Leonardo-Barton (1992) for more details.

Citicorp Inc.:
Learning to Innovate[1]

*We are really becoming a world bank in a very
broad sense and I am perfectly confident that it
is open to us to become the most powerful, the
most serviceable, the most far-reaching financial institution that there has ever been.*

—James Stillman
Senior Executive
Citicorp, 1915

*We have to build a smart organization, not just a
responsive organization. A smart organization
has shared wisdom and perspective, a textured
competence that shapes the behaviour of
individual practitioners.*

—John Reed
CEO
Citicorp, 1990

THE BACKGROUND

Citicorp (the name was adopted in 1974 for its non-consumer
operations) was established in 1812 as the National City Bank of
New York. It is the largest American bank, with assets exceeding
$210 billion, a shareholder equity of $11,181 million, and a profit
growth rate of 258 per cent. In 1993 it ranked as the fifteenth
largest in the world, accounting for 35 million outstanding charge

and credits worldwide. While it is headquartered in New York in the US, its reach is global; in 1990, 40 per cent of its revenue came from non-US operations. It has over 2,000 branches in 93 countries, with more than 90,000 employees. It has been operating in Europe since a long time: the London branch was set up in 1902 (the same year it launched its operation in India), the Paris office in 1906, and the German office in 1926. Today, it has over 700 branches in Europe, operates in 11 countries, and serves 3 per cent of all European households.

The bank has the reputation of being a fast-growing, competitive and customer-oriented organisation. For years, it has won accolades for being among the most professional banks in terms of services and solutions offered. In 1993, for the fifteenth consecutive year, it was polled the best bank for arranging foreign exchange by *Euromoney*; it has access to 140 currencies, and made a record-breaking profit of $1 billion in forex operations. In 1993, it was also among the top ten investment banks, and was voted second best for trading and arranging syndicated loans. In 1992, it was voted the best bank for providing information service. During the last decade, it has consistently featured among the top ten banks for its profits, ability to arrange loans and note facilities, developing new financial solutions, pricing sophisticated transactions, and so on.

In this case, we will trace the origins of Citibank's reputation and performance, both in its history and unique practices and procedures. (Citicorp is the bank holding company of which Citibank is the largest unit; the two names are often used interchangeably.)

BUILDING THE MOMENTUM

Throughout its long history, Citicorp has shown the potential for taking risks and being innovative: it was amongst the first banks to start global operations at the beginning of the twentieth century; in 1921, it was the first commercial bank to extend its lending activities to individuals; in 1951, it launched the first credit card— Diner's Club—in collaboration with Bloomingdale; in 1961, it created and introduced certificates of deposits, and so on. However, the changes that transformed its functioning and made it a market leader started in 1970 when Walter Wriston took over as its CEO. At that time, Citibank was the third largest American bank, Chase Manhattan and Bank of America being first and second, respectively.

Wriston was a visionary, who visualised Citicorp's future beyond merely operating within the boundaries fixed by the regulators and by the prevailing banking norms. In many ways, Wriston's style was confrontational and iconoclastic. As an article in *Fortune* described him: 'A man with a mission, he steamrolled his way to success.' During his tenure as CEO, Wriston gave the bank an aggressive stance and a unique identity in the banking community. He insisted on achieving an annual growth rate of 15 per cent for returns on assets. To achieve this, he demolished or got around the regulatory barriers to keep Citicorp expanding into investment banking and across state lines. In the process, he managed to transform the bank from a traditional commercial lender into an innovative organisation offering a wide array of services ranging from mortgage financing and insurance to electronic banking.

By the time Wriston handed over charge to John Reed in 1984 Citicorp had become the number one bank in America. In 1986, its net assets were $200 billion (the next largest bank was Bank of America, which had assets worth $95 billion). It ranked first in its profits, in 1981 and 1982; and between 1973 and 1983, the earnings per share increased from $2.11 to $6.48. It had also gained a reputation for being a fast-paced innovative trendsetter (in 1984, a *Fortune* survey of the 'most admired companies' gave it top rank for 'innovativeness'). What is more, the company has maintained this lead, and reputation, to the present.

To help implement his vision, Wriston brought in a group of young managers from outside the traditional banking fraternity to manage key posts. These newcomers, known at that time as the 'young tigers', also ushered in fresh perceptions and approaches about how Citicorp's operations should be organised, and how the bank should be run. These people were of diverse backgrounds and alien to the conservative banking profession. To take some significant examples, this group included:

- John Reed, the present CEO, an American literature, metallurgy and management major from MIT, known as a 'paradigm shifter'. He wanted to run banking as a 'focused factory'—a metaphor he carried from his previous work experience at the Ford Motor company—to liberate human resources and focus them outward on the customer and environmental scanning.

- Lawrence M. Small, who became head of the commercial banking operations, was a classically trained guitarist and had spent time studying the Flamenco guitar with Spanish gypsies. He was also recruited from Ford.

- Pei-Yuan Chia, a one-time brand manager of Brim decaffeinated coffee from General Foods, he headed Citicorp's Credit Card division. He is currently head of its global consumer banking business.

- Steve Price, who was one of the creators of the Citibanking concept, was also a General Foods marketer. His work experience before coming to Citibank included working with *Newsweek*. Price's boss, James Johnson, was a former packaged goods marketer with R.J.R. Reynolds (he has since returned to that company as president of its tobacco division).

- Richard S. Braddock, who was president and head of individual banking (Citicorp's term for its consumer and retail banking operations) till 1992, had past experience in selling Tang (the powdered drink) as the product manager with General Foods. His team consisted of two ex-General Foods managers, and one who started his career as a systems analyst.

The injection of new blood did change Citicorp's way of working. Reed, for instance, established his credentials in the 1970s by streamlining the functioning of the 'back office'—a name given to the operating group that processed check transactions. According to a Harvard Business School study, the long-term profitability of the bank depended on bringing the back office costs under control. Reed went about doing so by implementing a model of working which he had brought with his past experience. Reed's vision was to transform the back office into a factory producing high-quality products. In his own words, as Executive Vice President, Consumer Banking, in 1976: 'It should be pretty clear that we are creating ... a fundamentally new business.'

He recruited several executives with production background, and initiated system-wide changes. The division was reorganised on the model of a factory, processing transactions as if one was making cars. He automated, redesigned the work-flow and control systems, and brought down the headcount from 2,400 to 600 (in the process, gaining a reputation for being ruthless and brash—he was known as 'the brat'). Nevertheless, he managed to bring down and stabilise costs, achieving at the same time, an annual growth rate of 15 per cent in transaction volume.

During this period, Citicorp not only grew, but also became a market leader in defining the trends by developing and offering new services. In a way, through its innovative offerings, it started defining the rules of the business for others (a trend which it still continues to maintain).

- It extended banking operations beyond the traditional boundaries of corporate lending, inter-bank lending and foreign exchange, and developed and offered new services for corporate and institutional clients (such as currency 'swaps', commercial paper, hedging).

- In 1978, Citicorp became the first bank to launch automatic teller machines (ATMs) on a large scale.

- Around the same time, it also became the first bank to offer credit on checking account deposits.

- It moved ahead with interstate banking in the early 1980s.

- It was also the first bank to cash on information technology by establishing an elaborate satellite network for electronic banking.

In fact, during the 1980s, the rate of innovation was so high, that 50 per cent of the bank's earnings were coming from services that had not existed five years earlier. What is more, its innovations were not limited to banking operations alone; it innovated even in redefining itself. One of its 'inventions', the bank holding company, allowed it to circumvent regulatory barriers to operate outside traditional banking.

HOW CITICORP DOES IT

Over the years, fast-paced innovativeness has become institution-alised in Citicorp, enabling the company to successfully deal with the discontinuities of environmental changes. As we will see in the following sections, underlying this innovative and competitive stance is the ability of the organisation to learn from its experi-ences, and to foster an atmosphere in which not only is learning encouraged, but it even becomes a ruthless necessity for personal survival.

Orchestrated Diversity and Contradictions

One distinctive feature of Citicorp is the way in which it accom-modates, builds in, and encourages diversities, deviations and internal contradictions. This is nowhere more apparent than in its employee profile. We saw some notable examples of this diversity earlier. Similarly, the Policy Committee, which consists of the top 30 executives, has people of diverse backgrounds and nationali-ties. This is a multinational multilingual group, of whom three-fourths have experience of working in different cultures. This diversity, besides providing a pool of corporate talent, also facili-tates the organisation in having a more holistic approach to its business. Commenting on the cultural diversity represented in Citicorp, Reed remarked: 'Our global human capital may be as important a resource, if not more important, than our financial capital.'

The variety in profiles (and the consequent variety of orienta-tions and viewpoints) is not limited to key posts at the strategic apex. It cuts across all levels and functions in the organisation. Unlike many other organisations, Citicorp recruits people from diverse backgrounds. In applying for a job at the lower entry levels, it does not make a difference what school one went to or whom one happens to be related to. One advantage of such a system is that it does not allow an old-boys' network to form (who can form a political nexus to resist change). Citibankers, however, are similar in one way. They are all competitive, action oriented and individualistic (exceptions probably leave or are weeded out). According to Braddock (the individual banking chief): 'All our recruiting starts from the view that we are a different business from a traditional bank. The skills required to make it successful are also different, more oriented to management and marketing.'

The diversity contributes much to the state of perpetual dynamic instability which characterises Citicorp. In fact, the organisation actively and consciously encourages this disequilibrium. One researcher has described Citicorp as 'living dangerously', sustaining a precarious balance between powerful and mutually contradictory forces. The following examples of how Citicorp is organised and operates provide a reasonable appreciation of these inherent contradictions:

- Citicorp encourages risk-taking, initiative and innovativeness; managers are generously rewarded with pay increases and promotions for their creative efforts. But, simultaneously, it is also a system-driven result-oriented organisation that allows for no excuses, or qualitative rationalisations of failures. For instance, without exception each year the managers are expected to achieve each of their five mandatory MBO targets.

- Citicorp has a comprehensive human resource function, which very effectively drills the 'soft' skills of motivating, communicating, giving constructive performance feedback, conflict resolution, and the like, into the first-line and middle-management ranks. This training is not merely 'one of those things which organisations do' (since Wriston's time human resource function has been headed by fast-track line managers). These are skills which managers genuinely need to master in order to survive. Side by side, however, the organisation expects managers to take hard decisions and instil cold discipline to achieve results (many of its divisions still practise a system of bi-annual forced ranking of all its employees by the respective managers, after which the bottom 10 per cent are culled out).

- In many ways, Citicorp is a hierarchical organisation. Asking the managers to take hard decisions about their subordinates' performance encourages them to play god with them. One's survival depends on the boss's evaluation. According to one observer: 'One wins by anticipating what the bosses will ask for.' On the other hand, Citicorp also excels in moving decision-making levels down. There is a high degree of decentralisation, and individuals with just a few years experience are handed major accounts and clients. The pressure to perform, and the stringent evaluation criteria also ensure that young individuals take decisions. In many instances (such as corporate banking) this is also a business necessity, as Reed explains: 'Our professional competence sits down low in corporate bank, with people on the frontline who deal with customers and advise the transactions. We can't develop products at the center and push them out. Good corporate bankers are walking product development departments.'

- Against all classical principles of management, Citicorp has a propensity for assigning tasks with overlapping jurisdictions, which forces executives to compete against, and negotiate and/or collaborate with their colleagues (in any case it does not allow them to become complacent in their jobs). Often, 'specialist' divisions, such as treasury, investment management, new issues and forex management, may find themselves dealing with the same customer for overlapping services. The director of human resources explains:

There is a lot of creative tension here over jurisdiction. Things are organized by function, market, or product. Many of these impact on the same customer. No one here has a clear territory, or clear ownership of a total activity. This tends to keep people on their toes. You're aware that all of your colleagues are nibbling at opportunities too, and if they can come at what you do from another direction and do it well, and make a buck, they're going to get license and permission to pursue that.

- These contradictions, which are part of the Citicorp culture, are manifested in the socio-political aspects of its functioning as well. It might sometimes be difficult to assess the causes underlying actions and events; many organisational happenings are ambiguous, equivocal, even self-contradictory. For instance, in 1982, Wriston's creation of a separate investment banking division was strongly resisted by a senior member of the strategic apex, Thomas C. Theobald (who was also Reed's chief rival in the succession battle). During Reed's time, however, it was Theobald who took charge of the investment banking division and made it a success (in 1993, Citicorp was polled the world's tenth best investment bank by*Euromoney*, and second best in trading and arranging syndicated loans). One can guess the kind of political uncertainty such shifts in alignment would create for the lower cadres. Similarly, when Reed became CEO in 1984, he changed from the brash confrontative 'brat' of the 1970s and adopted a much softer stance (people commented on his having become magnanimous, accommodating and cooperative). At the same time, Lawrence Small, Reed's closest associate (and therefore perceived as conveying Reed's message), circulated a somewhat threatening note to the top management group. The note said:

> We have too many people doing too much unnecessary bureaucratic activity, too many studies, too many reports, too many management information systems, too many staff functions, too many unprofitable relationships. ... No one here is getting paid to have an easy way ... we have to become flatter and leaner.

Meritocracy and Entrepreneurship

The concept of 'meritocracy', that is, pay and promotions are not linked to seniority but to performance, was institutionalised during Wriston's tenure. Citicorp nurtures talents and allows them to bypass others and jump rungs. However, the practice of meritocracy goes beyond mere compensation and promotion. The organisation makes conscious efforts to seek out and support high-track talent. High-flyers are identified early in their careers, and get special attention for development. According to one report:

> Behind locked doors on the fifteenth floor of Citicorp's Park Avenue headquarters sits a room devoted to what is called 'Corporate Property'. Pinned on a board in the office are the photos and biographies of about 75 managers, considered to be [the] bank's up-and-coming superstars. The only people permitted entry into the room are the bank's top two dozen senior executives. They make sure the superstars get special attention and job transfers to acquire a broad-based experience at the bank.

However, this does not actually amount to the building up of a culture of haves and have-nots, which separates the blue-eyed boys from the lesser mortals. Rather, the opportunity to create one's unique career path is open to anyone who aspires after it. Wriston used to tell prospective employees. 'Each new job I've accepted (except the one I now hold) didn't exist before I took it.'

In some ways, the philosophy of encouraging individualistic initiative influences the bank's recruitment as well. Citicorp often hires above its baseline requirements. It expects that the working together of so many over-achievers will create new jobs and opportunities for them as well as the bank. Job changes and horizontal movements are popular and frequent across levels, partly because people are expected to create their own niches. Moreover, as mentioned earlier, Citicorp culture provides enormous autonomy to take initiative. Instead of large departments, in which one may become an anonymous figure, the bank is organised as small, more or less autonomous 'enclaves', providing enough opportunity for independent action. A senior vice president of the consumer bank division has commented:

> Citicorp moves decisions down. This is an extremely important aspect of the bank, and its impact is far-reaching. An individual in his or her late twenties is handed major responsibility. You can run your business, your department, or be on a team that's running business. With this strong tradition of pushing decision-making down, young individuals have to take decisions and are weaned on that tradition. Here is our engine of innovation. We genuinely empower them. We don't get in their way and undermine them with bureaucracy and excessive financial controls.

It is not surprising that Citicorp has a reputation for being innovative and enterprising. Commenting on this organisational tendency, a senior Citicorp executive said:

> We're encouraged to break away and defy parameters. You really have a bunch of kite fliers, and like kites, they tend to go where they please and catch different currents. . . . It's so competitive and culturally diverse that without a strong leader with a strong vision, we have strong centrifugal tendencies.

Experimentation and Action Learning

Citicorp's strategy for countering environmental turbulence has been to pre-empt changes. Instead of reacting and adapting to environmental changes, it experiments and proactively enacts and creates an environment for itself (and often for others). This was most apparent in the manner it went about developing and implementing the ATMs.

Citicorp began investing in ATMs almost a decade before many of its competitors. In 1971, it bought Transaction Technology Inc. (TTI), a California engineering and software company, and set up 'the lab' in the basement of a New York office building. The sole function of this facility was to develop and test new products and services. Headed by the chief of consumer bank's development division, Lawrence Weiss (another marketing man with previous experience of selling Hungry Jack pancake mix at Pillsbury and Cycle dog food at General Foods), this venture helped Citicorp understand the customer's response to a non-human teller. Observing and talking to customers in the lab provided useful clues for solving such mundane design problems as how high the machine's keyboard should be and how hard the buttons should be pressed. These issues were critical to making ATMs user-friendly, and in attracting the less gadget-prone customers. In 1977, when Citicorp deployed ATMs on a large scale, it was TTI's sixth-generation prototype. The first five were designed, built, tested in the lab and scrapped. This ATM (christened Suzy by the affectionate researchers) did not frighten the customers away with brusque command phrases such as INSERT CARD NOW (as the machines of the competitors did), but asked warm, friendly and helpful queries, such as 'May I help you with something else?' This automation also proved to be the single biggest factor in Citicorp's success in grabbing a large chunk of the New York market—one of the most competitive ones in the US. In a short time, about 80 per cent of Citicorp's customers started using ATMs for more than half their business transactions. Over the next decade or so, Citicorp tripled its share of deposits and its share of customer loans went from 1 to 21 per cent.

Citicorp's learning from experiments, however, is not merely limited to such safe settings as 'the lab'. It also creates learning experiences for itself from what social scientists would describe as 'field experiments'. For instance, Citicorp's Credit Card division (which includes Visa, Master Card, Diners Club, Carte Blanche, and Choice, a card offered to Washington, D.C. residents) periodically takes a few thousand applications at random and approves them without performing any credit evaluation beyond verifying that the applicant is not bankrupt. Many of these, naturally, are bad risks. But Citicorp lets them default on payment in order to get a better statistical picture of how defaulters behave. The information derived from such experiments goes into Citicorp's credit-scoring system, which is used for monitoring the behaviour of the existing and future cardholders. The system is considered among the most sophisticated ones in the world.

Of course, such learning comes at a cost. In one experiment, for instance, the card division loses something between $1 and 5 million. In fact, between 1979 and 1981 Citibank's card business lost $516 million. But, then, the bank hopes to capitalise on this learning and recuperate the losses by more precise control in future. This attitude is reflected in Braddock's comment: 'Failures are part of the landscape if you're trying to change things and grow.' Citicorp has changed the landscape; today it is the largest card-issuer, with more than 36 million cards in circulation globally.

This somewhat reckless attitude of shooting first and aiming afterwards is to some extent part of Citicorp's tradition and culture. The organisation encourages speed in action and decision-making. An informal rule is to take quick decisions, even if the solution is less than perfect. Citicorp culture discourages the tendency to study things for too long or to stand in the way of action. As a result, the failure rate of initiatives is rather high. There have been times when Citicorp has had to backtrack on its actions. For instance, in 1983, the bank insisted that customers with a balance of less than $5,000 should transact only through ATMs. This created quite an uproar among the customers. Citicorp's competitor Chemical Bank took advantage of the dissatisfaction by putting out ads saying, 'Our Tellers Love People'. Citicorp had to quickly reverse its decision.

This maverick (and apparently impulsive) approach to doing business, however, does not mean that organisational actions are not rooted in any deliberately designed strategy. On the contrary, the strategy is to be impulsive, to experiment, and to learn both from successes and failures. This is clear from the fact that Citicorp has always shown as much alacrity in reversing a losing strategy as it has in implementing it. In 1987, when it was planning to launch Citi Stations (modelled on the concept of familiar gas stations, and equipped with ATMs that would rise and fall to the height of the customer's car), it also had a plan ready to quickly cancel this if it did not work. One of the consequences of such a strategy is, of course, a high redundancy of efforts. According to one insider:

> This place is organized chaos. We start a lot of things and only ten to twenty per cent of them survive. A lot don't work out. A lot of other companies with a more rigorous management style wouldn't allow that. But around here, we build things, blow them up, then start again.

Customer Responsiveness

Customer focus is not new to Citicorp. It has been part of the bank's strategy for nearly a century. A part of its mission statement reads: 'Our financial objective is to build shareholder value through ... a continued commitment to building customer-oriented businesses worldwide.'

This is not just rhetoric. It is built in in the way the bank operates and organises itself. One of the underlying beliefs which guide Citicorp's operations is that clients value the quality of the relationship (i.e., the service and responsiveness) more than the cost of the relationship (i.e., the interest rate and charges). And it has not been misguided in this belief. For instance, during the mid-1980s, it charged an exorbitant interest rate of 19.8 per cent on credit card balances; and yet, between 1983 and 1987, its credit card accounts increased threefold, from 3.2 million to about 10 million. The reason was that Citicorp, supported by its computerised systems, offered the most efficient service in the retail banking sector. Its credit card service centre handled 60,000 calls every day, many of them between midnight and 6.00 a.m. ('The Citi that never sleeps'). More than 95 per cent of the problems, such as billing errors and lost and stolen cards, were resolved in the course of the customer's initial call.

Similarly, in its mortgage business (described later), while the Gallup Poll results showed that consumers prefer best rates and reputation over quick processing of loan applications (rank 4), Citicorp succeeded by focusing primarily on the service aspect.

Citicorp realised long before its competitors that for service organisation in a highly competitive and changing business environment customer focus is a basic necessity for success and survival. As Julian Simmond, Managing Director of FX and money markets in Europe, explains: 'You can't have just a product and not customer focus. It's the combination that makes us unique.' Citicorp has always taken initiative in offering innovative services and financial options, and has succeeded because these offerings were designed to meet emergent customer needs. Often, the efforts to satisfy customers appear, at first glance, to be unnecessarily risky. A closer examination, however, shows that underlying the recklessness is actually a smarter way in which the organisation has applied its collective learning knowledge.

Take, for instance, Citicorp's operations in mortgage financing. At a time, when the normal time taken by banks to process loans was around 45 days, Citicorp entered the market (in 1983), offering to approve loans in 15 days. With such a tempting (and to many, foolhardy) offer, naturally, Citicorp catapulted into the market. Mortgage originations from the bank grew from $756 million in 1983 to $5.5 billion in 1986. When it created Mortgage Power in 1986, they jumped to $14.8 billion in 1987. To outspeed itself, in February 1989 Citicorp announced that it promised to decide on mortgage loans in 15 minutes!

Was Citicorp recklessly trading risks for quick growth? Apparently not. The strategy was largely based on a thorough understanding of the nature of the market and customers' needs. Mostly customers needed large loans for purchasing a house, for which they had signed an agreement. Since this agreement normally closed in 60 days, the time between applying for the loan and its sanctioning was filled with uncertainty and anxiety (for, who knows, the mortgage company may, as they were wont to, ask for more documents or clarifications at the last moment or worse, deny the loan). Citicorp's quick-response offer was focused on meeting this need of the customers. However, it had also significantly covered its risks by working smarter than its competitors. First, it accepted only applications with a loan-to-value ratio of 80 per cent or less, which was a reasonable estimate of the minimum price a property would sell for, in case of default. Second, its application form was designed to preclude the necessity of extensive document enclosures (thereby reducing the time required for verification). It also circumvented some of the time-consuming activities by redesigning procedures (e.g., instead of asking for mortgage insurance and losing time in verifying its validity, it chose to self-insure its mortgages). Third, its system of electronic data transmission saved as much as about a week of processing time. Lastly, and most significantly, unlike other banks, it treated real estate agents as much its customers as the real applicants (the majority of whom in any case apply only through an agent) and focused its efforts to enlist them. The MortgagePower programme offered membership to real estate agents for $2,500, in return for a discount on loan interest rates, and a promise of a loan decision within 15 days. The relationship with the agents ensured that they screened the applicants before forwarding their applications to Citicorp: Quality customers were directed to Citicorp, while the high-risk customers were sent to traditional sources of money.

The bank, however, does not define customer focus as mere selling of specific services; for it, customer focus means developing a long-term relationship with clients (note that customer is defined as 'client'; customers buy products off-the-shelf, whereas the relationship with a client is deeper and longer lasting). If an organisation has managed to build stable relationships with its clients, then, in many ways, it has succeeded in creating stability in a changing environment (as it did by stabilising its relationship with real estate agents). Linc Hoffman, who heads the Citicorp's World Corporate Group (WCG) in the UK, explains: 'Managing relationships is a marathon, not a sprint. A relationship properly developed will transcend my lifetime. It takes years to build and seconds to destroy the trust and confidence for a relationship. ... A short-term point of view just won't work.'

Correspondingly, Citicorp invests a lot into developing specific long-term relationships with clients. For instance, WCG, which was set up in 1986 to focus on the top global companies, has a specific post of 'relationship manager'. These managers are assigned to specific accounts (clients). Relationship managers generally stay with the account for a minimum of five years, which helps them in getting to know the client and his needs well, and to develop, what is called in Citicorp a 'relationship-continuity'. Learning about the client's requirements is an essential element of the relationship-building process. Clients are visited on a regular basis (often once every two months), and the visits are not confined to any particular level (e.g., director) or department (e.g., finance). Discussing issues with people not necessarily linked to the banking process helps the bank in understanding the client's business as a whole.

In addition to the visits, the various departments of the bank conduct a yearly survey called 'relationship review', which seeks feedback from clients about how the bank is handling their accounts in different product areas. The client's perceptions are used by the relationship managers for two purposes. First, they are used for coordinating the services that different product areas are offering to the same client (this is essential also, given the overlapping nature of services and jurisdictions). For instance, in WCG, relationship managers organise periodic internal meetings of all those on the account. The agenda of these meetings is not necessarily to solve specific problems, but to discuss and understand what the bank is doing (or should be doing) with the client. Often, these meetings include clients so that their views can be sought in setting objectives and checking the congruence between the bank's and the client's objectives.

Second, the information is used for designing, innovating and customising a solution (a blending of different financial techniques) which fits the client's requirements. In fact, developing a customised solution is an essential part of developing enduring client relationships. A senior executive from the corporate banking division pointed out: 'We're a problem-solving unit. If you haven't solved the company's problem, you won't get the repeat business.'

Citicorp develops customised solutions in a variety of ways. The feedback and the clients' expectations are identified from different sources and integrated in the planning process. They are also used as the basis for generating internal knowledge through brainstorming sessions. A study on Citicorp describes one such case:

For one client, the WCG organised a full-day session which brought together relationship managers and product specialists. One executive narrated his experience: 'We sat down and thought about the company (after having done our homework) and in the brainstorming session, came up with 32 ideas. We then tried to narrow them down into categories. Five representatives from the company were invited to dinner that evening and placed at five separate tables corresponding to five different categories of ideas that we had developed for them. . . . They told us that we had a better understanding of their business strategy than anyone else they had talked to.'

One unique feature of Citicorp's functioning is the way in which it manages an 'intangible' like service performance. This process comprises two overlapping activities: the scrutiny of and control over the quality of service, and the codification and measurement of performance. Internally, a solution goes through a thorough screening before it reaches the client. The system of regular internal meetings and periodic discussions with client facilitate this process. In addition, Citicorp has a system of 'cross-selling': the specialist divisions are required to sell their services to the relationship managers (thus, a high premium on 'presentation skills' within the bank). The process entails tough internal criticism and successive stages of refinement of an idea before presentation to the client. Similarly, many departments of Citicorp have a system of looking at, and learning from, past mistakes. Weekly meetings are held to discuss and analyse failures and derive constructive lessons for the future. Such systems ensure that only client-relevant learning is used in developing solutions and ideas.

Citicorp has developed its own ways of codifying and measuring the effectiveness of customer responsiveness. Revenue and profit are much too myopic an indicator of customer relations, when one is trying to develop a long-term relationship with the client. Customer surveys, of course, provide a conventional means of assessing this responsiveness in a tangible manner. There are other more innovative methods the bank uses for translating intangibles into tangibles. It has, for instance, a system called 'tier-positioning', which helps it assess where it stands vis-à-vis corporate clients. If the bank is among the client's top three banks, it is in tier one; tier two means that the bank is one among the first six; and below this is tier three, which means that the bank is one among the many others which the client uses. If, over the year, a department has increased the number of clients for which it is in tier-one position, it has made progress. Similarly, some departments monitor the number of calls made per product area to the client annually, and the level of contact and the time spent with the client to keep track of the nature of customer contact maintained by the bank. There is also a 'global relationship' award for the team which achieves the greatest growth in client activity.

Management of Information

Citicorp was the first bank to use information technology as a competitive weapon. In fact, it was Wriston's vision to make the bank capitalise on the vast potential of this technology. During the 1970s and 1980s, Citicorp's incursions into information technology were in the field of the related technologies of data processing, telecommunications, office and professional systems (MIS), decision support and production control. By the end of 1986, Citicorp had more than 200 data centres, operating within a worldwide communications network comprising over 125,000 terminals, 85,000 of which were located in customers' offices and homes. It had become the world's largest non-government information-processing operation outside the data-processing industry. In fact, in 1989, its annual expenditure on info-tech was close to $900 million. According to some researchers: 'On a scale of 1 to 10, when it comes to willingness to invest in technology-based business ventures, Citibank is a 10—and few others score higher than a 7.'

This not only helps speed up the bank's operations, but also binds its widespread operations in a network. For instance, all branches of the bank in the US are connected through a wide area network (WAN). This permits sharing of daily news among branches, and teller transaction times and cash difficulties, and of giving and seeking help during emergencies. The technology has given it an edge even in training its workforce. Since 1988, many product extensions and new launches have been 'taught' to the branch staff through interactive Macintosh colour diskettes. This permits branch managers to schedule staff training around slower periods, and allows junior employees to access the same learning (classroom training is reserved for more difficult human issues, e.g., negotiation).

Information technology is only one source of gearing up for knowledge-based competition. Citicorp puts a high premium on information inputs from clients to learn more about them (and about its own business performance). It also subscribes extensively to financial sectoral studies done by external consultants and organisations (e.g., Greenwich Study in the UK) as important inputs in its planning and problem-solving activities. What is significant, however, is the way in which it leverages its isolated instances of knowledge resources into innovative and competitive strategies, products and services. For instance, after the October 1987 New York Stock Market crash, Citibank had a new supermoney market product developed and priced, together with powerful market promotion, aimed at capturing dollar deposits from investors fleeing the capital market. The whole process was prepared in a 72-hour marathon, made possible only by the bank's ongoing ability to scan the market-place at the lower levels: the branch network, the Citibankers, and the events in the external environment.

In spite of Citicorp's highly individualistic (and for some, dog-eat-dog) ways of working and stringent individual performance standards, the emphasis on sharing of expertise and knowledge is built in into its systems and practices. Indeed, there are numerous awards based on a system of sharing and working as a team: the 'best partnership' award for the relationship between managers and product specialists, the 'best transaction' award for increased activity between two or more countries, and so on. According to Reed:

> You create the demand for sharing with a strong and consistent drive from the top. In the early days, a few of us were catalysts, flying all over the world and urging people to work together. You create the supply by showing people what has been done elsewhere. Exposing people to success gives them the courage and drive to persist. It's a known fact in scientific literature that if you tell one lab that another lab has succeeded at an experiment, the first lab is much more likely to succeed as well. The same dynamics works in the bank.

There are a variety of ways in which the bank approaches the process of 'success transfer' (a term coined by Singapore

Citibanker, Rana Talwar). Many of the organisational systems and practices facilitate this process, even though they might not have been designed with this explicit purpose in mind. One such widely practised system is the frequent rotation and transfer of personnel on a regular basis. While this does produce discontinuities—probably the system is designed to do precisely that—it also ensures that people develop a common perspective and vocabulary, and that the expertise of one gets transferred to others. Only in isolated cases does the bank initiate horizontal movements with the clear motive of transferring expertise from one place to another (e.g., someone who understands the card business in Brazil is moved to a place where he or she is needed); mostly, moving people around is just the way the organisation operates.

Knowledge transfer is further facilitated in Citicorp by internal meetings and conferences. As noted earlier, the system of cross-functional meetings helps people exchange their understanding of clients' needs and requirements. In addition, Citibank organises conferences with the specific purpose of people sharing their experiences. Reed has described these:

> We've always had lots of meetings organized by function or lines of business. We might get all the credit card people in the world together and let them tell war stories—what works in Australia, what is working in Germany. We also carefully track performance around the world. We would take auto loans, for example, and organize a conference to compare revenues, expenses, write-offs, staffing levels, and so on. ... We would learn from what they were doing and transfer those insights around the world.

Besides facilitating contact between people, Citicorp has systems for circulating information on a regular basis. It uses its electronic information transmission system to circulate and keep people posted on the new ideas and solutions developed by Citibankers around the world. Also, it publishes a monthly in-house journal. Every issue contains ten to 15 innovative solutions, permitting ideas to be drawn from solutions developed by others. Such systems are designed to disseminate ideas and information, and to convert local solutions to global competitive advantage.

Notes

1. Citicorp is a much written about company. This case was developed on the basis of published magazine and newspaper reports, and studies by academic researchers. Readers may refer to Boyer (1986), Cobb *et al.* (1992), Horovitz and Panak (1992), Levering *et al.* (1984), Meehan (1990), Norton (1987), Pascale (1990), Stalk and Hout (1990), Tichy and Ram Charan (1990), Urban and Star (1991), and a report in the *Wall Street Journal* (18 March 1992) for more details.

General Electric: Learning as Cultural Transformation[1]

This is one of the biggest planned efforts to alter people's behaviour since the Cultural Revolution.

—Professor Len Schlesinger
Harvard Business School

We want ... GE as a place where people have the freedom to be creative, a place that brings out the best in everybody. An open, fair place where people have a sense that what they do matters, and where that sense of accomplishment is rewarded in both pocketbook and the soul. That will be our report card.

—John F. Welch
CEO, General Electric

THE GROWTH

To say the least, General Electric (GE) is a remarkable organisation, both in its history and stature. One of the world's largest companies, with a revenue of $65 billion, it is the world's leading producer of items from light bulbs and dishwashers to locomotives and power plants. It manages more credit cards than American Express, and owns more commercial aircraft than American Airlines. Its salary bill of $13 billion (for 300,000 employees) is large enough to change the balance of trade of many countries. This case describes the successful cultural transformation of GE.

GE evolved from a company founded by Thomas Edison in 1877 to manufacture electric light bulbs. In 1892, Charles Coffin, who was one of the investors in Edison's venture, purchased Edison's patents and founded the General Electric Company. GE's growth came because of its strategy of working along the US government policies, which recognised electricity as a major factor in the industrialisation of America. GE, along with its major competitor, Westinghouse, virtually monopolised the power generation, transmission and distribution market. In time, Coffin and his successors diversified GE's product portfolio, ranging from products that generated or transmitted electricity to appliances that used it. Thus, by the mid-1930s, the company was producing small and large electrical appliances (e.g., bulbs, toasters, heaters, refrigerators), as well as power generation and transmission equipment. It had licensed its technology throughout Europe, China, Japan, and Latin America, where it also had joint ventures. It also owned equity in companies like Seimens and Philips.

The Second World War, and the post-War boom in the demand for reconstruction of Europe, further increased GE's operations. This period also saw GE entering many wartime technologies, such as aircraft engines, nuclear energy, and aerospace. With its philosophy, to make rather than outsource, GE's business integrated vertically. The opportunity to diversify, combined with the tendency towards self-sufficiency, created a huge organisation. There were, of course, some less successful ventures too, such as computers and mobile communications; nevertheless, the company continued to grow.

By the early 1980s, GE's empire had spread across some 350 products and businesses, many of which were leaders. It was manufacturing a dazzling array of products from bulbs and refrigerators to locomotives and power plants. It had the third largest manpower in the US, totalling some 367,000 employees, and, in spite of its size and diversity, it managed itself successfully. Its revenue (more than $25 billion) ranked fourteenth highest in the world (and eleventh in the US), and it was the fifth most profitable US corporation. Over the years, on average, it had earned a 15 per cent return on investment— an achievement not many companies can boast of in this time span. It is nost surprising that Harvard

Business School wrote over 90 extremely flattering cases on this organisation.

THE RENEWAL

Given its success, there appears to have been no reason for GE to have attempted to change and renew itself. However, there were two reasons for its doing this. One, behind its apparent success there lurked the seeds of potential failure. In integrating itself vertically during the post-War period, and by subsequent attempts to streamline its activities, GE was becoming a bureaucratic mammoth, difficult to manage. During this period, GE's CEOs decentralised powers to businesses, and fixed profit and loss accountabilities with them. This increased the bureaucratic needs for financial accounting, audit and control. GE's 'invention' of strategic planning put further emphasis on compliance to planning and reporting procedures by the business units. Moreover, while GE's revenues grew, in real value, they merely doubled between 1958 and 1981.

The second reason for GE's change was that, in 1981, it got a new CEO, John Francis Welch, who was aware of the realities mentioned above. Jack Welch was a surprising choice, being very different from past CEOs; also, aged 45, he was the youngest CEO in GE's history. But as one observer has noted: 'GE's genius has been in its choice of successive CEOs, each of whom tended to counter the extremes of his predecessors.' Jack Welch, with a doctorate in chemical engineering from the University of Illinois, was known as a maverick, often abrasive, and entrepreneurial—a complete misfit in the GE of the day. However, his performance record in turning around and building businesses was excellent. He started his career in GE's plastic division, and built it into a 2 billion business, with an average earning growth of 33 per cent a year. Promoted as a group head, he made GE's fledgling medical diagnostic business into a world leader in CAT-scan imaging. And then, as vice chairman, he transformed GE's financial arm, GE Capital, into the fourteenth largest lending institution in America.

One can identify two distinct phases of GE's self-renewal and revitalisation under Welch. According to Welch himself:

The decade of the 1980s imposed two distinct challenges. In the first phase, through 1986, we had to pay attention to the 'hardware'—fixing the businesses. In the second phase, from 1987 well into the 1990s, we have to focus on the 'software'. Our sustained competitiveness can only come from improved productivity— and that requires the bottom-up initiatives of our people.

Correspondingly, the first phase of Jack Welch's initiative focused on the restructuring of portfolios. During this time, GE organised itself along three interlocking circles representing its businesses: the core businesses (e.g., lighting, major appliances, turbines), the high-technology products (e.g., plastics, aircraft engines, medical appliances), and the high-growth services (e.g., financial and information services). Businesses which fell outside these circles (e.g., coal mines, computer chips, mobile communications, consumer electronics, housewares) were sold off. New businesses, such as RCA, Employee Reinsurance Company, and Peabody Kidder, were acquired to further strengthen the existing portfolio. Between 1981 and 1987, GE acquired companies worth $16 billion and sold operations worth $9 billion. Through layoffs, attrition and sale of businesses, GE eliminated over 100,000 jobs (Welch acquired the nickname of 'Neutron Jack', after the neutron bomb, which eliminates people but leaves the building intact). Through the reshuffling, divestures, and acquisitions, GE's 43 strategic business units (SBUs), consisting of about 350 businesses and product lines, were consolidated into 14 business divisions. GE's corporate aim was to focus energies and to become a world leader ('number 1 or 2') in these businesses.

The second phase, which started in the later part of the 1980s, focused on corporate cultural renewal. It comprised a programme of infusing the organisation with new ideas about managing itself, of empowering people, and breaking the mental and organisational boundaries to bring out the creative energies in the organisation. Although we will be discussing the second phase in this case, it is worth keeping in mind that, in a way, the two phases are not really different from each other. They are part of an overall strategy. And strategy, according to Welch, is 'not a lengthy plan of action, but the evolution of a central idea through continually changing circumstances'.

Also, these efforts did appear to succeed. By 1989, after adjusting for inflation, the real earnings per share rose to an average of 7.6 per cent, as compared to 4.9 per cent and 1.6 per cent during the times of Welch's two predecessors. Further, between 1983 and 1993, GE's sales more than doubled, from $26.5 billion to $62 billion. GE ranked as the world's largest company in terms of assets, and its market value shot up from $12 billion in 1980 to $765 billion in 1991 (second only to Exxon). It became the world's fourth most profitable company (its profits exceeded the total sales of more than 180 companies in the *Fortune Global 500* list).

CREATING A BOUNDARYLESS COMPANY

'For a large organisation to be effective,' according to Welch, 'it must be simple.' However, he also says that it is quite difficult to be simple. But simplicity is essential for the organisation to be alert and agile in meeting challenges. Achieving this simplicity was the focus of Welch's efforts to transform GE, based on the vision of, what he described as, 'a boundaryless company'. Boundarylessness has myriads of meanings, and a far-reaching significance. According to James E. Noel, manager of GE's Crotonville Management Development Institute:

> What it basically means is that there are artificial boundaries that you create within your organisation, and those boundaries create all sorts of problems for you. They are boundaries of a hierarchical nature between levels and layers within the organisation; there are boundaries that you create for yourself between functions; and all those boundaries get in the way of your doing work, of being effective, of creating an organisation that can move fast, that has the characteristics of speed and simplicity.

It is interesting to note that while Welch embarked upon changing GE's historical traditions, he also had the advantage of building on that history. New concepts and visions were not new to the company. Many management concepts—decentralisation, market research, action learning, portfolio planning, management by objectives, strategic planning, etc.—which have now found their way into textbooks, were either invented in GE, or were for the first time systematically applied there. Thus, in a way, the new vision of boundarylessness was only a continuation of that tradition.

As will be seen later, this concept also extends to GE's relationships with its environment—to its customers, suppliers, and to the countries in which it operates. In the following sections, we will discuss how GE has attempted to operationalise this 'boundarylessness' in its day-to-day functioning.

Busting Up the Corporate Bureaucracy

I have mentioned earlier the growth of the bureaucracy in GE during the 1960s and 1970s. Welch has described it as 'the cramping artifacts that pile up in dusty attics of century-old companies: reports, meetings, rituals, approvals, and forests of paper that seem necessary until they are removed'.

It is necessary to elaborate this point to understand its implication for the company. An understanding of GE's bureaucracy and its growth also provides the rationale behind the many changes which were to come in the 1980s.

The post-War period was a period of growth for GE. The company diversified and entered into many new businesses, partly because of the opportunities, and partly because of its in-built philosophy of self-sufficiency. Its growth also created a greater need for control and coordination. This need was met by decentralising and treating each unit as a profit centre, and allocating resources and control on the basis of returns. This enhanced and strengthened the power of finance executives at the corporate level. In fact, over a period of time, by the 1970s the 12,000-odd finance cadre of GE had become, according to one observer, the most 'formidable example of an elite cadre in corporate America' which exerted an inordinate amount of influence on corporate activities. A member of the finance cadre could easily overrule his peers, and even a superior, in the line function.

Even at the business-unit level, the finance manager was more or less independent of line control. The line manager could not hire, select, remove or fire the finance executive without the chief financial officer's review and concurrence. Later, when the 43 SBUs were created to consolidate the growing diversity, they added to the management overload—and GE solved the problem of coordination by regrouping them into six sectors.

These measures also had positive outcomes. Greater focus on controls, return on investments and cash flow, staff reviews, demand for clear-cut strategies from the business units, etc., improved GE's financial situation. GE went from a chronic cash shortage to immense financial strength, which further enhanced its strategic flexibility.

Conversely, these measures resulted in increasing the layers of hierarchy and creating bottlenecks. The management structure grew to nine layers and 29 salary levels. Moreover, the need for financial accounting and coordination was gradually replaced with compliance and control. Planning procedures, routine reporting, and selling one's plans to top management took precedence over the more core-line activities. In the early 1980s, an informal poll of GE line managers showed that over two-thirds of them considered the financial elites as overemphatic in their demand for perfection and compliance. One business journalist reported the excessive bureaucratic emphasis in GE's functioning:

> The computers in one GE business spit out seven daily reports. Just one made a stack of paper twelve feet high, containing product-by-product sales information—accurate to [the] penny—on hundreds of thousands of items. The bureaucracy routinely emasculated top executives by overwhelming them with useless information and enslaved middle managers with the need to gather it. Old timers say that the mastery of facts became impossible, illusion sufficed.

One of the challenges in rejuvenating GE was to remove excessive, obstructive bureaucracy. Realising that the various levels between the CEO and the business heads filtered the communication and increased the decision cycle time, Welch started from the top. He eliminated levels of corporate staff and sector and group heads, and dramatically reduced the controls and reports which did not add value to work. The management structure now comprised just five broad bands.

An example of the exercise of simplifying the organisational routines was the restructuring of the apex body, the Corporate Executive Council (CEC). By eliminating the intervening sectors (in 1985), this small group now ensured direct communication among the 14 business heads, the top staff people, and the CEO. The group would meet for two days every quarter to review progress, and to share information and ideas (which included the programme that had failed). Moreover, instead of a formal, long-winding strategic review, the business heads now worked on a much simplified framework. In 1986, each of the business heads was asked to prepare a one-page answer to five basic questions:

1. What are your market dynamics globally today, and where are they going over the next several years?

2. What actions have your competitors taken in the last three years to upset those global dynamics?

3. What have you done in the last three years to affect those dynamics?

4. What are the most dangerous things your competitor could do in the next three years to upset those dynamics?

5. What are the most effective things you could do to bring your desired impact on those dynamics?

The five charts for each business, which would be updated regularly, were easy to understand, communicate, and manage. They became the guidelines for strategic decisions and actions for GE, ensured that everyone in the CEC had a comprehensive and holistic understanding of GE's business, and reduced the cycle time for decision-making. Investment decisions which would otherwise have taken months or years, now could be made and implemented in days. For instance, when GE swapped its consumer electronics business with Thomson's medical equipment business, the process took just five days. Similarly, it took GE only three days to negotiate and finalise its joint ventures in gas turbines, medical equipment, circuit breakers, and appliances with GEC, Britain outsprinting rivals like AT&T, Plessey, Thomson, and Northern Telcom.

Empowering the Grassroots

The CEC model percolated down to the executive and operating committees of individual business. Here, multifunctional groups would meet monthly or weekly to thrash out problems, exchange information, communicate with each other about their prospects and programmes. The communication process ensured that people in different functions had access to a common database, so that it was easier to arrive at common understandings and decisions. As Welch expressed in an interview in 1989: 'The problem is, we don't get the same information. We each get a different piece. Business isn't complicated. The complications arise when people are cut off from information they need. That's what we are trying to change.'

These changes were not merely cosmetic and limited to the top; they had a real and genuine impact on the operational efficiency on the shop-floor as well. Freed from bureaucratic and control-oriented barriers, they empowered the ground-level workforce to take entrepreneurial initiatives in solving problems without bothering about approvals from the top. The following are some examples of the nature of these changes:

- GE's Bayamon factory in Puerto Rico, which makes arresters (surge protectors that guard power stations and transmission lines against lightning), is designed to be a high-performance workplace. It employs 172 hourly workers and just 15 salaried 'advisors', and a plant manager—there are only three layers—but no supervisors or staff. They work in a team of about ten, and each team 'owns' a part of the work, for example, assembly, and shipping and receiving. The members come from all areas of the plant, so that each group has people from both upstream and downstream operations. The team meets weekly to take decisions and solve problems. The advisor sits in the back of the room and speaks only if the team needs help.

- In a more or less assured market, GE's light-bulb business grew complacent, over the years, with a productivity growth rate of only 2 per cent. In the mid-1980s, when companies such as Philips invaded its turf, it started slipping. A new management team, and the initiative to solicit employees' ideas for solving low-risk problems saw a turnaround of the business. Employees' contributions were small and incremental—for instance, they found a way to load more boxes of bulbs into trucks increasing the payload, thus effecting a saving of $16,600 per year—but they enhanced worker commitment, and boosted the productivity growth to 9 per cent, the highest in GE.

- At GE's Plastics division, for over a decade researchers had been working on Ultem, a durable, heat-resistant plastic which could be used in everything from circuit boards to auto parts. Without seeking or getting approval from corporate headquarters, they invested $1 million to build a pilot plant. The corporate management was brought in only when they started making samples, and had discovered close to 200 applications for the product, ranging from airplane interiors to packaging of microwaveable food. Ultem grew into a business worth hundreds of million dollars.

- In the early 1980s, GE's circuit-breaker business was threatened by a stagnant market and by competitors like Siemens and Westinghouse. A multifunctional team, consisting of manufacturing, design and marketing experts, overhauled the manufacturing process and consolidated manufacturing operations of six plants into one. They redesigned the circuit breakers to reduce 28,000 unique parts to just 1,275 (while still giving the customers a choice of 40,000 different sizes, shapes, and configurations). More remarkably, they did away with all line supervisors and quality inspectors on the factory-floor, and reduced the layers between the plant manager and the worker from three to one. The workers were divided into self-managing groups of 15 to 20 and they shared the responsibility for quality, work rules, vacation scheduling, etc. The only 'managerial communication' with workers was through the electronic sign boards in the shop indicating their target for the day, how much they have achieved, and how much time they are taking to make the items. Result: GE reduced the order-to-delivery cycle from three weeks to three days.

Work-Outs

The technique which became a major vehicle for empowering employees and stimulating their entrepreneurial zeal is the Work-

Outs. This unique technique was an offshoot of Welch's regular meetings with the course participants at the Crotonville Management Development Institute. Since becoming CEO, Welch had made it a point to visit Crotonville every month and engage in a frank, and often rough-and-tumble, debate with the participants on GE's functioning. These sessions were fruitful for him as well as the participants, providing significant insights, solutions, and commitments for improving GE's operations. The Work-Out technique was conceived—and announced to GE's 500 top executives by Welch himself in January 1989—with the aim of transferring it into the day-to-day functioning of the businesses. As Welch explained it:

> The point of Work-Out is to give people better jobs. When people see that their ideas count, their dignity is raised. Instead of feeling numb, like robots, they feel important. They are important. ... With Work-Out and boundarylessness, we're trying to differentiate GE competitively by raising as much intellectual and creative capital from our work force as we possibly can.

What is Work-Out? Essentially, it is a forum which allows the employees to eliminate the extraneous elements in their jobs, and to work out problems together. The aim is to get the bosses to join the subordinates in identifying inefficient processes and practices, and to make a commitment to eliminate them. A typical Work-Out meeting starts with assembling a group of 40 to 100 employees representing different levels and functions, often somewhere outside the workplace. The boss addresses the group, reviewing the business, its strategies, the major opportunities and threats facing it, and the existing gaps and the current efforts to bridge them. He stresses that the agenda of the Work-Out is to eliminate wasteful and unproductive work practices.

After this he leaves, and the group forms smaller teams to list out the wasteful practices. With external facilitators, the teams review and discuss these practices. The participants work in functional as well as cross-functional teams to identify the problems and develop solutions. They also make contracts with each other to solve the problems that can be solved at their own levels.

In the last session of the Work-Out, which is presided over by the boss, the employees present their findings and proposals. The boss is expected to agree with the proposals; if he declines, it should be for clearly stated reasons. Specific commitments from employees and the superior are made with clear-cut deadlines. Since many problems are of a cross-functional nature, Work-Outs often commission task forces from different functions, but around the same business process, to solve them. The recommendations are compiled in a summary report. After a couple of months, the group reassembles for a follow-up of its work.

At GE, Work-Outs served to empower employees and release their creative energies. It gave them the power and responsibility to solve problems, which otherwise were in the domain of managerial prerogative and obstructed by bureaucracy. Moreover, it became an effective means of eliminating wasteful work practices and improving on others. For instance, at a Work-Out at the GE aircraft engine factory, workers proposed building a new protective shield for grinding machines. The design was conceived by an hourly worker and drawn on a brown paper bag during the session. They spent $16,000 on building it, as against $96,000 quoted by an outside vendor.

Similarly, at one of the GE Plastics plants, workers took up the task of increasing the percentage of resin, which ends up as saleable pellets, without its having to be melted and run again through extruders. They installed a computer terminal on the extrusion floor to give early warning to workers about problems upstream where resins are made. They realigned the pipes to reduce spillage, rewrote the procedure manual, and, after three months (and an expenditure of $10,000) they could reduce the waste by 37 per cent.

It is also worth noting that, for many GE bosses, Work-Outs subverted the control-and-command structure. The experience of employees solving problems, and negotiating commitments from them in face-to-face encounters was new and threatening. In accepting employees' proposals, they were, in turn, forced to negotiate upwards with *their* bosses. Nevertheless, Work-Outs became quite prevalent in GE.

According to one estimate, as many as 40,000 GE employees attended at least one Work-Out session in 1991. One of the reasons for this was the support they had from the top. Not only did the corporate headquarters bear the expenses, but Welch also made it clear that the thwarting of the efforts of the Work-Out teams by a superior would be a 'career-limiting move'. This was because Work-Outs were not mere problem-solving mechanisms; they were also ways of changing the organisational culture. According to Welch:

> [What] we want to achieve ... begins by putting the leaders of each business in front of 100 or so of their people, eight to ten times a year, to let them hear what their people think about the company, what they like and don't like about their work, about how they are evaluated, how they spend their time. Work-Out will expose the leaders to the vibrations of their business—opinions, feelings, emotions, resentments. ... Ultimately, we're talking about redefining the relationship between boss and subordinate.

Harnessing Internal Capabilities

Needless to point out that such far-reaching changes can only be successful if they have the support of middle-level management. In most organisations, It is the middle management cadre which resists changes and does not want to deviate from the bureaucratic norms on account of the security offered by them. According to Welch:

> Insecure managers create complexity. Frightened, nervous managers use thick, convoluted planning books and busy slides filled with everything they've known since childhood. People must have the self-confidence to be clear, precise, to be sure that every person in their organisation—highest to lowest—understands what the business is trying to achieve.

To support the process of change managers must feel secure and self-confident; that is, they must acquire and develop the new skills and competencies relevant to managing change.

GE Crotonville Management Development Institute played the enabling role in developing these skills and competencies. Established in the mid-1950s, it has since acquired the reputation of being 'the Harvard of Corporate America'. A host of external experts from Harvard Business School had a hand in shaping its curriculum. It is headed by James Baughman, who gave up his professorship at Harvard to take up this job. Every week, Crotonville brings 120 GE executives in contact with the latest management ideas, and provides them the opportunity to learn these directly from luminaries like Peter Drucker, Chris Argyris, John Kotter, and Andre Laurent. Crotonville also provides an arena where executives can have a face-to-face dialogue with the top management. Every year, approximately 60 per cent of GE's top management executives, including Jack Welch, participate in the courses at Crotonville, as teachers, discussion leaders, role models.

Crotonville offers pre-entry and entry-level courses in leadership, manufacturing, finance and sales, advanced courses in functional areas, special courses for high-potential candidates, and business management programmes. Though the academic content of these courses is as sound as that of any good business school, what makes the courses more effective is that they are focused on GE, and are practise oriented. After taking over as CEO, Welch emphasised that executives not just learn management concepts; they must also learn how to apply them. Thus, Crotonville introduced actual GE problems and their potential solutions in its curriculum. The emphasis shifted to action learning, in which participants worked in teams, applying concepts to solve real problems. Not only did this simplify transfer of learning from classroom to workplace, the company also benefited from their efforts in solving business issues. An article describes one such course:

> Formats vary. But generally, two teams of five to seven people each work on a single project, which is provided by a senior business development manager from one of GE's separate businesses. Participants come from diverse businesses and functions within the company; no team member is from the business being studied. Participants spend the first seven to ten days of the course receiving instruction and taking part in team building activities. In the next stage, they conduct 40 to 60 interviews . . . with customers, suppliers; analysts, and GE employees. In the final week of the course, participants make their recommendations in the form of a presentation to the business leader who provided the project.

As can be seen, Crotonville's courses define another kind of boundarylessness—the permeability of boundaries between the classroom and business setting, between learning and working.

Another initiative of GE to disseminate new learning among its cadres started in 1988, and came to be known as Best Practices. This project started by posing the simple question: How do other companies achieve a higher productivity growth than GE? A team of GE business development executives scrutinised an initial list of 200 organisations and identified about two dozen which had achieved a faster productivity growth than GE, and sustained it for at least ten years. After screening out direct competitors, and those whose achievements would not be credible to GE employees, the list contained some well-known corporations, such as Hewlett-Packard, Xerox, AMP, and Chaparral Steel, and some Japanese companies. These were the companies GE needed to emulate.

The Best Practices project was more than just benchmarking. Of course, GE did benchmark—for example, its teams studied how AMP does the purchasing, and how the UN and Citicorp move supplies and equipment in congested Manhattan—but it also looked at these organisations as a whole, at their attitudes and management practices. Studies found a remarkable similarity in the reasons underlying their success. These organisations emphasised not functions but processes: they focused more on improving upon the method of doing rather than on managing what got done; they treated their suppliers and customers as part of the process and worked along with them. As a result, they had lesser working capital tied up in inventories and could be therefore swift in responding to the market with new products.

GE used this learning to implement changes in its way of working and managing business. For example:

- Crotonville converted the Best Practices findings into a course for GE executives emphasising managing processes and encouraging process ownership. In fact, this course also provided a base for Work-Out teams to improve business processes

- The composition of the corporate audit staff changed. Instead of having people only from a finance background, now half were operations or information systems experts. Their work included tracking inventory on the shop-floor and identifying ways of improving the process to bring it down.

- Process mapping—that is, creating a flow-chart showing every small and big step which goes into making or doing something—became a companywide standard method for analysing work, and identifying and eliminating extraneous steps. For instance, at one of GE's component manufacturing plants, process mapping helped to achieve a $4 million drop in inventory. Similarly, GE Appliances could cut down its production cycle by 75 per cent and reduce inventory by $200 million while increasing product availability by 6 per cent.

- At GE's locomotive paintshop, inspection of the process showed that one of the reasons for delay was the inconsistency of the paint. In one of the Work-Outs, the team enrolled the chief chemist from a supplier firm. Together they wrote the standards for colour and consistency, eliminating the need for double inspection. This helped reduce the paint job from 12 shifts to ten.

- Many divisions started making attempts to organise their functioning around the business processes. The GE lighting business, for instance, scrapped its vertical structure, and adopted a horizontal design with more than 100 processes and programmes.

The internal initiatives and changes also fed on themselves. Successful experimentations within GE became internal benchmarks for other businesses to emulate. For instance, when GE Appliances reduced its cycle time and inventory to achieve a turnaround, it attracted executives from other divisions to visit and study the changes. The large size and free flow of communication became a vehicle of learning for GE as a whole. As Welch has remarked: 'The enormous advantage we have today is that we can run GE as a laboratory for ideas. We've found mechanisms to share best practices in a way that's trusting and open.'

Co-opting Customers

The concept and practice of boundarylessness in GE extends to include customers in planning and implementing business strategies. Like many other responsive organisations, GE learned that working with customers is a useful way of anticipating and meeting their needs. For instance, working with BMW helped the company innovate the first thermoplastic car-body panel for the Z1 two-seater. Similarly, GE's Credit Service division worked with Montgomery Ward to cut down the time for opening a new account from 30 minutes to 90 seconds.

GE, however, extended this process further than just working together. It started customer education programmes, which helped it in not only understanding its customers better, but also in shaping their future needs. In an article, Noel *et al.* state:

> When a company involve customers in its management development programs, it begins to share a managerial competence with the customer. GE learns more about how customers think because GE has influenced the process. With this insight, GE is seen as a supplier who is more able to anticipate needs, not merely serve needs.

What makes GE's customer education courses different from other customer-training programmes is that these did not focus only on making the customers aware of its products. It also aimed at building an understanding and a long-lasting relationship between the customers and their counterparts in GE. These courses were attended by both the customers and GE employees, and were so designed that both found value in them. They helped them understand each other's processes and requirements and build relationships of trust and familiarity based on shared experiences. Moreover, they provided an opportunity to GE to look at itself, its processes, strategies and plans, from the customers' point of view.

For instance, in 1990, GE Appliances conducted a business–customer Work-Out with its largest customer, Sears. The programme aimed at identifying and resolving various business system issues and increasing their understanding and communication at all levels about business-related topics, and improving the relationship between GE and Sears. The Sears participants included buying teams for ranges, home laundry, refrigerators, microwave ovens, and dishwashers, and they were matched with their GE counterparts. Like most GE customer education courses, the programme started with team-building sessions in which the 'real' vendor–buyer teams worked together. The teams reflected on their experience of the exercises, and tried to incorporate their learning into their working relationships. In the process, they questioned the existing Sears–GE Appliances relationship and deliberated on what could be done to make it more effective. At the end of three days the teams had worked out plans to improve the relationship, and made commitments at their respective levels to implement them.

Such programmes were particularly effective when entering into new and unknown markets. Working with potential customers in management development programmes proved to be a source of valuable insight and information for GE. For instance, when GE was negotiating with the erstwhile Soviet Union to re-engine the Soviet-built airliners for Aeroflot, it was necessary to develop a knowledge-base of the Soviet ways of working. A successful business relationship required an understanding of the difference in product design, process flow, role of government and ministries, and the relationship among designers, manufacturers, and operators of the aircraft.

To build this understanding, GE organised a course at Crotonville and invited participants from Aeroflot and the Soviet Ministry of Civil Aviation, and a Soviet airframe manufacturer, along with their GE counterparts. The interaction during the course (and during the visit of the Soviet participants to GE's plants) provided useful information about the Soviet aviation industry. For instance, in a discussion of a case of the American aviation industry, the Soviet participants were asked how their industry operated. Their presentations provided a major learning of the market and how it operates. What is more, it was communicated directly to the GE people who were going to manage the entry into that market.

Similarly, GE's China Management Training Programme, which was initiated in 1986, was conducted once a year, and involved a one-month classroom session, followed by a two-month visit to the plant. The Chinese participants were selected by the six GE businesses represented in China, and consisted of senior Chinese officials and managers from these industries. The programme helped GE not only in building a lasting and strategically valuable relationship with its Chinese counterparts (e.g., for receiving recommendations for joint ventures), but also in gaining useful insights and learning about their businesses. For instance, through their various presentations and interactions, the Chinese participants suggested how GE could enter the Chinese market and gave information about the appropriate ministries to be contacted, the marketing strategies for operating in China, feedback and recommendations which would make GE operate more effectively than its other global competitors in China, and so on. In addition, GE would also hold alumni meetings of different Chinese batches in Beijing, where it would gain an update on different industries.

POSTSCRIPT

Over the past decade GE has emerged as a benchmark for the transformational organisation. But organisational cultures do not change overnight—much less of organisations of the size and with the history of GE. Rather then trying to measure the quantum of change, what would probably be worth considering is the nature of the processes which have led to these successes.

According to Welch himself there is still a long way to go:

We're not that far along with boundarylessness. It's a big, big idea, but I don't think it has enough fur on it yet. We've got to keep repeating it, reinforcing it, rewarding it, living it, letting everybody know all the time that when they're doing things right, it's because their behaviour is boundaryless. . . . I think any company that's trying to play in the 1990s has to find a way to engage the mind of every single employee. Whether we make our way successfully down this road is something only time will tell—but I'm as sure as I've ever been about anything that this is the right road.

Notes

1. Much has been written about GE in business magazines as well as in academic literature. To understand GE better, readers may refer to Pascale (1990), and some of the most informative articles which have appeared in *Academy of Management Executive* (Tichy, 1989), *Business Week* (Smith, 1993), *Harvard Business Review* (Tichy and Charan, 1989), *Human Resources Management* (Downham, Noel

and Prendergast, 1992; Keller and Campbell, 1993; Noel and Charan, 1988; Noel, Ulrich and Mercer, 1990), *Fortune* (Dumaine, 1989; Labick, 1989; Petre, 1987; Sherman, 1989; Stewart, 1991, 1992; Welch, 1993), and *Training & Development* (Noel and Charan, 1988).

Xerox Corporation: Learning to Cope with Environmental Turbulence[1]

*It is self-evident that our future growth must
come from products and services which are far
more complex than these which are our present
heartland. Therefore, we must learn to be
different people than we have been.*

—Joe Wilson
CEO, Xerox Corporation, 1996

*The technology is changing quickly. The
demands of the marketplace are also changing.
... They are going to continue to change. So we
have to change the company itself.*

—Paul Allaire
CEO, Xerox Corporation, 1992

BEGINNING OF THE END

William James in his classic book, *Varieties of Religious Experiences*, makes a distinction between once-born and twice-born souls. The once-borns go through life with an un-self-conscious attitude, happily ignorant of their own human frailties and mortality. They accept life as it comes, and suffer and prosper without pausing to self-reflect on their own role in charting their destiny. The twice-borns, on the other hand, have experienced the taste of death, and emerged the wiser and humbler to face life. Having become aware of their own mortality, they are acutely conscious of themselves, and constantly reflect upon, and critique and question their own choices.

In many ways, Xerox is a 'twice-born' organisation. But for its phoenix-like resurrection in the mid-1980s it would have made an excellent study of how successful organisations fail and die. To understand how Xerox functions now, it is important to trace the history of its meteoric rise in the 1960s and 1970s and subsequent fall. The crisis, which all but finished Xerox, and the learning therefrom, also became the basis for its moulding itself into one of the most unique organisations of the corporate world.

Xerox was earlier Haloid Corporation, which was founded in 1906 to make photographic paper. Its fascination with new technologies is apparent from its history: in 1947, it bought Chester Carlson's patent for electrography technique, which had already been refused by many well-known organisations (e.g., IBM, General Electric [GE], Remington Rand). Some even conducted a market survey and concluded that since not more than 5,000 machines could be sold, it was not worthwhile investing in its development. Battelle Institute, a contract research centre, agreed to invest in developing Carlson's idea, and was looking for corporate sponsors for the project. For Haloid, and particularly its then CEO, Joe Wilson, the concept of electrography held the promise of a new, even if uncertain, market. During the 1950s, the company invested a large proportion of its profit into developing the technology into a commercially viable product, and launched Model 914, the world's first plain paper copier, in 1960. In 1961, it changed its name to Xerox Corporation. (The name Xerox comes from the Greek words 'xeros', meaning dry and 'graphien', meaning writing; the trade name was initially printed as XeroX.)

The new product, as Xerox had envisioned, created a new market for itself and zoomed the company to success. During the 1960s and 1970s, Xerox kept introducing new and more efficient models (813, Xerox 2400, Xerox 3600, Xerox 7000, etc.), and held an almost complete monopoly in the reprographic market. Its revenues increased from $37 million in 1960 to $698 million in 1966, and to $4.4 billion in 1976. Its profits too grew almost five-fold between 1966 and 1977, from $83 million to $407 million. For a decade it maintained 20–30 per cent return on equity, and in 1972 its stocks commanded an enviable price of $172 per share (its market value was $11.8 billion).

The reason, of course, was that Xerox had the advantage of an early start, and a virtual monopoly in the office copier market (while it had licensed to IBM, GE, RCA, Bell, etc., to work on xerographic process, it was only in areas other than office copiers). Rapid success and prosperity, however, made Xerox complacent and arrogant. The company did not give sufficient strategic thought to the changes occurring in the market and their implication for it. It also ignored the new entrants in the market (Ricoh, Canon, Sevin, IBM, etc.) who were establishing their stronghold in the lower end of the market and in certain specialised segments. When, between 1971 and 1975, the company's pre-tax profit margins dropped from 27.2 per cent to 18.7 per cent it was officially attributed to worldwide inflation and depressed economic activity. Moreover, the stupendous growth made the company very large, from 3,000 (in 1960) to about 100,000 employees spread worldwide. Nevertheless, it continued to operate on functional lines. Its operating costs (and therefore, the prices of its products) were high, and it was offering products of poorer quality than its competitors. The decision-making process on crucial strategic and product decisions was centralised, often resulting in changes in the positioning of the product by the time it was finally developed and launched. As one of its CEOs, David Kearns (who became its president in 1977, and led Xerox as its CEO from 1982 to 1990), expressed it: 'We were becoming a dinosaur that couldn't get out of its own way.'

The late 1970s and early 1980s were bad years for Xerox. Its real competition, interestingly, came not from giants like IBM and Kodak, but from small innovative Japanese companies. These companies nibbled away at Xerox's market by offering better quality machines at lesser cost, and with the features customers desired. Xerox's market share, which had dropped between 1970 and 1975 from 100 per cent to 81 per cent, crashed to a mere

13 per cent in 1982. Between 1980 and 1981, its profits plummeted from $1.15 billion to $600 million, and then further to $290 million in 1984. In the first half of the 1980s its annual sales revenues kept stagnant around $8.5 billion. For many, Xerox was in the process of becoming the prototype of the corporate Icarus.

THE SECOND BIRTH

What jolted Xerox back to reality was the discovery that Japanese companies were making profits by selling better quality midsize copiers for just $9,600—a price considerably less than Xerox's manufacturing cost in the US. It brought home the fact that there was something fundamentally wrong in the way the company managed its activities, and that to survive it must improve its efficiency. Luckily for Xerox, the way to make this possible lay in its own Japanese joint venture, Fuji-Xerox. Fuji-Xerox had encountered competition from other Japanese companies in 1976, and had achieved a remarkable turnaround through a total quality process effort (in 1980, it won Japan's coveted Deming Prize for quality). In 1979, a team of Xerox line managers led by its manufacturing chief went to benchmark Japanese business practices. They encountered some shocking truths: Xerox took twice as long as its Japanese competitors to bring a product to the market; used five times the number of engineers; made four times more design changes; and had three times their design costs. Yet, the product had over 30,000 defective parts per million, which was 30 times more than that of its competitors. What the low quality of products and processes also amounted to was that Xerox was spending about 25 per cent of its revenue (and, therefore, one-fourth of its facilities, equipment, space, and people) redoing what had not been done right in the first place. Moreover, the benchmarking also revealed that as against the targeted 8 per cent annual productivity growth rate (when the industry average was 3 per cent) Xerox would need an 18 per cent annual productivity growth rate for five consecutive years to catch up with the Japanese.

It was facts such as these that forced Xerox to start considering some very basic changes, which were not limited only to its operating structure, but aimed at transforming the company's basic philosophy, culture and processes. In an article, its then CEO, David Kearns described the revolutionary nature of this transformation:

> Building a strong corporate culture means getting everybody to think and do things in a certain way—consistently. It's a long, arduous, and sometimes frustrating process. . . . Now, imagine, if you will, what it's like to reverse that process. Imagine making everybody in the company unlearn a particular set of rules and learn a new one. Imagine completely changing the culture of the entire company. . . . [Faced with competition] we had to make several fundamental, long-term changes. First, develop more disciplined ways of working. Second, find ways of getting and staying closer to our customers. Third, make better use of the ideas and talents of our employees. And fourth, make a solid commitment to quality in everything we do.

The focus on fundamental corporate change took the shape of Xerox's 'Leadership through Quality' programme in the early 1980s. This initiative defined quality as fully meeting the requirements of customers; that is, defining who the customers are, within and outside the organisation, understanding precisely what their requirements are, and devising ways of meeting these requirements in the most innovative, efficient and effective way. While the inspiration for this effort came from Fuji-Xerox, it was translated into operational form taking into consideration the global nature of Xerox's operations. A task force consisting of entrepreneurial vice presidents and staff was set up. Working over six months in 1982–83, it came out with a 92-page blueprint for action detailing the guidelines for implementation of the Leadership through Quality programme.

Its implementation created new and different structures, forums and processes in the organisation. Xerox formally and systematically established benchmarking as a core function; it set up a Customer Satisfaction Management System to regularly sample, collect and study customers' opinions about the company's products and people; its huge sales force was integrated so that a single Xerox employee could represent the company's entire range of products and services: over a period of five years, a Quality Training Task Force of 140 professional trainers trained all Xerox employees in small-group activities and problem-solving techniques, and so on. Efforts were directed towards empowering employees and seeking their involvement and expertise in solving organisational problems. Multifunctional teams were established at all levels to solve problems (by 1988, there were 2,000 problem-solving teams operating in the company worldwide).

The efforts did yield results. By 1989, Xerox had closed the 50 per cent cost gap that had existed between it and its Japanese competitors. Through quality improvement, and through refocusing its product-market strategy (it started importing low-end copiers from Fuji-Xerox, and personal copiers from Sharp), it was even able to win back some of its market share from the Japanese. In 1989, it went on to win the Baldrige Award for quality. Its revenue started increasing again. Between 1986 and 1993, its turnover more than doubled, from $8.95 billion to $18.26 billion, and its assets grew threefold, from $9.82 billion to $34 billion. Its ranking in the *Fortune 500* list went up from 42 in 1982 to 21 in 1993. In other words, Xerox had remoulded itself and made a comeback.

THE ARCHITECTURE OF A NEW ORGANISATION

Not many companies have the capability to survive the kind of crisis Xerox had to face. Atari and People Express, for example, could not. Moreover, its turnaround took place not only in the face of tough and increasing competition, but also at a time when the very definition of its market and competitive environment was undergoing radical changes.

Xerox's past success was built on its mastering electro-optical and mechanical technology and producing light-lens copiers and duplicators. In the 1980s, however, the developments in digital technology were changing the meaning of copying and the duplicating process itself, making it more economical and efficient to electronically scan and capture the image before transferring it. They also provided opportunities to network photocopiers and duplicators with other digitised equipment, such as computers and communication instruments. For Xerox these changes implied the necessity to compete and win in a competitive environment, which itself was shifting its base. The company had to change its technology base from electro-optical and mechanical to digital; it had to acquire technology and expertise to develop and produce networked, instead of traditional 'stand-alone' products; and it had to develop skills to offer to customers not products but innovative solutions for handling documents and information.

Xerox is unique not only in that it survived these changes, but also because it emerged as a better and stronger organisation. To achieve this Xerox had to redesign itself in ways which are ingenious, intangible and path-breaking. According to its present CEO, Paul Allaire: 'In fact, the term "reorganisation" does not capture what we are trying to do at Xerox. We are redesigning the "organisational architecture" of the entire organisation.'

The following sections describe some of the significant processes and mechanisms which have made the emergence of this new architecture possible.

Enacting Envisioned Futures

Xerox is a vision-driven organisation. Throughout its history of meteoric growth, followed by crisis, decline and a comeback, the vision of possible futures has played a vital role. This was apparent even in its initial investment in the development of the xerography process. When the company committed itself to finance Carlson's efforts, his ideas were still nebulous and undeveloped (in fact, many companies refused to buy Carlson's patent, because his crude apparatus would often fail to function during a demonstration). It was only the vision of the revolutionary potential of the new technology that steered Haloid, a very small company, to start investing as much as $100,000 annually in the development of the process, and that too, for more than a decade.

This visionary perspective is what guided the organisation and held it together in the face of incapacitating competition, product life-cycle declines, and turbulent changes in the technological environment. What is also remarkable about this envisioning process is that it aimed at creating new environments to operate in, rather than merely focusing on mastering the already existing ones. Consider, for instance, Xerox's first message to its shareholders in 1961. It was written at a time when information technology was limited to calculations and technical applications; large, stand-alone mainframes were the main modes of computing and electronic data processing; networking was an unknown concept; and fax was yet to be invented (by Xerox, in 1964)—and Xerox was just a small organisation, trying out a new product whose real potential was still largely unknown and untested. The message, however, read:

> Our goal is to be a leader throughout the world in graphic communications, concerned primarily with copying, duplicating, recording, and displaying images. *Today's machines work from visible characters. Tomorrow they may work, at great speed, from electronic impulses and invisible signals.* So long as there is a need for man to send information and either to copy directly or to convert the language of computers or other electronic devices into [a] form which other men can understand, there will be need for making images. This is our field. [emphasis added]

The impact of this vision and its long-term perspective is evident across the history of all Xerox's ventures. Even while the xerographic process was in the process of being developed in the late 1940s, Joe Wilson, Xerox's then CEO, realised that some day Carlson's patents would expire. To protect its competitive position, it was imperative for the company to continue to invest in technology and maintain its technological edge. As a result, by the end of 1950, Xerox had acquired 30 new patents; by 1975, this number had grown to 1,700.

Similarly, in the mid-1960s, although Xerox was riding high on success, there was a growing concern in the organisation about its excessive dependence on reprographic. The general feeling of the management was that success cannot be sustained by remaining confined to the 'reprographic heartland'. The new vision came from its president, Peter McColough: Xerox must focus on creating 'architecture of information' in the office. This was the vision that provided integrated information systems, which linked all office equipment (computers, printers, data storage and transmission devices, etc.) to one single network. In one of its recruiting brochures, Xerox defined its role as 'the architect of information':

> What we seek is to think of information itself as an undeveloped environment which can be enclosed and made more habitable for people who live and work within it. Our goal is to identify their discriminate needs for information and to build structures of information which they will find flexible, functional, and effective.

The vision also got translated into several of the organisation's strategic/operational activities. It led to the setting up of the Flevin Committee, which helped identify eight business areas for Xerox's information goals. During the late 1960s and 1970s, Xerox made forays into the computer and word-processing field by acquiring Scientific Data Systems (makers of time-sharing and scientific computers), Daconics (which made shared logic, word-processing systems utilising minicomputers), and Versetec (producers of electrostatic printers and plotters). In 1969, it opened its corporate R&D facility, the Palo Alto Research Center (PARC), with the aim of developing in-house technologies for furthering its goals.

It is also worth noting that Xerox's envisioning processes, and the technological capabilities they nurtured, were often far ahead of the existing reality. The reason for its crisis in the period 1975–85 was not that the organisation had not anticipated the future; rather, it was that, working for a future so far ahead, it lost sight of what lay immediately ahead. Also, its vision gave it a charter so broad that often its researchers and product developers would be working on technologies and products peripheral to the company's own product-market strategy. Its technological innovations outpaced its marketing competencies.

For instance, in 1964, Xerox introduced the world's first commercial fax, or what it called the Long Distance Xerography (LDX) system. Xerox's marketing strategy was based on its experience with copiers, which was to rent the machine and charge for its use and service. But to do that with the LDX system one had to either link the machines with coaxial cables (which was too expensive), or own telephone lines (which Xerox did not). Finally, it settled for joining with Magnavox Corporation to use ordinary telephone wires for a 'telecopier system', which was slower but cost much less than the LDX system. Interestingly, Xerox's own long-term solution to the problem was to link faxes with copiers and computers in one giant metered network. And so, by 1980, when Japanese fax machines were flooding the US market, PARC researchers were working on integrating the three machines into a complete document-processing system. These developments, too, started bearing results in the 1990s, when Xerox modelled itself as a 'document' company; but in the meanwhile in 1989, 25 years after inventing the fax, Xerox's market share in fax sales in the US was only 7 per cent.

Xerox's visionary practices further resulted in its acquiring and developing computer and word-processing capabilities, which formed the basic building blocks of the future personal computer revolution. In establishing PARC, Xerox had created the seedbed for research in modern computing. It hired some of the leading scientists and gave them abundant funds to pursue their ideas of how complex organisations use, and can use, information (Xerox's expenditure on R&D is 7 per cent of its revenue; even during the 1980s, when it was struggling for survival, it ploughed back more than $3 billion in research.) The hands-off policy of headquarters gave sufficient freedom to the researchers to explore and innovate new concepts.

It is not surprising that the work at PARC culminated in many seminal ideas, concepts and products, which were to revolutionise the future markets. In 1973, it developed its first prototype of the laser printer—which became a multibillion business for the company by 1990; its innovations in custom design chips, and local area networks, and its distinctive computer interface designs proved crucial in meeting Japanese competition; and, it keeps feeding the organisation with innovations such as Paper Works, a software which allows users to access their personal computers from any fax machine in the world.

Ironically, the extent of Xerox's technological vision proved to be far ahead of its capability to exploit new markets. There were many revolutionary outputs from the efforts at PARC which, despite becoming the cornerstone of personal computing, could never be utilised by Xerox. In the early 1970s, PARC championed the 'bit map' display computer screens that made easy-to-use graphic interfaces possible (and which could be found in IBM and Apple computers ten years later); it created a software for 'windows' for working on several documents at the same time, as well as a pointing device, or 'mouse' (both found their way in Apple's Lisa PC); in the mid-1970s, it even developed a prototype of the personal computer, Alto, which relied on its own processing power and memory, and was 'open' to independently written software (a design attribute that fuelled the future PC explosion);

and its text-processing software, Bravo, developed for Alto, found its way into evolving into Microsoft Word. At the time these innovations were taking place, Xerox was still focused on the copier market. Many of the researchers working on these projects became discouraged and left to join other organisations, taking their knowledge with them.

Nevertheless, PARC was, and has remained, the embodiment of Xerox's vision of 'inventing futures'—a vision clearly spelt out even in the letter that is sent out to new researchers:

> Our approach to research is 'radical' in the sense conveyed by the word's original Greek meaning: 'to the root'. At PARC, we attempt to pose and answer basic questions that can lead to fundamental breakthroughs. Our competitive edge depends on our ability to invent radically new approaches to computing and its uses. ... If you come to work here, there will be no plotted path. The problems you work on will be ones you help to invent. ... [You] will have an opportunity to express your personal research 'voice' and to help create a future that would not have existed without you.

Continuous Self-reassessment

From a distance, and with the wisdom of hindsight, Xerox appears to be an organisation which got trapped in its own vision. In many respects it is true that the crisis it faced in the 1970s and early 1980s was partly due to its getting swayed by its own technological visions, and becoming complacent and losing touch with the current market realities. On the other hand, however, there is also sufficient evidence that Xerox has a strong tradition of regular soul-searching and reassessment of its own goals and directions. As will be discussed in this section, apparently, it was the ability to regularly rethink and remodel itself that gave it the internal strength to face the crisis and emerge a winner.

Xerox's history reveals the evolution and unfolding of a number of ways in which the company envisioned itself and its future. Each of its successive leaders articulated a new vision, each built upon the previous one while simultaneously questioning the status quo of the organisation. The visions were not mere slogans, but portrayed, and got translated into, the strategic and operational practices of the time. Initially, the entrepreneurial company grew from the vision of its first CEO, Joe Wilson: 'Our company is a cluster of enthusiastic, innovative people who have a dream that they are building an institution which will make a mark on our society.' As noted earlier, its next two CEOs, Peter McColough and David Kearns, gave a new and potent direction to the organisation by articulating new goals and aims: McColough's 'architecture of information' provided Xerox the impetus to acquire computer and software capabilities, and Kearns', 'Leadership through Quality' helped the organisation, as one journalist put it, in 'beating the Japanese at their own game'. In 1990 when Paul Allaire succeeded Kearns as CEO, he gave a charter of creating a new 'organisational architecture' for Xerox, organised around 'productive work communities' (discussed later).

These visions are unique in that they were not pushed down by the leaders; rather, they evolved from an organisationwide process of search and enquiry. These enquiries, which are a regular part of the tradition of Xerox, not only expressed the views and feelings of its members, but also incorporated and dealt with the existing business realities. More often than not, they encouraged (even forced) people to question the very basics of the way in which Xerox functions.

For example, in 1974, Xerox formed a committee headed by Michael Hughes, who was also the head of planning at Rank-Xerox, its joint venture in the UK, to broadly comment on the corporate strategy. The team comprised members who could voice concerns and views, even if they were unpopular. They were told to ignore all explicit and implicit company objectives, and to not limit their deliberations only to areas like 'reprographics', 'architecture of information', and 'high technology', but consider issues like energy conversion, ecology, the plight of the world's undernourished, and questions like 'should Xerox aim at acquiring American Motors?' The committee worked across national boundaries, interviewed Xerox's managers, analysed why other companies had succeeded or failed in their strategic thinking and implementation, employed external consultants to carry out studies, sought assistance from professors, worked out multiple scenarios for Xerox, and projected various options for the next 15 years. The recommendations of the committee served as critical inputs in Xerox's later internal developments and acquisitions in building competencies for the information systems business.

A somewhat similar process was repeated in 1990, when a group of six young middle-level managers, with a successful track record as line managers, were formed into a team called the 'Future Architecture Team'. They were given the task of re-examining the fundamental operating principles of the organisation. Following a participatory design, which involved other Xerox managers, this team worked out various options, and presented recommendations for redesigning Xerox. This exercise was followed by the formation of the Organisation Transition Board, which consisted of 20 senior managers and staff, for working out, by involving other managers, the details of the new organisation (e.g., the relationship between the new business areas, the role of the head office, the nature of the new managerial skills required). The culmination of this 15-month exercise is Xerox's current efforts at implementing a design which can align and integrate the formal and informal aspects of employee behaviour.

Xerox periodically uses committees and meetings as mediums for its soul-searching efforts. The other, a more continuous method, is the practice of 'competitive benchmarking'. The company pioneered the practice of benchmarking in the US. As mentioned earlier, Xerox first undertook its benchmarking mission in 1979. Benchmarking has since become a regular function in the organisation, with a benchmarking manager, and a standard ten-step method of benchmarking.

Two aspects distinguish Xerox's benchmarking efforts from simple competitive analysis or mere imitation. First, Xerox studied not only what the competitors were doing, but also how they function. That is, it focused on the processes and mechanisms which made others perform better, and then tried to emulate them. Second, Xerox benchmarked good business practices even if they were practised by companies in other industries. For instance, it studied American Express for its billing and collection procedures, American Hospital Supply for its automated inventory control, and L.L. Bean for its distribution, warehousing and order-taking practices.

One major impact of the imminent collapse on Xerox was that it became more externally focused, and more active in soliciting feedback from its customers. When Paul Allaire became its president in 1986, 'customer satisfaction' became the topmost priority for the organisation (even above market share and returns). Corporate staff started meeting the major customers regularly, and noting and sharing their feedback. Similarly, the various divisions started conducting product- and region-wise customer-satisfaction surveys, and doing internal benchmarking of the best practices, based on the feedback. With the aim of encouraging greater contact with the customers and developing new goals, practices and products consistent with the market needs, Xerox linked profit sharing and bonuses with customer-satisfaction surveys.

A likely reason for Xerox's openness to new ideas and its feedback from outside is the diversity of its senior management profile. Xerox has never relied only on its internally bred managerial talent; it has recruited, at senior levels, from as diverse industries as chemicals, automobiles, information, telecommunications, and finance (besides, of course, from its competitors). During the late 1960s, the company hired managers from companies such as Ford, General Motors, IBM, Eastman Kodak, and DuPont for the positions of president, executive and group vice president, vice president and treasurer. While often creating differences and problems in arriving at a consensus, this heterogeneity also made the management more open to diverse ideas and orientation. The trend has continued since, and a large number of senior positions are held by former managers of other companies.

Tapping the Organisational Unconscious

One of the most unique efforts of Xerox, particularly since the 1980s onward, has been to integrate its informal 'software' aspects (the informal networks and practices which link people together, value systems, organisational culture, etc.) with its formal 'hardware' structures, and mechanisms for planning, control and coordination. According to Paul Allaire:

> A successful organisation is one where the formal organisation and the informal one work together, rather than always working against each other. When there isn't a good fit between them, too much energy and creativity gets wasted simply in making the organisation work. But when you align the formal and informal, most of your energy can be externally focused on achieving the objectives of the business.

One way of achieving this alignment is by empowering people and increasing their participation and involvement in decision-making processes. This, of course, Xerox had practised even in the 1960s. John Dessauer, who played a pivotal role in Xerox during the tenure of Joe Wilson, noted that, 'Xerox management realised that the personal success of the individual was closely allied to the total success of the company'. Correspondingly, even in its earlier years, Xerox shared strategic information with its employees; its policies were formulated through a consultative process; the pay system included stock options and bonus plans; and the company would bear full tuition expenses of an employee studying for a masters degree or a doctorate.

Xerox's new approach, to align the formal with the informal, however, goes beyond mere employee involvement. The traditional empowerment and consultative practices aim at aligning the informal with the formal. Xerox's approach is to reverse the process; that is, it aims at changing the formal to synchronise with the informal. It is based on studying and understanding how its people, groups, customers, and even machines, actually function and interact, and then developing more effective systems around these informal practices. These efforts aim to study the 'technology in use'. That is, they focus on understanding the interaction between technology and the people who use this technology; and, based on this understanding, innovate and prototypes new work practices. In fact, this approach also defined a new role for PARC in the 1980s. In the words of John Seely Brown, Xerox's corporate vice president and director of PARC:

> The most important invention that will come out of the corporate research lab in the future is the corporation itself. As companies try to keep pace with increasingly unstable business environments, the research department has to do more than simply innovate new products. It must design the new technological and organisational 'architecture' that make possible a continuously innovating company. Put another way, corporate research must reinvent innovation ... [it] must prototype new mental models of the organisation and its business.

Naturally, some of the most important researches within the last decade or so have been conducted by PARC anthropologists (besides the traditional research professionals like computer scientists, physicists, and engineers, during the 1980s PARC also started employing anthropologists, linguists, sociologists and psychologists on a large scale). One such study, which probably set the tone for many others that followed, was done by the PARC anthropologist Lucy Suchman. In 1979, Suchman started studying how Xerox accounting clerks do their jobs. One of the most startling findings of her research (even though most employees in all organisations implicitly know it) was that while people described their jobs according to the formal job manual, they rarely followed it in practice. Rather, they actually relied on a variety of informal practices, impromptu innovations and improvisations in the crucial areas of their jobs. What the findings also highlighted was that these innovative practices were essential for coping with unexpected exigencies, and therefore, were essential for the organisation's responsiveness. But since they were outside the legitimate business procedures (as described by the formal manual), they remained invisible and officially unrecognised, and eventually got lost in course of time. The implication of these findings was that an effective work technology must tap invisible innovations, and provide a work environment in which people can legitimately improvise. PARC designed and provided people with easy-to-use programming tools, which permitted people to customise the information system for their own use—and, in the process, also capture these localised innovations into software for dissemination and use across the organisation.

Studies like these have converted Xerox into a large field site for anthropological research, which focuses on how work gets accomplished in Xerox: how clerks in the account office issue checks to suppliers, how technical representatives repair copiers, how designers develop new products, how customer-focus teams co-produce with customers, how users use Xerox's products, and so on. Xerox has used the insights from these 'institutionalised introspections' to improve and redesign its work practices as well. For instance, in the early 1980s, Xerox was receiving a lot of complaints about the 'unreliability' of its new copiers. Anthropological studies showed that the problem was not breakdowns, but that customers were finding it difficult to use the machine: the instructions were too complicated and detailed to follow. On the other hand, the designers were resisting change of design, because, after all, they had tested it against all human errors. They blamed the problems on the way in which customers used the machine . It was only when the researchers shared their findings (including a video recording of how some smart users, for example, Xerox's own computer scientists, get frustrated in using the copiers) were they able to break the resistance. The study also helped define the actual problem and, as a result, Xerox introduced design changes to make the copier more user-friendly.

Another widely quoted study, which also had implications for Xerox's new 'orgaisational architecture' of the 1990s, was conducted by Julian Orr, a former Xerox service technician, who later graduated in anthropology. In 1984, PARC was asked to research on developing less time-consuming and more cost-effective ways of training Xerox's 14,500 service technicians. Orr took up the task of finding out how the technical representatives actually learnt and did their jobs. He discovered that the actual learning took place not in the training classrooms, but while working on real problems and informally discussing them (in the canteen, near the water-cooler, or while working) with other technical representatives. Moreover, these conversations were more like story-telling sessions than technical discussions. The stories were used as 'expert systems', which circulated vast amounts of information among the technical representatives' community about past problems and diagnoses, and provided them with a template for constructing a theory about the present problem. PARC's approach was to think of alternatives (e.g., use of multimedia, videoclips, etc.) for making this collective memory available to others in the organisation.

Besides tapping the tacit and informal wisdom latent in the organisation, these innovative efforts have another implication for Xerox. They ensure a continuous process of self-critiquing and revaluation. In becoming aware of its own processes and improving upon them, Xerox has also come nearer the aim of practising the business solutions it intends to sell. In the words of Paul Allaire: 'If we intend to sell our customers our expertise as designers and implementers of new, more effective, and more productive business processes, then we had better make sure that our own organisation is a showcase for better ways of working.'

Creating Communities-of-Practice

One of the implications of Orr's work was that people work best in natural communities. Most organisations create an artificial segmentation of work (between working and learning) by creating barriers in exchange of ideas and knowledge. Natural communities on the other hand, he argued, allow people to share relevant information and learn from each other:

> The fact that work is commonly done by a group of workers together ... and the usual presence of such a community has not entered into the definition of work ... Occupational communities ... have little hierarchy; the only real status is that of [the] member. ... The work can only continue free of disruption if the employer can be persuaded to see the community as necessary to accomplishing work.

Orr's findings and recommendations while probably not influencing directly, did become the forerunners of Xerox's new 'architecture'.

Till the end of the 1980s, despite several attempts at restructuring, Xerox continued to be organised around discrete, hierarchically structured functions, such as sales, marketing, personnel, manufacturing, and finance. However, it was also beginning to realise that this structuring was contributing to a narrow, segmented focus of business, delays and inefficiencies, inordinately long cycle times, and, ultimately, to customer dissatisfaction. For instance, one study looked at the total process, defining the Customer Order Life Cycle, that is, everything that an organisation does from getting the order to installing, billing and maintaining the machine. One thing that became clear was that this business process cut across functions: sales made the proposal and received the orders, the legal department validated the contract, manufacturing built the order, distribution scheduled the despatch, customer service installed and maintained, and administration billed the customer. Most revealing was that about 80–90 per cent of delays, errors, and duplications occurred at the crossover points between functional boundaries. These findings could be virtually generalised over all business processes. As Richard Palermo, Xerox's Vice President, Quality and Transition, describes his 'Palermo's law': 'If a problem has been bothering your company and your customers for years and won't yield, that problem is the result of cross-functional disputes, where nobody has total control of the whole process.'

To overcome these problems, in the 1990s Xerox started redesigning itself around its business processes. According to Paul Allaire, the new architecture can be understood as consisting of three basic elements: 'hardware', 'people', and 'software'. The hardware was the new structure, implemented in January 1992, which divided the company into nine more or less independent business divisions, each with its own profit and loss responsibilities, and specific products and markets. The relationship of these divisions with the, now much-thinned, head office was that of an entrepreneur with a banker or a venture capitalist. In addition, to present a common face to the customers, a Customer Operations Group, with three geographic divisions, was formed to integrate the sales, shipping, installation, service, and billing activities.

However, these businesses also shared a common technology, and sometimes even the same customer. They needed a larger focus so that they could work in an integrated manner and collaborate with each other. This is where the second element, the 'people', came in. To manage these divisions as independent entrepreneurs, while maintaining a total corporate focus, Xerox needed people with more than only functional expertise. The Organisation Transition Board (mentioned earlier) identified 23 characteristics—ranging from strategic thinking and implementation competencies to teamwork and the ability to empower subordinates—to select (not promote) managers for the top posts. By this process of selection a lot of new talent was brought in at the senior levels (three of nine presidents of the divisions were with Xerox for less than a year, and about a third of the top 40 people less than three years). The process of selection was repeated within the divisions and the Customer Operations Group for selecting the business team general managers with the right 'software' qualities.

The uniqueness of this new horizontal organisation lay in its view of business as consisting of 'processes' instead of functions. The ultimate criterion of defining the business process, and when it has been successfully completed, was identical, irrespective of the *process*, namely, meeting the requirements of the customer (internal or external). Since all business processes require inputs from more than one function, Xerox started organising all work around multifunctional 'self-directed/self-managed work teams', consisting of people who work most closely with customers. A highly empowered team, they had the authority to completely own and manage their activities. The self-directed work team (SDWT) in Xerox was formally and specifically defined as:

> A self-directed work team is a highly trained group of employees [6–12] fully responsible for delivering a well-defined segment of finished work [a product or service]. It is chartered to assume management responsibility in addition to performing its specific jobs. The work team learns and shares jobs usually performed by a manager. In a fully functioning SDWT, controls come from within the group, rather than from [an] outside source. Even though the SDWT is [a] self-governing body, all SDWTs report to company management to ensure congruence with business strategy and goals.

To enable the teams to work more professionally and competently, Xerox also updated its training efforts in problem-solving, which had started in 1982. It developed a detailed six-step problem-solving process, and trained its people in relevant problem-solving and statistical techniques. The training was done 'on the job' with real problems and in 'family groups', and consisted of imparting the skills to generate ideas and collect information, reach a consensus, analyse and communicate data, and plan action.

The aim of these efforts was to create the organisation as an inter-related cluster of 'productive work communities', and to organise work in a way that helps people to learn and develop while working. They also brought into focus the new vision of Xerox, as articulated by Paul Allaire:

> We have to create a new organisational architecture flexible enough to adapt to change. We want an organisation that can evolve, that can modify itself as technology, skills, competitors, and the entire business change. . . . I envision a time when this company will consist of many, many small groups of people who have the technical expertise and the business knowledge and the information tools they need to design their own work process and to improve and adapt that process continuously as business conditions change.

Notes

1. Information for developing this case was collected from articles written on Xerox's unique history and turnaround. Readers may refer for more details to Brown (1991), Brown and Duguid (1991), Chapman (1988), Dumaine (1991), Garvin (1993), Garza (1991), Howard (1992), Kearns (1988), Main (1992), Norman (1989), Pantling (1993), Quinn (1984), Smart (1993), Stewart (1990a, 1992), Uttal (1983), and Walker (1992).

PART III

Building A Learning Organisation

5

Architecture of a Learning Organisation

*. . . the concept of 'order through fluctua-
tions' . . . involves a distinction between states
of the system in which all individual initiative is
doomed to insignificance . . . and . . . bifurcation regions in which an individual, an idea, or a
new behaviour can upset the global state . . . be
responsible for the destruction of this same
order, eventually producing a new coherence
beyond another bifurcation.*

—Ilya Prigogine

UNDERSTANDING ORGANISATIONAL ARCHITECTURE

Any discerning reader would have noticed that the six companies
described in Part II hardly share any similarities in their 'hardware'.
They are different from each other on virtually all parameters, such
as size, age, strategy, nature of business, formal structure, operating systems: Asea Brown Boveri (ABB) is an electrical equipment
manufacturer, while British Airways (BA) is an airline; General
Electric (GE) is a large multi-business global organisation, while
Chaparral is a small steel plant in the US; Xerox and BA are cases
of turnaround, while ABB and Citicorp are studies of remarkable
organisational growth; Chaparral has a diffused horizontal structure, while in Citicorp and ABB the structure is clear and precise . . .

The differences highlight one of the most critical issues in the study and practice of organisational learning: *how does one design a learning organisation?*

Unfortunately, conventional concepts of design process organisation have little to offer in this regard. Discussions on organisational design are often limited to the formal components of organisational structure and systems, such as centralisation-decentralisation, control systems, departmentation, and span of control. Useful as they may be, these concepts are grossly inadequate for providing insights for building a learning organisation.

Recent works (Nadler, 1989; Nadler, Gerstein and Shaw, 1992; Nevis, DiBella and Gould, 1995) on strategic organisation design have found 'architecture' as a superior explanatory metaphor for an understanding of large, complex organisations (it must be noted that the commonly used term 'structure' is also merely a metaphor). The reason for this superiority lies in the definition of architecture. Janson (1991) has defined an architecture as: 'something higher that ordinary "tecture" (that is, "construction" or "building") ... a structure distinguished from the merely practical, everyday kind by its scale, order, permanence, or solemnity of purpose. ... [It is] the art of shaping space to human needs and aspirations.'

In a penetrating analysis, Gerstein (1992) derived four insights from the concept of architecture that can be utilised for designing more effective organisations:

1. Architecture is a 'practical art'; its ultimate test is in terms of its utility to people who have to live and work in it.

2. A good architecture does not provide rigid specifications about how life should be lived; rather, it guides, facilitates, and provides a framework for living.

3. An architecture endures and inspires only when it is ahead of its time when planned. More than meeting the immediate functional concerns, it represents the aspirations and potentials of people who will use it.

4. Architecture evolves; it is not imposed. It is produced by a large number of people working together to achieve

a vision. Thus, architecture is, by definition, a social rather than a solitary activity.

Thus, organisational architecture is not just a description of the 'hardware' of the organisation; it also describes the 'software'—the people and processes who create it, and operate within it. According to Nadler (1992), the concept of organisational architecture

> includes the formal structure, the design of work practices, the nature of informal organisation or operating style, and the processes for selection, socialisation, and development of people. . . . Organisational architecture can be a source of competitive advantage to the degree that it motivates, facilitates, or enables individuals and groups to interact more effectively with customers, the work, and each other.

The metaphor of architecture is relevant for an understanding of the nature of a learning organisation. As seen in Chapter 4, the basis of the ultimate knowledge-based competition is invisible, that is, it is rooted in the knowledge embedded in the social architecture—the processes—of the organisation. Organisations are able to leverage on their knowledge resources not just through their 'hardware' (financial investments, strategic plans, structure, etc.), but also by designing appropriate internal 'software' to support the 'hardware'. Thus, in order to understand the dynamics of transformational learning, it is important to appreciate the features of social architecture.

Here we will discuss the processes and practices that characterise the architecture of learning organisations. As will be seen, this architecture comprises three mutually complementary components that promote transformational learning (Figure 5.1).

1. The leadership processes which create the *strategic intent to learn*.

2. The *learning mechanisms* which facilitate creation and acquisition of knowledge.

3. The *supporting structures and processes* which encourage learning activities in the organisation.

The following sections, using examples from the six cases in Part II, will examine how these components find shape in the practices of learning organisations.

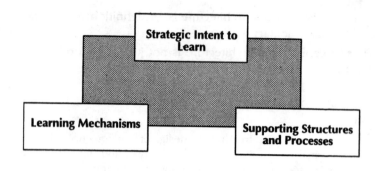

Figure 5.1 **The components of the architecture of a learning organisation**

STRATEGIC INTENT TO LEARN

The most critical part of the architecture of a learning organisation is its ability to define learning as a strategic necessity. Learning organisations visibly and formally communicate their commitment to learning to their members. More than in their vision and mission statements, this commitment is evident in the processes initiated by them. They learn because their leadership processes and strategy make it necessary for people to acquire new capabilities and knowledge, and to review and change their existing mental models. The following sections outline three ways in which organisations communicate their learning intent.

Transformational Leadership

Perhaps the most critical factor in achieving organisational transformation is the leadership process. Several researchers (Singh and Bhandarker, 1990; Tichy and Devanna, 1986) have observed that change-oriented values are transmitted through transformational leaders. Kotter (1990) made a crucial distinction between the styles of 'managers' and 'leaders'. Managers respond to changing environmental conditions by adapting and adjusting; they make incremental adjustments to achieve optimisation of resources. Leaders, on the other hand, respond more radically to problems and issues; they aim to create new environments by altering the organisational situations. In these terms, transformational leaders are less of managers and more of leaders. All successful 'frame-bending' changes 'are characterised by an individual leader who is able to serve as a focal point for the change, and whose presence, activity, and touch have some special feel or magic' (Nadler, 1988).

Often, this magic of the transformational leader is rooted in his/ her past career history of achievements. Most studies (e.g., Lant, Milliken and Batra, 1992; Virany, Tushman and Romanelli, 1992) show that successful organisational transformation and strategic reorientation invariably starts with changes in the top leadership. A study (Gopinath, 1991) of successful turnarounds found that in 20 of 22 cases a new CEO had been appointed in the company. A new leader with the reputation of being a change-master communicates the message of change and stimulates new aspirations among employees. For instance, when Percy Barnevik (ABB), Jack Welch (GE) and Colin Marshall (BA) took over the leadership, they already had a previous record of having achieved dramatic turnarounds and of building up new businesses.

The reputation of the leaders, however, forms only a minor part of their influence. It merely creates the right conditions for transformational processes to germinate. The strength of these leaders actually lies in the nature of the processes they promote. As Rolls (1996) has noted: 'These transformational leaders provide the critical set of conditions under which employees can unfold, transform, grow and flourish in uncertainty. They model and teach skills needed to build a learning organisation.'

What is distinctive about transformational leaders is their visionary ability. This ability consists of three kinds of skill: envisioning, energising, and enabling (Tushman, Newman, and Nadler, 1988). *Envisioning* skills help articulate a credible and clear vision of the organisation which leads to the formulation of new and difficult goals, and reshaping of history to generate pride and enthusiasm for the current mission. We saw many examples of such visions across the cases, for example, 'becoming a borderless organisation' (ABB), 'The Airline of the Future' (BA), 'Boundaryless Organisation' (GE). The power of such a vision lies in its definition of a reality resonant with the aspirations and perceptions of the members of the organisations. As Smircich and Morgan (1982) noted: 'Successful corporate leaders who give direction to organisations in a strategic sense frequently do so by providing an image or pattern of thinking in a way that has meaning for those who are involved.'

Energising skills are necessary for unleashing the energy and enthusiasm of people for achieving new goals. Leaders achieve this by demonstrating personal excitement about and active involvement with the goals and processes of transformation (e.g., Jack Welch's interactions with participants during training, the personal involvement of Percy Barnevik and Paul Allaire in interviewing people for new positions), and by modelling the behaviour requisite for organisational transformation (e.g., Colin Marshall's workaholic schedule and concern for details of the service).

Enabling skills are manifested in the leader's ability to support, motivate and reward the efforts towards transformation. As exemplified in the cases, leaders use their skills to build innovative systems and practices to empower people to participate in the process of transformation. For instance, GE's practice of Work-Outs permitted employees to question work practices and develop new solutions; Chaparral institutionalised 'sabbaticals' for supervisors to enable them to learn; Citicorp allowed people to experiment and take risks; ABB, Xerox, and Citicorp practised meritocracy to the extreme, and so on.

Stretch Goals and Vision

Visionary skills promote the creation of knowledge in the organisation in two ways: first, by articulation of high, and often seemingly, impossible, goals to stimulate people to review their assumptions about work, and to reconceptualise their tasks and practices (Nonaka, 1988). Also, they amplify the discrepancy between the present and the desired levels of performance, and provide a direction to the problem-solving efforts in the organisation. According to Sheldon (1980): 'Only if there is sufficient concern over the shortcoming of the existing paradigm will an exploration of alternative new ones become possible.'

That is why knowledge-creating visions often lead to the formulation of stretch targets. Chaparral Steel, for instance, kept itself humming with tension by articulating goals that called for continuous outpacing oneself: it countered Pohong's threat by fixing its target as 'to get our labour costs below the per ton of the ocean voyage from Korea'. Similarly, GE's goal 'to be number one or number two', Walter Wriston's insistence on achieving 15 per cent return on assets, Xerox's target to regain its market from the Japanese competitors are all examples of stimulating and challenging goals.

Second, these visions are often consciously ambiguous and open to multiple interpretations, which leads to divergence and dialogue in the organisation. According to Nonaka and Takeuchi (1995):

> When the philosophy or vision of top management is ambiguous, that ambiguity leads to 'interpretative equivocality' at the level of the implementing staff . . . can lead to a reflection or questioning of value premises as well as of factual premises upon which corporate decision making is anchored.

In essence, effective vision building stimulates an organisation-wide process of reflection, discussion and questioning, and often results in a redefining of the organisation's operating paradigm. For instance, when organisations define their corporate goals in terms of becoming a TQM company, of a learning organisation, or of leveraging on core competence, these goals (provided they are perceived as credible by the employees) often become the vehicles for self-reflection, self-reassessment, and self-renewal (Box 5.1).

Rocking-the-boat Factor

To develop learning-oriented practices and strategies, it is necessary for the organisation to become open to the idea of continuous change and transformation; that is, a learning organisation must develop processes and mechanisms that do not let it slide into inertia, but, instead, keep it in a state of perpetual 'unfreezing' (Lewin, 1947).

BOX 5.1

THE POWER OF VISION AND STRETCH GOALS: SOME INDIAN EXAMPLES

Arvind Mills[1]

Till 1986, Arvind Mills was part of an ailing industry. Though it had earned the highest profits that year (Rs 430 million on a turnover of Rs 1,100 million), the industry was witnessing an increasing onslaught from the unorganised powerloom sector. In a proactive stance, Arvind decided that the only way to survive in the future would be to become globally competitive. Moreover, it also decided that its global competitiveness would be based not on low labour costs, but on value addition and technological superiority. The company named this new strategic initiative Renovision, that is, a continuous renovation of vision.

Its first task was to align the senior management and workmen with this vision, which was done through extensive communication exercises. It was essential for the workers not only to become aware of the new vision, but also to accept it as their own. To encourage questioning and discussions of the vision, workshops were held for the entire workforce to bring the vision down the line. People were made aware of the challenges facing the company and that there was no option but to change. The vision was also communicated through corporate advertisements and stickers, and by making it part of the new year theme party.

The new vision brought about more concrete and visible changes too. For example, the company premises were given a facelift, a suggestion scheme was launched, the top management team was overhauled by bringing in professionals from other industries (e.g., Hindustan Lever, Citibank, Asian Paints, and Pepsi), the compensation structure was revamped threefold, the hierarchical levels were slashed down from 18 to nine, and a voluntary retirement scheme was introduced to reduce the flab (Arvind was able to reduce the numbers of workmen by 5,300 and officers by 405).

The impact of the new initiative was most visible in Arvind's strategic reorientation. The company used Porter's framework to analyse its competitive strength. This analysis helped it to shift its focus from conventional textiles to the denim market. Denim had a large global—and an increasingly expanding domestic—market: it was less affected by seasonal variations, and had high entry barriers due to the investments required in technology and quality.

However, to compete globally, Arvind needed to enhance the quality of its products, maintaining, at the same time, a cost advantage. To achieve this goal, Arvind leveraged on its research infrastructure. Even as far back as in 1977, the company had invested Rs 60 million to set up one of the largest R&D facilities ever to be attached to a single mill, consisting of 55 researchers. Arvind now increased its focus on research and brought it in line with its strategic intent. This facility helped Arvind Mills make indigenous breakthroughs in denim-making technology. For instance, it could modify the air-jet looms to substitute projectile looms for making denims; this not only cut down capital cost by almost 50 per cent, but also improved operating efficiency. Similarly, the company was able to reduce the dyeing process from a four-stage operation to a single-stage one, and hence achieve substantial reduction in drying time and in cost.

By 1995–96, Arvind emerged as the largest denim manufacturer in India, with a market share of more than 75 per cent. Between 1988–89 and 1995–96, the company's revenue increased from Rs 1,910 million to Rs 7,500 million, while its net worth increased from Rs 420 million to more than Rs 10,000 million. It became the fifth largest denim producer in the world, with production facilities in Sri Lanka and Mauritius.

Core Healthcare Limited[2]

When Core Parenterals Ltd (now Core Healthcare Ltd) was set up in 1988, it was just another small-scale industry in the IV fluid market along with 200-odd small- and medium-scale regional players. Core, however, decided to aim at becoming a global player in the world market. This meant high-quality low-cost manufacture of large volumes of IV fluids. Core translated this vision into a demanding agenda for itself: (a) to invest in technology and research with simultaneous increase in its capacity, (b) to aim at manufacturing 'reject-free' products, and (c) to reduce costs every year equal to the increases expected on account of inflation and other factors.

To achieve these goals, Core accessed technology from established global players like Rommelag of Switzerland, Neste, BASF, and Pall. In 1992, the company started an independent R&D unit at an initial cost of Rs 30 million, which was more than the investments required for setting up a standard conventional IV fluid plant.

Core started the process of continuous improvement of its basic business processes by benchmarking the best in the world (e.g., BASF) on specific performance parameters, and fixed the goals for improvement. Realising that cost improvement can only be achieved through the participation of employees, the company launched a unique initiative called 'half-inch programme'. Under this programme a number of cross-functional teams were formed to work concurrently on various ideas suggested by employees. The focus of the efforts of these teams was on improving all aspects of the company's operational or administrative procedure (e.g., reducing costs and rejection rate, energy conservation, improving process control, reducing manufacturing leadtime, decreasing machine breakdowns). As a result, by 1995, Core managed to *decrease* the manufacturing cost of a bottle from Rs 100 in 1989 to Rs 98. Similarly, it was able to reduce the rejection rate from 7–8 per cent to less than 2 per cent in the corresponding period.

In addition, the company invested heavily in improving the skill- and knowledge-base of its personnel. Besides hiring professionals from other companies (e.g., Hoechst, Hindustan Lever, and Ranbaxy), Core also paid considerable attention to the training of its people by devising focused, need-based programmes for them. By 1994, the average time spent by an employee on training was 45 hours, and the company was investing 4,868 mandays on training.

By 1996, Core emerged as Asia's largest, and the world's fifth largest, IV fluid manufacturer, with a turnover of Rs 2,250 million. It had captured 20 per cent of the domestic market. Forty per cent of Core's production (which was 90 per cent of the country's total IV fluid export) was exported to about 60 countries. With one offshore manufacturing facility in Sri Lanka, it had plans to put up factories in China, Vietnam, Dubai, Ukraine, Uzbekistan, Malwai, and Zaire.

Mahindra & Mahindra Ltd[3]

During the 1990s, M&M, manufacturer of jeeps and tractors, started facing new challenges. Liberalisation had opened the door to competition from global players. With capacity increases in the industry, the market was shifting in favour of the buyer, and technological advancements were forcing a shift in the product and process parameters. The company realised that it was not geared to meet these emerging demands. There were a number of issues that needed to be addressed, for example, low productivity levels, too much complacency and segmentation within the company, large variations in technology across locations, duplication of manufacturing activities, fragmented supply base, and a lack of customer focus.

The initial efforts to rectify the situation were limited to initiatives like introduction of JQI, Kaizen, quality circles, ISO 9000 pursuits at individual sites, etc. But these efforts were isolated, and the results not very impressive. For instance, at a point of time the company had 127 quality circles, involving 1,200 employees, yet improvements did not seem to be forthcoming because these quality circles were still working within segmented functional boundaries, whereas most of the critical problems were of a cross-functional nature. M&M realised the need for a more radical approach.

It was then that M&M decided to set some tough goals for itself: to increase the production of tractors from 40,000 to 60,000 per annum; to reduce customer complaints by 90 per cent; to increase sales per employee by 175 per cent; to increase productivity by 100 per cent; to increase stock turnover fourfold; to achieve 100 per cent adherence to schedule, and so on. What made these goals even more challenging was the decision to achieve them without adding any new equipment or personnel to the existing infrastructure.

Having fixed the target, M&M was forced to work backward to identify the areas that could be improved. The company benchmarked the systems followed by its suppliers, Lucas Engineering and Sundaram Fasteners, and found that their work practices were superior. This, too, helped the company identify its inefficient operating systems and non-productive work practices.

What followed was one of the largest re-engineering exercises in India. M&M redefined itself in terms of its three core processes: logistics, strategic sourcing, and manufacturing. To create a process-based organisation, the tall hierarchy was flattened to reduce flab; at the factory level, the number of layers was crunched from eight to three. Additional manpower was retrenched and/or redeployed. The factories were re-engineered both in terms of physical layout and work-flow processes. The shop-floor was restructured into manufacturing cells which were part of the autonomous product units. Each cell, which consisted of many machines, was now to be responsible for a complete process, and product unit for the complete product.

M&M was aware that these were more than just structural changes, the successful implementation of which required a mind-set change and a sense of ownership among the workmen. To achieve this, the company took many initiatives; for instance, teams of both workers and managers were sent abroad for training and industrial visits. This provided first-hand exposure to the viability of change. When these teams returned, the members were asked to make presentations to their peers, which helped in dissemination of knowledge.

The other initiative to increase the sense of ownership was the formation of teams at the shop-floor level. In the new work design, each cell was managed by a team of workers, who set their own targets. To create greater flexibility within the team, people were trained in multi-skilling and multi-machine manning. The product units too were managed by cross-functional teams, responsible for interacting with customers, and responding to their feedback. This way each unit could interact with the customer and supplier and get a feel of the market-place. For instance, the shop-floor engineers would visit customers across the country twice a month, videotape their interactions, and play them back to the workmen. Thus, a customer's complaint or reaction that would have reached the shop-floor via internal memos, could now be heard live by the technical staff.

The results of these changes soon started becoming visible. For instance, during April–June 1995, the production of tractors increased by 50 per cent. The flat and team-based structure also helped in reducing the bill-processing time from 12 days to less than three. Similarly, productivity increased from 1,100 people producing 85 tractors per day to 670 employees producing 120 tractors per day.

Canon's president, Kaku, once remarked (Nonaka, 1988):

> There are two things which the top management must keep in mind in order to guarantee the continuing existence of the company. The first task of the top management is to create a vision that gives meaning to the employees' job. The second task is to constantly convey a sense of crisis to their employees.

Kaku's remark reinforces one of the essential conditions for organisational learning: that is, stability and complacency are not conducive to learning. Even though this contradicts traditional organisational wisdom, a learning organisation, must value the norm of 'rocking the boat' as a more viable operating norm than maintaining stability (Shukla, 1994b).

Such a state of disequilibrium is essential for creating the degree of freedom a system requires for adapting itself to turbulent environmental conditions (Cameron and Zammuto, 1988). Instabilities and crises shake up people, force them to question the status quo and to focus on the essentials. Dumaine (1993) quoted a study of 40 companies which found that in each case a major strategic and organisational change was preceded by some form of crisis. Nonaka (1988), too, in his study of self-renewing companies, noted that crises create opportunities for growth and innovation:

> In order for an organisation to renew itself, it must keep itself in a non-equilibrium state at all times. . . . A crisis, of course, can mark the start of a company's demise. But, in general, some form of crisis is needed to generate an entirely new, innovative product concept or to abolish a company's existing patterns and replace them with a new order.

As can be noticed in the cases, one element common across the six organisations was the propensity not to let the company settle into inertia. The practice of keeping the company in a state of perpetual 'dynamic equilibrium' is quite apparent from a comment of the production manager of Chaparral Steel (Leonardo-Barton, 1992): 'In other companies, the word is—don't rock the boat. Here we rock the hell out of the boat. We don't know the factory's limits. We want it to change, to evolve.'

These companies, however, also knew how to manage 'rocking the boat' in ways that enabled them to use stress creatively. Nadler (1988) has termed this as 'Management of Pain Principle': 'Successful long-term changes seem to be characterised by creation of a sense of urgency right at the limit of tolerance— just at the point where responses may start to become defensive.'

One of the most common ways in which companies, and their leaders, create a sense of impending crisis is by implementing swift structural and/or strategic changes. In the cases, major transformational processes started with massive shake-ups that involved down-sizing, divestments, and acquisitions, changes at the apex level, restructuring, etc. (Box. 5.2). What made these actions a force for 'unfreezing' the organisation and shaking it out of its complacency was the speed with which they were implemented. The swiftness and magnitude of such actions serves to communicate signals of change across the organisation, and prepares people to align their expectations and actions with change. As we saw, this emphasis on swift action was one of the distinctive features of the organisations studied in the cases. In the words of Percy Barnevik (Taylor, 1991): 'You have to be factual, quick and neutral. ... I'd rather be roughly right and fast than exactly right and slow ... because the costs of delays are vastly greater than the costs of occasional mistakes.'

Thus, it is evident that an organisation's intent to learn is embodied in specific kind of leadership processes that create the momentum and direction for learning to take place (Figure 5.2). However, the vision and actions of leaders provide only the thrust for learning. To translate the thrust into learning, organisations need to evolve the mechanisms necessary for the creation and acquisition of knowledge.

BOX 5.2

BENNETT COLEMAN & COMPANY[4]

Changing the Rules of the Game

When Samir Jain took over as joint managing director of Bennett Coleman & Co. in the mid-1980s, he realised that the company was hardly running like a business. The over two dozen publications (e.g., *The Times of India, The Economic Times, The Illustrated Weekly of India, Femina, Filmfare, Dharmayug,* and *Science Today*) of Bennett Coleman were considered benchmarks of the publishing and editorial standards in India. And yet the group's PBT (profit before tax) was just Rs 11.8 million for 1983–84, which was less than 2 per cent of the turnover.

The reason was that (as in most other publishing houses) newspapers and magazines were considered the domain of editors, and not part of a business. In fact, the world of media was more like a club than a business. Rival publications were referred to as 'contemporaries' instead of as competitors. For most newspaper barons, the dailies were just 'objects of influence' for political purposes, while the money was in other businesses. In such a scenario, the editors were left to manage the publications outside the mainstream corporate structure.

In the span of just a decade, Samir Jain shook up the company and changed its personality beyond recognition. Many of his unconventional ideas emerged from the experience he had gained during his apprenticeship with *The New York Times* in his earlier years. He redefined the business of publication, in contradiction to some of the established tenets.

Jain viewed publishing like any other business—which implied that it should make profits. So far, a paper's success had been judged in terms of its market share of readership (which depended on its editorial content) or by its revenue (which was a function of circulation and of advertising space sales). Jain changed this criterion and shifted the focus on gaining the market share of the profits. He defined the goal as 'the ownership of the market', that is, Bennett Coleman's profits should exceed the combined profits of all others in the market. The company started judging its performance in terms of its growth rate of profits as compared to that of its rivals. ·

To achieve this goal, the company redefined its product portfolio, repositioning some of its publications and killing others. It discontinued many of its well-known magazines (e.g., *The Illustrated Weekly of India, Filmfare, Dharmayug, Parag, Sarika, Indrajal Comics, Vama,* and *Science Today*), since they contributed only marginally to the group's profits. Some others (e.g., *Femina* and *Filmfare*) were repositioned, while forays were made into new markets. For instance, Bennett Coleman started Times FM, a new medium for radio advertising for the young, and built Times TV into a viable business by marketing Doordarshan programmes. Also, the company identified the *Times of India* and the *Economic Times* as the mainstay of its business.

Simultaneously, the company reconceptualised its business management. One of the sacrosanct tenets to be challenged by the company was the role of the editor in bringing out a publication. Most publications were identified with their editors, who ran them like their own fiefdoms. Jain did away with the post of editor. Although the Press and Registration of Books Act (1987) prescribes the post of editor, who is supposed to be responsible for the content of a publication, Jain managed to circumvent these structures. The *Times of India*, for example, has no post of editor. Instead, the post of managing editor was created, and a former cigarette company executive was brought in to head it. The executive editor, responsible for the news, was not included in editorial meetings. Similarly, with the *Economic Times*, the post of editor was replaced by that of chief executive. News operations were looked after by an associate editor, while the editorial page was managed by a consulting editor; both reported to the CEO.

To create better business focus, the company appointed brand managers for its publications. Each publication was defined as a brand and these executives were responsible for the profitability of each brand. They decided on issues such as pricing, product mix, and brand extension or modification, and had the power to vet and review an editor's proposals. The new system ensured that the editorial department worked in conjunction with the commercial objectives of the publication. Brand management also ensured that the editorial, circulation, and space selling departments worked in tandem.

In defining new paradigms for the publishing business, Bennett Coleman generously borrowed ideas from other spheres of business. For example, the idea of variable rates for a newspaper came from the rates of admission in a zoo. Most zoos have reduced entry fee on one day in a week. The company experimented with this concept with the *Economic Times*. The Delhi edition of the *Economic Times* slashed the price of its Wednesday edition from Rs 4.50 to Rs 2.00, with a compensatory price increase in the weekend editions. While regular readers had to pay the same amount for the month, new readers could try it out once a week. This helped increase circulation from 100,000 in the second half of 1990 to 360,000 for the corresponding period in 1994.

Bennett Coleman borrowed the idea of marginal onward pricing from airlines. Just like a passenger flying Bombay to Bangkok can hop to Singapore on a marginal fare, the company offered add-on advertising rates for extra publications. Thus, advertisers of the *Times of India* were offered a discount for advertising in the *Economic Times*.

To improve the quality of publications, the company developed systems to increase reader–editorial interface. In Delhi, for instance, readers from particular areas were invited to meet journalists to give a feedback on the shortcomings of the Delhi edition of the *Times of India*. Many new features and editions were launched on the basis of these feedbacks.

These changes were by no means taken well by all. Many well-respected editors left the group. But Bennett Coleman had achieved what it had intended to achieve—a paradigm shift—and emerged as one of the country's most profitable companies. Within a decade its profits had gone up by 11,000 per cent (i.e., 111 times!), from Rs 11.8 million to Rs 1,299.4 million (27 per cent of the turnover). Its performance was better than that of some of the corporate gaints (e.g., Telco, Ranbaxy, and Ballarpur Industries). During the same period, its sales rose seven times, from Rs 685 million to Rs 4,795 million, and the reserves multiplied by a factor of 21. With the focus on profits the circulation of its publications soared. The company's flagship paper, the *Times of India*, emerged as the largest selling paper in India, and the sixth largest read daily in the world!

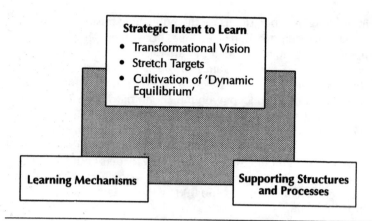

Figure 5.2　Elements of the strategic intent to learn

LEARNING MECHANISMS

The strategic intent to learn merely makes the organisation more open towards acquiring new knowledge and capabilities. However, for learning to actually take place, this intent must get translated into specific systems and mechanisms which enhance organisational learning. This is a very critical step in building a learning organisation, since it requires managerial action and implementation skills. The following sections discuss some of the important learning mechanisms that determine the specific manner in which organisations go about acquiring and generating new business-relevant knowledge.

Recruiting for Diversity

Learning, as already noted, requires a fresh perspective and a certain amount of disequilibrium. Though leadership processes create this condition, organisations also introduce variety and a constructive disorder in their functioning by recruiting individuals with diverse experience—often even unrelated to the company's basic business. This practice ensures the availability of a diversity of skills in the organisation, helps inject new perspectives in the organisation, creates a polarity of views, and facilitates the process of questioning. According to Pascale (1990):

> A system requires 'internal variety' to cope with external change. The trouble is, 'internal variety' is most experienced within organisations

as contention. The central thrust of this thinking is that internal differences can widen the spectrum of an organisation's options by generating new points of view. This, in turn, can promote disequilibrium; under the right condition, self-renewal and adaptation can occur.

As we saw in the cases, the organisations were both serious and unconventional in their recruitment procedures. Chaparral Steel, for instance, made it a policy to not recruit people with previous experience in the steel-making industry, but to recruit those who had 'a twinkle in the eyes and a zest for life'. Similarly, at Citicorp, recruitment was based on 'the view that we are a different business from a traditional bank'.

Such recruitment practices are particularly effective when they influence the composition of the top team (Bantel and Jackson, 1989). According to a study of 59 minicomputer companies (Virany, Tushman and Romanelli, 1996), high-performing companies responded to environmental turbulence by changing the executive team, whereas in failing firms there were either no changes or too many changes at the top. The study concluded:

> CEO succession and executive-team changes are fundamental levers for triggering second-order learning. Executive succession is associated with new competence and a shift in executive-team demography as well as revised executive-team processes. While second-order learning produces less consistent and reliable outcomes than first-order learning, this increased variability has enhanced ability to deal with uncertainty and/or crisis conditions.

This pattern of manning top positions is apparent in all six cases. At Citicorp during Wriston's tenure, the process of change started with the recruitment of senior executives from companies engaged in totally unrelated businesses, such as Ford, General Foods, Newsweek, and R.J.R. Reynolds. Similarly, BA brought in people from industries as diverse as Hertz, ICI, Mars Candies, etc. Xerox traditionally recruited managers at senior positions from diverse industries (besides, of course, from its competitors), such as chemicals, automobiles, and finance. In the late 1970s, it also started recruiting people with entirely new—and, for some, unrelated—professional skills, for example, anthropologists, linguists, and psychologists, in addition to engineers, metallurgists, and computer professionals.

This trend is also evident among many of those Indian companies which could successfully transform themselves. For instance, in its attempts to strategically reorient itself and achieve a turn-around, Arvind Mills generously employed people with no background in the textile industry at the senior positions (Box 5.1). It hired, for instance, from companies as diverse as Pond's, Citibank, Hindustan Lever Ltd, Asian Paints, etc (Kelkar, 1994b). The 'internal variety' helped the company think through its strategies from a new and different perspective. As Slywotzky (1996) has observed:

> Hiring primarily from within your industry leads to the in-breeding of ideas that makes it difficult to see how the customer has changed. Deliberately hiring talent from outside will generate different perspectives. The debate engendered by a flow of new ideas can be irritating and uncomfortable, but may save the company.

Openness to Learn from Others

Learning organisations approach the environment with the humility and curiosity of a learner, always willing to adapt insights to their use. This is natural because a learning orientation must thrive on receptivity to ideas and solutions in the environment. This attitude is essential to enable organisations tap and creatively leverage on bits of migratory competitive knowledge. A study commissioned by Ernst & Young (Prusak and Matarrazo, 1992) found that such a learning orientation was highly prevalent among Japanese companies. The study reported:

> Japanese companies have a preoccupation with the actions of their competitors. . . . Japanese companies' strategic planning process places more of an emphasis on competitor comparisons than do firms in United States, Germany, or Canada. The same holds true for information about foreign nations, and global industries. . . . Japanese management reads. This simple fact is significant. We observed many senior executives actually reading in their corporate information centres and libraries—something one rarely sees elsewhere. At one large library, we saw an executive with ten years' worth of annual reports from an American competing firm. He was reading the report's annual letter from the CEO because he 'wanted to get an unfiltered sense of how their CEO thinks'.

Benchmarking practices of this kind are quite common among learning organisations, and enable them to learn from their competitors. Competitive benchmarking provides not only realistic goals for the organisation to aspire for, but also knowledge about how these goals can be realised (Bogan and English, 1994). We saw how Xerox benchmarked against its competitors' products to gain an insight into its own operations. Similarly, starting January 1987, AT&T sent teams to do benchmarking studies in order to compare the rates of product introductions, length of product-realisation cycles, value–price relationship, etc. Its new knowledge of industry practices helped AT&T reduce its product development process from two years to 12 months (Hanley, 1990).

Underlying such practices is the belief that a good business practice is a good business practice, and is worth emulating, irrespective of who practises it—one's customers, suppliers, competitors, collaborators, other units of the company, or even organisations in unrelated industries. For instance, when Amtrex Appliances found that its service response time was more than that of others in the industry, the company benchmarked its processes against Modi Xerox (Ganguly, 1996).

However, organisations can benefit from such practices only when they build an open architecture, that is, when they align their internal processes and practices with the external reality. Correspondingly, learning organisations are designed to ensure a strong linkage between their significant internal work processes and practices and the external environment.

It is important to note that benchmarking may not necessarily be limited to one's own industry rivals. There are several examples of such open organisational architecture among the six cases. All these organisations had developed work practices and processes that could cross organisational boundaries to create learning partnerships. For instance, companies such as Chaparral, Xerox and GE had a system of benchmarking the best practices from organisations in different, and often completely unrelated, fields (e.g., how American Express clears bills, how McDonald's manages its burger business, how L.L. Bean organises its warehousing operations, how the UN moves files and equipment through the congested streets of Manhattan). Chaparral had the unique practice of sending its employees on 'sabbaticals' to travel, visit other steel mills, work with suppliers, customers or in technical labs, and bring back ideas to implement. Likewise, ABB, BA, and Citicorp used their size and geographical diversity to share and benchmark the best practices.

Open architectures permit organisations to learn more effectively from strategic alliances and collaborations. Although most alliances are supposed to take place because partners want to minimise their risk and investment, it is also true that the gains to the partners from alliances and collaborations are far from equal. Apparently, those who gain have more effective learning practices, and are better able to assimilate the strengths of their partners. A study of nine international alliances concluded that (Hamel, 1991): 'When collaborating with a potential competitor, failure to "out-learn" one's partner could render a firm first dependent and then redundant within the partnership, and competitively vulnerable outside it.'

In US–Japanese collaborations, for instance, the Japanese companies almost always emerged with greater competitive advantage than their partners. Based on their study of 15 strategic alliances, Hamel, Doz, and Prahalad (1989) found that the Japanese companies made more conscious and concerted efforts to learn and acquire the knowledge assets of their partner. They noted that: 'Successful companies view each alliance as a window on their partners' broad capabilities. They use the alliance to build skills in areas outside the formal agreement and systematically diffuse new knowledge throughout the organisation.'

They found that in many Japanese companies the collaboration managers regularly made rounds of all employees involved in the alliance, collected information and then passed it on to the appropriate departments. In some others, regular meetings were held where employees shared new knowledge and determined who was best positioned to acquire additional information.

Aligning with Customers

Another mechanism which enhances an organisation's learning is that of aligning its activities with the customers and the market. Learning organisations are invariably customer focused. For instance, BA used information from customer-feedback surveys to develop new services; Citicorp had relationship managers; at Chaparral, everyone was a member of the marketing department;

GE co-opted customers in market creation; and Xerox linked customer satisfaction with rewards for performance.

Sinkula (1994) noted that for an organisation to learn, the way in which information is processed (i.e., how it is acquired, translated into problems, shared and utilised for critical decisions) must take precedence over the use to which it is put. Appropriate customer/market focus enhances the creation of knowledge in the organisation in many ways. First, customers provide useful feedback to the organisation about its own functioning. Learning organisations use this feedback to create a better match between their offerings and the needs of different segments of customers. As we saw, in companies such as ABB, BA, Citicorp and Xerox there were regular systems to seek customer feedback, which was then shared across the organisation and used for developing more effective practices.

Second, customer orientation provides useful knowledge about competitors' strengths and weaknesses. In the ultimate analysis, customers are in the best position to evaluate and compare the relative merits of competing products and services. For instance, in the late 1970s, when Xerox found that customers preferred competitors' products, its engineers began to routinely tear apart photocopiers offered by Canon, Ricoh, etc. and study them component by component.

Lastly, working along with customers can be a major source of new ideas for products and services (Box 5.3). Competitive organisations use customers as major partners in their research efforts and processes of technological innovations: 'The research department's ultimate innovation partner is the customer' (Brown, 1991). GE, for instance, worked with their customers, BMW, to innovate the first thermoplastics car-body panel for their Z1 two-seater.

This correspondence between the marketing and internal work processes and practices also forms the basis of 'expeditionary marketing' (Hamel and Prahalad, 1991), that is, it allows organisations to discover new markets by converting the latent needs of customers into concrete products and services. For instance, when

BOX 5.3

PRAJ INDUSTRIES

Customising Research

Praj Industries was established in 1985 as an entrepreneurial venture by four technocrat friends to supply high-tech process solutions for setting up fermentation and distillation plants (Karnani, 1993; Majumdar, 1995b). At that time, Larsen & Toubro (L&T) and Alfa Laval were established as the leading suppliers of technology to the process industry. Praj chose its market in the process industry (comprising businesses such as pharmaceuticals, food, breweries) because sugar factories and distilleries had been the most neglected segment by the established players. Praj aimed to create its niche in this segment.

Soon after starting, Praj realised that to remain competitive it must have access to technological knowledge more superior than its competitors'. It signed a collaboration with Vogel Busch of Austria, the world leaders in continuous fermentation technology. As it grew, and identified new markets, the company continued to access new technology through collaborations, for example, with Reheat of Sweden to manufacture plate heat exchangers, and with DAB of Germany for setting up breweries with the latest know-how.

However, Praj's success was not built solely on a parity in offering 'international technology'. Rather, right from the beginning it followed a conscious strategy of learning from the environment and of offering customised solutions to meet specific client needs. For instance, when Praj started there were very few players in the market. These companies supplied distillation plants as equipment. They took responsibility neither for the construction, nor even for fabrication of some of the equipment, which was to be done by the customer. Praj saw the opportunity and created a market for itself by becoming the first company to offer a plant on a turnkey basis with a systematic project-engineering approach. Similarly, Praj bagged many contracts because it offered to help customers with complete solutions, even those of a non-technical nature (e.g., processing a license, arranging finance, and getting pollution clearance).

Realising that technological superiority was necessary to drive and exploit the market, Praj invested in creating a strong research and development base. At a time when companies were investing in research to save on taxes, Praj established a research centre which was linked to the market and could serve the company's strategy of speed and flexibility in offering its products.

Praj leveraged its research strength in many ways. For instance, when Praj entered into collaboration with Vogel Busch, it realised that environmental conditions in India, as well as the quality of molasses in different parts of the country, were very different from those found in Europe. Praj used its research capacity to adapt the technology to Indian conditions. In fact, this gave it a decisive edge over its major rival, Alfa Laval, who was offering only off-the-shelf technological solutions.

Its strong research facilities also helped Praj create new solutions for existing or emerging market conditions. For instance, it experimented with raw materials other than cane sugar molasses (e.g., tapioca, potato, and corn) to produce alcohol. These experiments helped it to set up the country's first starch-based plant to produce alcohol from tapioca in Kerala. Similarly, in 1986, when government imposed stricter pollution control regulations, Praj noticed an absence of solutions in the distillery industry, which was identified as one of the most polluting. From its research base, Praj was able to develop its own technology for pollution control. It also developed a machine called Spranhillator, which not only completely incinerated the spentwash, but was also energy-efficient since it did not need additional heat input.

The research function at Praj interfaced with business development. The business development managers scanned and identified potential customer needs, and identified and shortlisted the latest available technologies. These were then passed on to the research centre. Following this lead, the researchers visited prospective client sites to find out the applicability of the technologies, clients' exact needs, adaptations which would be required to meet these needs, and so on. Thus, Praj started customising technology to customer needs even before the selling process had started.

This strategy helped Praj in two ways. First, it speeded up the adaptation process, and, second, when the company's product managers approached clients, they already had a string of options, with quantitative and experimental findings, to support their claims. Intensive research backing and engineering skills not only allowed Praj to create and sell customised solutions, but also helped it respond to the market with greater speed and minimum cost.

In addition, Praj invited its existing and prospective clients to test their processes at its research facility. While the clients could get the analysis facility without any capital investment, Praj built new tie-ups as well as got access to clients' needs. Praj also started monthly training courses for executives from customer companies at its R&D centre. This helped in creating a more educated and sophisticated customer base, which could appreciate the value of new technological solutions.

By 1995, Praj had cornered 85 per cent share of the distillation and fermentation market (the rest was with Alfa Laval). Its turnover had grown from Rs 4 million in 1985 to around Rs 660 million. It had also started diversifying into other businesses (e.g., breweries) and product lines (e.g., solvent recovery systems, evaporators, dryers, decanters, and plate-heat exchangers).

Toyota introduced a new version of an existing commercial van, its engineers spent more than six months riding through the streets of Tokyo with the present users of its vans. These engineers were later made the project managers for the new van, and their knowledge of the customers' needs helped them develop a model that completely met market requirements (Shaw and Perkins, 1992).

Building Capabilities

Merely exposing people to external sources of knowledge, however, is meaningless unless they are alongside equipped with the skills and capability required to translate their experiences into decisions and practices. It is natural, therefore, for learning organisations to make a significant investment in the training of their people. However, as discussed earlier, organisational learning is more than just the sum of the learning of the organisation's individual members. Hence, two critical issues that learning organisations need to address are: (*i*) how to ensure effective learning of its members, and (*ii*) how to disseminate the learning of individuals and small groups into the collective learning of the organisation.

As we saw in the cases, all six organisations attached great value to human resources, and made conscious efforts to identify and develop their skills and capabilities. There was an implicit understanding that successful learning and strategic reorientation can only be engineered around the skills and expertise of employees. There were, however, three areas of difference between these efforts to build competence and change attitudes and the conventional training initiatives.

First, these were massive, companywide efforts, aimed to build a critical mass of people who would think and act in similar ways. For instance, BA puts all its 35,000 employees through the 'Putting People First' programme, followed by the 'Managing People First' course for its 2,000 managers; at Chaparral, all employees undergo a rigorous 7,280 hours on-the-job apprenticeship (in addition to courses on areas such as safety, programming, metallurgy, and basic mechanical maintenance, plus the mandatory 'Chaparral Process' course); Xerox trains all employees in small-group activities and problem-solving techniques; GE regularly trains its executives at its own management development institute at Crotonville.

Second, these efforts are distinctive in their sharp focus on the company and its problems, and pointed practice orientation. The underlying philosophy appears to be that training to impart 'abstract' knowledge has no meaning by itself; knowledge is useful and valid only when it can be practised within a context.

Learning . . . involves becoming an 'insider'. Learners do not receive or even construct abstract, 'objective', individual knowledge; rather, they learn to function in a community. . . . They acquire that particular community's subjective viewpoint and learn to speak its language. . . . Workplace learning is best understood, then, in terms of the communities being formed or joined and personal identities being changed. The central issue in learning is becoming a practitioner not learning about practice. [Brown and Duguid, 1996]

This orientation is evident in the practices of all six companies studied; they made greater use of the real-life context and internal resources in training. For instance, they designed their training programmes around real issues faced by them (e.g., ABB, BA, Xerox), used practising managers as training resources (e.g., Citicorp, Chaparral, GE), and incorporated application of theory to practice as a part of training (e.g., GE, Xerox).

Lastly, and probably most significantly, learning organisations seem to focus more on team learning than on individual learning (e.g., companies such as Xerox, GE, BA train their people in 'family groups'). They understand that, since individual learning in formalised settings usually has very little impact on the collective learning of the organisation, the unit for learning should be the team and not the individual. Moreover, when the team consists of 'people who need one another to act', the transfer of learning is much smoother and has greater impact (De Geus, 1988). Senge (1990) has noted that:

> Whether they are management teams or product development teams or cross-functional task forces—teams . . . are becoming the key learning unit in organisations. . . . Individual learning, at some level, is irrelevant for organisational learning. Individuals learn all the time and yet there is no organisational learning. But if teams learn, they become a microcosm for learning throughout the organisation.

SUPPORTING STRUCTURES AND PROCESSES

The preceding discussion highlights the critical learning mechanisms which are necessary for translating the corporate vision into a reality (Figure 5.3). The effectiveness of these mechanisms determines the quality and relevance of the organisation's learning. The effective execution of these mechanisms, however, also requires appropriate organisational structures and processes, which can sustain and encourage the learning activities. While the learning mechanisms facilitate learning and knowledge creation, supporting structures and processes ensure that the learning is productively used by the organisation. The following sections discuss some of the critical attributes of these structures and processes.

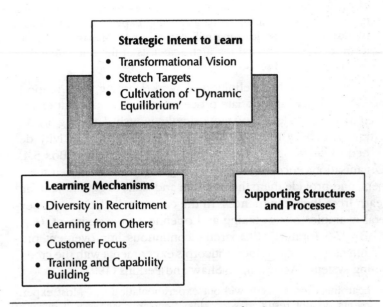

Figure 5.3 **Elements of the learning mechanisms**

Sculpting Learning Communities

In the conventional mind-set, 'working' and 'learning' are seen as mutually exclusive, sometimes even mutually contradictory. While learning is understood as an act by which knowledge is generated and acquired, working is regarded as the application of knowledge. This distinction is also based on the implicit assumption that, while working is a concrete and result-oriented activity, learning involves something that is abstract and detached from practice.

For viewing organisations as learning systems, however, this distinction is neither realistic nor conducive to organisational learning. An organisation that views itself as a learning community must reconceptualise the meaning of work and learning to incorporate learning as an essential component of its work processes and practices. Chaparral, for instance, described itself as a 'learning laboratory'; similarly, Xerox viewed itself as a cluster of 'productive work communities' that evolve and innovate as they work. According to Nevis, DiBella and Gould (1995):

If learning comes through experience, it follows that the more one can plan and guide experiences, the more one will learn. Until managers see organising ... as a learning experiment as well as a production activity, learning will come slowly. Managers need to learn to act like applied research scientists at the same time they deliver goods and services.

To implement this definition of work/learning, organisations need to develop appropriate processes and practices that enable their members to learn and work simultaneously. Learning organisations do so by treating work as an experimental activity designed to deliver results as well as create knowledge (Box 5.4). Organisations encourage a risk-taking attitude among their members, and provide them the freedom and skills to experiment and learn from their experiences. In the cases studied, there are several examples of risk-taking and openness to experiment. (e.g., ABB's '7-3 formula', Chaparral's continuous improvement programmes at the shop-floor, Citicorp's experiments with the credit-rating system). According to Shaw and Perkins (1992):

> Learning cannot occur without experimentation. . . . Most experiments do not result in successes. New approaches will occur if people feel they have permission to fail productively and that experimentation alone will be rewarded. . . . Learning-efficient companies set up experiments with clear objectives, ensure that experiments are executed well, and document the results. . . . [Many companies] provide training in statistics, experimental design, and problem analysis that enables employees to design, implement, and analyse experiments.

Enabling and Empowering

Developing an experimental attitude also necessitates creation of an empowering environment. Empowerment is essential for people to act and experiment (Denton and Wisdom, 1991). One of the conditions under which people are stimulated to act and take risks is when organisations clearly state their core priorities and show a bias towards results (e.g., Citicorp's target of 15 per cent return on assets, GE's aim 'to be number 1 or 2', Chaparral's aim to be the world's least cost producer of steel). Learning organisations empower people by giving them goals with personal accountability for delivering results (e.g., GE's Work-Outs, Citicorp's freedom

BOX 5.4

WORK AS LEARNING

Cipla Laboratories

From the beginning of the 1990s to the present, Cipla has grown from eleventh spot to rank third in the pharmaceutical industry. A factor which has aided its growth is the unique structure of the company which helps create a diverse set of capabilities among its employees. In Cipla, people do not have functional designations; they are given a set of responsibilities in a core area, but are expected to spend considerable time on assignments of a cross-functional nature. Thus, a cost accountant might also be involved in new product development and launches, pricing and costing, handling MIS functions, etc. (Gupta, 1995a).

PGR Corporation

At PGR (see also Box 5.5), continuous learning, knowledge sharing and improvement are part of the company philosophy, which is implemented through a variety of unique methods. For instance, it has innovated the concept of 'five-minute training' on the shop-floor in which an expert or an employee holds a short session on the dos and don'ts of a new technique. Employees are members of 'study circles' that meet periodically to discuss the books or articles read by the members. The company also distributes books and articles to employees on a regular basis. New skills are developed by a system of regular job rotation across departments. In addition, of course, PGR expects its employees to nominate themselves for eight days a year to external courses as well (Bohra, 1996).

Praj Industries

Praj Industries (see also Box 5.3) has evolved a unique process for learning and internalising new knowledge while working. Every year Praj adapts a theme (e.g., speed, quality, customer orientation, innovation), relevant to the company's effectiveness and the entire organisation works on this theme throughout the year. By the end of the year, this knowledge becomes internalised among the employees and the work processes. To ensure that the new competence does not dissipate, the chosen theme is converted into performance parameters, which are included in employees' performance appraisal (Majumdar, 1995b).

laced with the five MBO targets). As we saw earlier, democratisation of the workplace is supplemented with skill building and training so that people can use their freedom meaningfully.

An important precondition for empowered action lies in the nature of the organisation's formal structure. Tall hierarchies invariably stifle freedom at the lower levels. One of the ways of empowering members is by reducing the number of hierarchical levels, creating more autonomous business units, and decreasing centralised controls. For instance, ABB had just five levels from CEO to shop-floor, Chaparral had only three, GE reduced its 29 levels to just five broad brands, and so on.

An even more radical approach to restructuring for empowerment is the formation of self-managing teams (e.g., ABB, BA, GE, and Xerox). These teams are designed on the principle of minimum critical specifications' (Herbst, 1974), in that there are fewer external rules imposed on them; mostly, they are free to formulate their own rules and operating norms, as long as they meet their goals. The rules are replaced by broad guidelines and operating norms, which are reinforced and clarified from time to time, providing a great degree of freedom to the teams (Box 5.5). Having delegated responsibilities down the line, organisations do not require a multilayered centralised system to regulate and monitor performance. Morgan and Ramirez (1983) note that the principle of minimum critical specification

> facilitates such changes in structure by encouraging systems' designers to specify not more than is absolutely necessary for a system to begin operation, so that a system can find its own design. The minimum conditions are what might be understood as 'enabling conditions'—conditions that enable a system to initiate key processes necessary for its continued existence.

Correspondingly, self-managed teams share three features (Banner, 1993; Nonaka, 1988; Simmon and Blitzman, 1986):

1. They are autonomous in that they take many operational decisions, such as goal-setting, planning, monitoring performance, hiring, and peer appraisal.

2. They are responsible for achieving their performance goals regarding costs and profits.

3. They are mostly multidisciplinary, so as to achieve synergy through cross-fertilisation of ideas among members.

BOX 5.5

MANAGING WITH TEAMS

Amtrex Appliances Ltd

Since 1992, Amtrex, India's third largest air-conditioner manufacturer, has been redefining itself around teams (see also Box 6.3). By 1996, the company had almost 70 cross-functional teams to look after the key processes (e.g., order-to-delivery cycle, new product launch ratios, and quality). While the teams set their own targets, their performance is evaluated by the customer teams. To ensure transparency, the results are shared among all management staff. Moreover, an individual's performance appraisal is linked to his team's performance (Chhaya, 1996; Jain, 1996; Nair, 1994).

Otis India Ltd

Otis India's efforts to build a team-based organisation started from the shop-floor level. Having achieved success with teams for managing quality, manufacturing and safety standards, the company extended its team efforts to organisational levels. It created five cross-functional management teams at the senior level to virtually run the company. These teams, comprising seven members each, deal with all the issues pertaining to people, organisation, customers, environment and infrastructure, and report directly to the managing director. The teams are fully empowered to set and achieve their targets. Each team meets once a week, to review the performance of the team and its members and to develop plans. (Chhachhi, 1996a).

PGR Corporation

The shop-floors of PGR Corporation (see also Box 5.4) are structured as small autonomous groups, called 'Lakshya Prapti Samuh'. These groups are fully empowered, and meet weekly to set their own targets and review performance. In addition, any employee can initiate a cross-functional team, and co-opt members from other groups. An individual's performance is evaluated on the basis of his team's performance. This unique system has enabled PGR to enhance its productivity twofold, and reduce the waste and absenteeism by almost half between 1992 and 1994 (Bohra, 1996).

Tata Consultancy Services

At Tata Consultancy Services, teams are an essential part of working. They are formed and disbanded as per the life of the project. The members of a team are identified by the Manpower Allocation Committee and the human resources department, who keep a track of the talent in the company. Being a knowledge-based entity, seniority plays only a minor role in the team; it is quite common for members to report to a team leader who may be five years their junior. Once a team is formed and the project leader identified, the team is on its own to decide how it will function (Chhachhi, 1996b).

Overlapping Work Processes

In the evolutionary perspective, the richness and variety of a system significantly determines its capacity to deal with complexities in the environment (the recruitment strategies of learning organisations, as discussed earlier, also aim to create this variety). According to the principle of 'requisite variety' (Ashby, 1956; Morgan and Ramirez, 1983), in order to deal with the variety in the external environment, the system itself must possess at least an equal amount of variety. That is, the system must contain certain redundancies in order to remain flexible in meeting unforeseen situations.

Conventionally, organisations build 'requisite variety' into their designs by creating functionally specialised tasks, slack resources, just-in-case inventories, etc. These assets are activated and used whenever the organisation encounters demands that stretch its resources. However, since this kind of variety also decreases the efficiency of an organisation, the aim always is to keep it to a minimum.

Learning organisations, on the other hand, view redundancies as essential to a system's effectiveness. However, they do not mechanically design this variety into their structures, as is conventionally done. Instead, they tend to build variety (and therefore, redundancies) into their processes and people. The advantage here is that diverse resources are made available at the point they are directly required. Such redundancy and variety

> encourages frequent dialogue and communication. This helps create a 'common cognitive ground' among employees and thus facilitates the transfer of tacit knowledge. ... Redundancy also spreads new explicit knowledge through the organisation so that it can be internalised ... when responsibilities are shared, information proliferates, and the organisation's ability to create and implement concepts is accelerated. [Nonaka, 1991]

Thus organisations encourage learning by consciously incorporating overlaps in their work processes, company information, business activities, and/or managerial responsibilities. As we noticed in the cases, practices such as multi-skilling, interfunctional job rotation, double reporting, cross-functional teams, parallel systems for information generation, use of multiple teams for the same project, etc., were quite prevalent in these companies. Although the specific modalities for introducing redundancies may have differed across companies (e.g., matrix structure of ABB, cross-functional teams in GE and Xerox, overlapping jurisdictions at Citicorp, extreme multi-skilling at Chaparral Steel), they all had practices which, in one way or the other, optimised the level of disorder in the company.

This disorder, when combined with a powerful vision, helps organisations develop self-designing and, therefore, transformational capabilities. It encourages debate and dialogue, constant questioning of assumptions, and creation of new alternatives. As Hedberg, Nystrom and Starbuck (1976) stated: 'A self-designing organisation can attain dynamic balances through overlapping, unplanned, and nonrational proliferation of its processes; and these proliferating processes collide, contest, and interact with one another to generate wisdom.'

Knowledge-connectivity Processes

As discussed in Chapter 3, the capability to communicate and distribute knowledge across the system is an essential requirement for a learning organisation. Only when knowledge is disseminated can it become the shared cognitive basis for individual action (Garvin, 1993). The knowledge-connectivity processes are the mechanisms that enable learning organisations to communicate and disseminate localised learning across the organisation.

These processes are relevant on three counts: First, in an organisation, knowledge and expertise is power, and power differentials can block freedom and synergy. Nonaka (1991) has observed that 'When information differentials exist, members of an organisation can no longer interact on equal terms, which hinders the search for different interpretations of new knowledge.'

By smoothening the flow of ideas and information, an organisation transforms itself into an interactive network, allowing people access to each other's knowledge, to exchange views and ideas, and to interact with each other to develop new concepts (solutions, services, products, etc.) on a regular, and often, on a real-time, basis. As the cases show, learning organisations make conscious efforts to make information secular across the organisation by building effective communication channels (ranging from computerised performance feedback to face-to-face discussions).

Second, systems for sharing information and expertise are normally not built in into the conventional organisational structures. The flow of knowledge and information within organisations is often inhibited and distorted by departmental, hierarchical and group boundaries. Thus, organisations require to innovate multiple channels for reaching relevant information across to people. According to a study of successful organisational changes (Young and Post, 1993):

> During times of crisis or major reorganisational change, the best response involves multiple communication devices—pulling out all the stops—to ensure that employees understand the action. . . . [Our research findings indicate that] most effective communication programs couple a liberal and imaginative use of high technology [television and e-mail, for instance] with a high-touch strategy that involves face-to-face and personalised communications.

All six organisations in the cases made generous use of both formal and informal mechanisms of communication and dissemination of information. BA, for example, coupled face-to-face meetings with the use of the house journal to keep employees abreast of the progress on nearly 200 corporate performance targets; Citicorp used its information network as well as regular meetings to keep people informed about the innovative solutions developed by Citibankers worldwide. ABB publicised the performance indices collected by Abacus and alongside created forums for interaction with the CEO and other senior managers ('We don't just inform we overinform'), and so on.

An emerging alternative to increase the flow of information, which gets blocked at the organisational boundaries is to redesign the work itself (e.g., Chaparral, GE, Xerox), that is, to completely 're-engineer' the work processes so that all relevant expertise is available at the point of work where it is required (Hammer, 1990; Hammer and Champy, 1994). Work is accomplished through autonomous multifunctional teams organised around specific business processes and outcomes, and not around functional tasks (e.g., representatives of research, engineering, manufacturing and marketing sit together, and not sequentially to create and launch a new product). This arrangement makes it possible to tackle work-related interfunctional problems in parallel and interactively. For instance, in 1989, Kodak re-engineered its business processes and organised its employees into multi- functional 'zebra teams' to manage the 'flow'. Each team was made responsible for making items for a particular internal or external customer. Being multifunctional, the teams could sort out diverse functional, but overlapping, problems (related to design, production, marketing, etc.) at the very point where they arose (Stewart, 1992).

Lastly, it is important to realise the value of informal networking and communication in a learning organisation. As discussed in Chapter 4, often the knowledge that makes an individual, team or department effective is tacit, personalised and deeply embedded in the specific context of the action (Badaracco, 1991; Nonaka, 1988; Nonaka and Takeuchi, 1995). Making this knowledge explicit requires more than just picking it off the shelf and distribu-ting it. Several studies (e.g., Brown and Duguid, 1996; Spender, 1992) have shown that tacit knowledge is more effectively communicated and updated through informal interpersonal processes (in the canteen, while working, through exchanging stories, etc.) than through formal meetings, training programmes, house journals, etc. Tapping this hidden knowledge and converting it into collective learning is largely dependent on close, personalised interactions. According to Spender (1992), learning is dependent on an activity whose social structure is not dependent on the knowledge necessary for the task at hand, but which arises from some other social patterning—such as 'old school ties', religious affiliation, family membership, or, most important, to Western organisations, professional affiliation, or membership of a creative team.

Learning organisations, as observed earlier, initiate many processes that help create an informal connectivity among their employees. For instance, the internal conferences in ABB and Citicorp on specific subjects brought together participants from worldwide offices so that they could share their experiences; BA used the advantage of the mobility of its manpower to intermingle with other staff; Chaparral ensured regular face-to-face communication by discouraging written memos and notes, and so on.

Some of the recent advances in information-communication technology have further facilitated knowledge connectivity (Andreu and Ciborra, 1996). The implications of an informationally wired-up organisation (i.e., networking among terminals, group softwares, expert systems, neural networks, e-mail) are diverse (Savage, 1992). Many companies (Citicorp, Xerox, etc.) use the potential of information technology to not only facilitate exchange of ideas among people, but also to enable themselves to make more efficient use of their own knowledge and expertise (Box 5.6). Interactive information systems affect the organisations in three ways:

1. The free flow of information empowers people and so helps create an equalitarian work culture (Clement, 1994).

2. The on-line communication and frequent exchange of ideas among employees build up group synergies and create new knowledge which would otherwise not have been available. As Zuboff (1985, 1988) pointed out, the use of computers is more than mere replacement of human efforts with smart technology. Computers do not just automate, they also 'informate', that is, they can simultaneously generate information about the underlying processes by which an organisation accomplishes its work. For instance, the microprocessor-based manufacturing process also generates information about the production process (on

BOX 5.6

NETWORKING THE KNOWLEDGE

Asian Paints Ltd

Asian Paints Ltd was one of the earliest exploiters of information technology in the country (see also Box 3.4). Besides tracking market information, its networking also extends to the shop-floors. Computer terminals are installed at each stage of the paint-making process. Whenever the worker adds an input to the process, he keys in this information. This availability of up-to-date information about the work in process has helped the company save on material loss, and improve productivity levels (Katiyar, 1994; Kelkar, 1993; Khanna, 1992).

Colgate-Palmolive

All 300 salespersons of Colgate-Palmolive are equipped with laptops and modems. As they travel to service the 600,000 outlets of the company, they book orders on the computer and electronically transmit them to one of the company's 19 computerised warehouses instantaneously. At the warehouse the order is processed promptly through the computer and stocking decisions are simultaneously taken. This information is daily aggregated at the headquarters and generates additional information, for example, about logistics, production planning, areas requiring thrust, high-performing salespersons, and emerging trends. It also helps the headquarters in guiding salespersons regarding specific field problems on a day-to-day basis (Gupta, Srivastava and Majumdar, 1995).

Parle Agro

Parle Agro is the maker of Frooti, which commands 86 per cent market share of the 12-million case Rs 1,500 million market of tetrapak drinks. The company uses a unique information gathering network, the Parle Agro Retail Barometer (PARB), through which it can continuously monitor every sale in 24,690 shops in almost 350 towns across the country. The system helps the company keep track of the width and depth of distribution of its own and its competitors' products, sales and stock levels, pricing and promotion data, etc. It also keeps the company abreast of information about its franchisees who pay a royalty for using the company's concentrate, brands and advertising campaigns, and contribute 16 per cent to the profit margin. Parle Agro uses this information to get the franchisees to respond quickly to market conditions. Further, this information is used to promote inter-franchisee rivalry by publishing their performance in the quarterly newsletter (Carvalho, 1994).

Precision Fasteners Ltd

Precision Fasteners Ltd manufactures over 4,500 types of fasteners, which are customised in terms of size, design, and material. The complexity of its operations (it uses 18,000–20,000 different tools) meant that the typical order–delivery cycle was a nine-step process involving half a dozen departments. An order to make a new bolt would go from engineering design to tools fabrication to production planning to materials purchase to finance, and so on, before the production could actually start. It would take a minimum of one month for an order to reach the production stage. In 1994, the company linked all the departments through a network of computers: This allowed simultaneous updating of information for various functions, such as materials management, sales and distribution, finance, production, and planning/control functions. Once an order was booked, different functions could start concurrently, such as materials planning, and scheduling of production and delivery. Hence, the one-month lead time was reduced to just four days (Gupta and Bhatt, 1995).

terminals and in printouts), which earlier either did not exist or existed only in someone's mind.

3. They help create a common reservoir of organisational knowledge and expertise readily available to all for solving organisational problems. Advances in systems such as neural networks, expert systems, and genetic algorithms make it possible for organisations to create intelligent problem-solving systems by pooling the best of all the relevant knowledge available in the organisation.

IMPLICATIONS

In this chapter, we looked at the basic anchors that define the architecture of a learning organisation (Figure 5.4). Three significant insights can be derived from the discussion:

First, unlike the traditional organisations, which rely on shaping their structures to improve efficiency, learning organisations focus on sharpening their processes to achieve excellence. This difference is most apparent in the way they organise their work. Conventionally, it is organised by dividing it—through division of labour, creation of hierarchies, departments and functions, with the aim of minimising the number of skills required to do a job.

In contrast, as noted, learning organisations aim at dissolving hierarchical and functional boundaries, and focus on designing work processes. They maintain optimum balance between the structured and unstructured, the planned and unplanned, consensus and dissension, which allows them to continuously reappraise and self-monitor.

Second, these architectures embody an entirely different view of the process of organisational change. The conventional view of this process is that change is an anomaly, or at best an infrequent incremental occurrence. Taylor's scientific management approach and Weber's bureaucracies, for instance, viewed organisations as mechanical clockworks, in which change did not feature. Correspondingly, organisations were viewed as instruments for minimising and eliminating uncertainties and, therefore, the need for change as well.

Later, the open-system model of organisation accepted the reality of change, but regarded it as an incremental adaptation to the environment, which must take place within the 'norm of rationality'. Managing change, therefore, involved creating slack resources and protecting the core functions, so that change did not shake up the organisation. Kindler (1979) described this kind of change as 'step by step movement or variations in degree along an established conceptual continuum or system framework. ... It is intended to do more of the same but better.'

Learning organisations, in contrast, are based on the premise that change is a discontinuous, transformational process. They involve the creation of crisis and disorder to enable a quantum re-

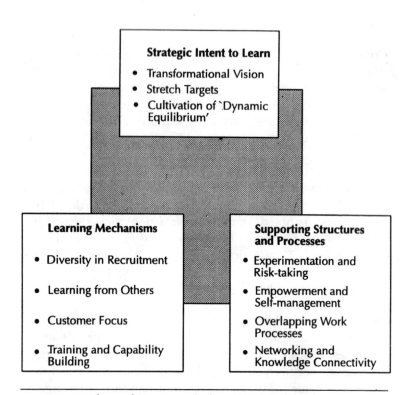

Figure 5.4   **The architecture of a learning organisation**

adjustment of their elements. In such organisations change is not an occasional occurrence that needs to be coped with once in a while. Rather, these organisations operate, and are structured, on the assumption that they consciously transform themselves by creating redundancies and increasing disorder within themselves.

Lastly, learning organisations differ from the conventional ones in terms of the very definition of an organisation. In the conventional framework, an organisation is an information-processing system (Galbraith, 1973). Here, the assumption is that organisationally relevant information is explicit, tangible, mostly quantifiable, and readily and systematically available for planning, decision-making and implementation. Organisations must, therefore, be designed to process and apply this information, which they can do effectively by reducing redundancies and contradictions.

A learning system, on the other hand, views relevant business knowledge as not always explicit, but often tacit, intangible, and deeply embedded in the way individuals, teams, organisations, and even environments behave. The primary task of an organisation, therefore, is to discover and create knowledge before starting to apply it (Nonaka, 1991; Spender, 1992).

It appears increasingly clear that the architecture of learning organisations represents an entirely new and different paradigm. An appreciation of a learning organisation would be incomplete without an understanding of the nuances of this new paradigm. We will analyse this in the next chapter.

Notes

1. Information for the caselet on Arvind Mills is taken from a number of published reports. For details, readers should specifically refer to Bhardwaj (1995), Kelkar (1994b), Lalbhai (1993), and Parekh (1991).

2. For more details on Core Healthcare Ltd, readers should refer to Arora *et al*. (1995), Jacob (1994), Jain (1996), Joseph (1995), Majumdar (1995a), Ray (1995), Sethi (1992), and Subramaniam (1994).

3. The transformation of Mahindra & Mahindra has been widely documented. Readers may like to refer to Chhachhi (1995), Gupta (1995a), Joglekar (1994), Lakshman (1993), Sarangdhar, Pednekar and Rajappan (1995), and Viswanathan (1994) for more details.

4. Details for the case on Bennett Coleman & Company have been taken from Kaul (1996), Rawla (1976), Roy (1995), and Srivastava and Gupta (1996).

6

The Learning Organisation: An Emerging Paradigm

*Evolution is open not only with respect to its
products but also to the rules of the game it
develops. The result of this openness is the self-
transcendence of evolution in a 'meta evolution', the evolution of evolutionary mechanisms
and principles.*

—E. Jantsch

DECONSTRUCTING THE ORGANISATION

Semco is a Brazilian group of companies that manufactures a wide
range of products such as pumps for oil tankers, dishwashers,
cooling units for air-conditioners, and mixers for rocket fuel (or
bubblegum), and sets up biscuit-manufacturing plants. Since
1982, when Ricardo Semler, the son of the founder, took over,
Semco has undergone some interesting changes (Semler, 1994).

To start with, Semco does not have any rule book ('the only
policy is to have no policy'). What it has is a 20-page booklet for all
its employees known as 'The Survival Manual', which contains
many cartoons. Its basic message is: Use your common sense.

There are no managers and workers at Semco; there are associates and coordinators. According to Semler (1994):

> Well, we don't have as many managers as we used to. . . . We have
> also reduced our corporate staff . . . by more than 75 per cent. We no
> longer have data processing or training departments. Everyone

vouches for his own work, so we don't need a quality control department either. . . . [We] whittled the bureaucracy from twelve layers of management to three and devised a new structure based on concentric circles to replace the traditional, and confining, corporate pyramid.

Factory and office workers manage the place. They come for work at the time that suits them and their teams, and take breaks when they think it convenient. They also fix their own production quotas, design the products they make, and formulate marketing plans. Even big decisions (e.g., the location of a new factory) are taken by vote—and everyone, including the CEO, gets a vote.

Before people are hired or promoted to leadership positions, they are interviewed and approved by all those who are going to work for them. These leaders have complete freedom to run their departments like independent business units, buying and selling services and products to one another. If it suits them better, they can even buy from and sell to outsiders. They fix their own salaries (these, of course, are made public), and workers decide on the share and distribution of their profit. Every six months the 'subordinates' evaluate their managers, and the results are posted on the board for everyone to see.

Over the years, Semco has emerged as an archetype of the new and successful form of organisation. During the 1980s, when the Brazilian economy was in a shambles, Semco registered a sixfold increase in its assets; its turnover grew from $4 million to $35 million; its profits rose fivefold; productivity increased seven times; the sales per employee increased from $10,800 to $92,000 (adjusted against inflation); it turned its inventory 17 times a year (as against the industry average of three times); and maintained number one or two position in all its markets.

Semco, however, is not an isolated example of a new breed of 'disorganised' organisations. There are points of similarity between Semco and some of the companies discussed in the cases, e.g., Asea Brown Boveri (ABB), Chaparral, General Electric (GE), and Xerox. In fact, Semco represents the growing numbers organisations of that are not only defying convention, but redefining the very meaning of organisation.

The prevalence of new forms is so widespread that within the last five years there has been a proliferation of new terms to describe this emerging breed of organisations, e.g., 'Virtual Corporation' (Davidow and Malone, 1992), 'Modular Corporation' (Tully, 1993), 'Horizontal Corporation' (Byrne, 1993), 'Starburst Organisation' (Quinn, 1992), 'Network Organisation' (Nohria and Eccles, 1992) and, 'Hypertext Organisation' (Nonaka and Takeuchi, 1995). What is common across these terms is the concept of organisation that turns conventional organisational logic upside down and questions the validity of the basic tenets of the organisation (Box 6.1).

BOX 6.1

THE DISORGANISED ORGANISATIONS

Dell Computers

Dell Computers is the fifth largest PC company in the US. However, it owns no plants and leases two small factories to assemble computers from outsourced parts. Unlike other companies, Dell sells its PCs, which are customised to customer specifications, directly to the customers through mail-order. In addition, Dell offers to its customers more than 650 softwares, a full range of modems and other PC accessories. But it neither makes nor stocks these products. It simply orders them from other companies who deliver directly to the customer (Tully, 1993).

Oticon

Oticon, a Danish hearing-aid company, responded to competitive challenges by changing into a 'spaghetti organisation'—an organisation without a centre. It razed walls, eliminated secretaries, erased job descriptions and specialities, and did away with formalised rules and procedures. The employees now formed project-directed completely autonomous groups; they decided their functions and targets and physically arranged themselves as they saw fit to get them done (Peters, 1994).

Reebok India

Reebok India, like Reebok's worldwide operations, is designed as a network organisation. It has outsourced shoe manufacturing

---

to Phoenix, Aero and Lakhani, retailing to Phoenix, logistics to Nexus Logistics, and warehousing to Bakshi Associates. Its stores will be designed by Aakar, and advertising will be managed by Hindustan Thomson Associates. Even selection has been outsourced to Prospects (Roy and Augustine, 1995).

UBEST

UBEST, a Calcutta-based telecom software company, is unique in many respects. It is a hierarchyless, flat organisation, in which no one has a designation. Its members work in overlapping project teams. The organisation follows the flexitime system and its members have the freedom to decide on their own workload, timing and pace of work, and work-related expenditures. There is no system of approvals, and written communication is discouraged (Gupta, 1995).

In this chapter we will discuss how the conventional 'Industrial Paradigm' is giving way to an emerging Learning Paradigm—and how this shift requires a transformation in our understanding of the concept of an organisation (Hodgetts, Luthan and Lee, 1994). Before discussing this shift, however, it is imperative to understand what a paradigm shift is.

PARADIGM AND PARADIGM SHIFT

In 1962, Thomas Kuhn (1962), a historian of science, published a small, path-breaking book, *The Structure of Scientific Revolutions*. Kuhn's book challenged the existing belief that science was a logical enterprise, representing a linear, incremental progress in an accumulating base of knowledge. Till that time, the history of science was described as if scientists across the ages had worked on similar sets of problems with similar sets of rules of thinking. Each scientist, thus, only added to existing knowledge, taking a 'logical step in a gradual approximation to an increasingly accurate description of the universe and the ultimate truth about existence' (Grof, 1985).

Kuhn pointed out that scientific advances progressed through periods of stability ('periods of normal science') followed by quantum discontinuous jumps ('paradigm shifts'). According to him, scientific activities most often are governed by a particular *knowledge paradigm*—a constellation of values, philosophical beliefs, and techniques—shared by the members of a given scientific community. This paradigm defines the basic scientific issues, such as what the legitimate scientific problems are and how they should be studied. In essence, the paradigm represents (Kuhn, 1962)

[the] collection of ideas within the confines of which scientific inquiry takes place, the assumed definition of what are legitimate problems and methods, the accepted practice and point of view with which the student prepares for membership in the scientific community, the criteria for choosing the problems to attack, the rules and standards of scientific practice.

During the period of normal science, one paradigm dominates. It is a time of stability, when the scientific community 'knows' what the universe is like, what problems are scientifically legitimate, what is the range of possible solutions, and how they need to be arrived at. Obviously, normal science is not the domain of scientific creativity and innovation. In fact, during this period, unconventional research designs and unexpected results are labelled as 'bad research' and rejected. That is why when Gregor Mendel published his laws of genetics in 1866, the scientific community failed to recognise them for the next 30 years. Or, in the nineteenth century, meteorites were thrown out of the Vienna museum as useless pebbles, because they did not fit the known description of the universe.

The change in the paradigm begins with the continual increase in the discrepancies between theory and observation. Over a period of time, the new findings and observations accumulate that cannot be explained within the existing paradigm. With this accumulation there is a corresponding increase in the number of scientists who gather information that requires new formulations to account for it. The anomalies cease to remain just another puzzle; they are increasingly viewed as a major challenge to the validity of the existing paradigm.

This is the period of 'extraordinary science', when new and competing theories proliferate, and there is a conceptual chaos. During this period, the inadequacies of the existing paradigm are more explicitly expressed, and there is greater debate over the fundamental assumptions of science. New frameworks and perspectives are proposed, tested, and critiqued in the search for a new vision of the reality.

It is from this debate and chaos that the new paradigm emerges. The new paradigm is not just an improved version of the older one; it is a quantum conceptual leap. It most often emerges from the creative insights of extraordinary individuals (such as Newton, Darwin or Einstein), who suggest a superordinate vision of the reality. The new paradigm is a more complex and comprehensive 'above the battle' vision; it synthesises competing perspectives, and stimulates people to explore new ideas instead of defending the older ones. The old paradigm does not vanish; rather, it becomes part of the new one.

Kuhn's insights are relevant to present-day managers, because something similar to a paradigm shift is happening in the field of management. This shift is forcing reconsideration of some of the basic assumptions about the concepts of business, strategy, organisational form, and managerial control. The following sections analyse this shift in detail.

CONCEPT OF BUSINESS: VALUE CHAIN TO KNOWLEDGE CREATION

Conventional business organisations are an offshoot of the Industrial Revolution. Their proliferation was stimulated by the emergence of the capital-intensive mass-manufacturing technology. Fuelled by technological advances (e.g., steam and electric power, engines, steel-making technology), manufacturing organisations became models of efficient application of scientific and technical knowledge to create wealth.

The mass-manufacturing technology created a parallel revolution in management activities. To manage the complexity and

Exhibit 6.1   The concept of business organisation

Industrial Paradigm	Learning Paradigm
* Organisation is a system of control * Organisation is a portfolio of product markets	* Organisation is a system for creating knowledge * Organisation is a constellation of competencies and capabilities

volume of work, the entire task was broken down into smaller and simpler activities, linked together in the value chain. To manage large factories, organisations required to ensure the reliable performance of these activities by hundreds of employees. Consequently, they developed a set of standard rules and procedures, and hierarchical layers of managers to see that these were adhered to. The purpose of these bureaucratic arrangements was to maintain control over the organisational activities that comprise the value chain.

As discussed earlier, many of the assumptions behind these control-focused organisations are becoming less and less applicable (Exhibit 6.1). In an era of information-intensive mass customisation, creation of knowledge is taking precedence over creation of wealth. More and more organisations are realising that creation of wealth is directly determined by the degree of efficiency of organisations to create, process, and transfer knowledge and information within the system. It is not surprising that, in 1991, US companies spent more on information-processing (computation and communication) than they did on buying mining, industrial and construction machinery (Stewart, 1994). Similarly, a study noted that in 1986 (Kodama, 1992), R&D expenditure in the top 50 Japanese companies exceeded capital spending. The study concluded that:

> The manufacturing company is traditionally a site for production, and the economist's formulation is a production function: capital plus labour equals output ... as R&D investment surpasses capital investment, the corporation shifts from being a place for production to being a place for thinking.

There is yet another shift occurring in the concept of the business organisation: the definition of a business organisation as a portfolio of product markets, managed through separate Strategic business units (SBUs), is becoming increasingly superfluous (Prahalad and Hamel, 1990). Defining a company in terms of its product markets was relevant when its environment, though complex, could be segmented in more or less well-defined sets. However, such a definition offers no meaningful guidelines for an organisation's success, in an environment marked by turbulence, radical changes in both the size and shape of market domains, shifts in customer tastes and preferences, and cross-industry competition (Slywotzky, 1996). It does not explain, for instance, the success of many Japanese and South Korean companies, or the failure of well-known ones like Remington and Gestetner (in spite of their market dominance, product positioning and brand equity).

That is the reason organisations are increasingly 'rethinking the corporation' in terms of their core competencies (Prahalad and Hamel, 1990), invisible assets (Itami, 1987), knowledge-based assets (Quinn, 1992), and such other concepts. Nevis, DiBella and Gould (1995) described the emerging definition thus:

> The value chain of any organisation is a domain of integrated learning. To think of the value chain as an integrated learning system is to think of work in each major step . . . as a subsystem for learning experiments. Structures and processes to achieve outcomes can be seen simultaneously as operational tasks and learning exercises. . . . This view is consistent with a definition of organisations as *complex arrangements of people in which learning takes place.*

STRATEGIC FOCUS: PRODUCT TO CAPABILITIES

The natural corollary to viewing the organisation as a bundle of knowledge-based assets is the need to redefine the nature, formulation and implementation of strategy. Conventionally, strategy is defined in terms of the SWOT of the company's products, markets and competitors. Three assumptions underlie such a concept of strategy:

1. Competing is essential for survival and growth.
2. Competition is based on the strength of one's product/ service portfolio.

Exhibit 6.2 **The concept of strategy**

Industrial Paradigm	Learning Paradigm
* Target focused	* Vision based
* Focus on competition	* Focus on collaboration
* Market dominance	* Market creation
* Shareholder returns	* Customer satisfaction

3. Maximising returns and a larger market share is the successful strategy.

These assumptions are becoming increasingly inadequate in explaining the nature of contemporary successful strategies (Exhibit 6.2). First, as the business environment becomes more complex (e.g., fragmentation of markets, emergence of new technologies, trade barriers, etc.), the ability to compete ceases to remain the sole criterion of success. Mere competitive focus does not always help companies gain entry into new markets, acquire technological and financial prowess, or develop fast-cycle manufacturing capabilities. Consider, for instance, Corning's success following 40 strategic alliances across the world, the strategy of companies such as Benetton, Nike, and Nokia of forming partnerships with suppliers and dealers or the entry strategy of Japanese companies through joint ventures with local partners. Such examples indicate that the capabilities to collaborate with suppliers, customers and (potential) competitors are becoming as important as those required for competing (Box 6.2).

Second, the assumption of product-or industry-based competition does not apply when the competitive threat comes from changing markets and technologies. To recall the examples of 'alien invaders' discussed in Chapter 1, the strength of strategy lies in the organisation's ability to meet competitive threat from unrelated industries, markets and technologies. Thus, just like the change in the definition of the organisation (from a portfolio of products to a collection of competencies and capabilities), the basis of competition, too, must shift from product to competencies. As Hamel (1991) noted:

> Conceiving of the firm as a portfolio of core competencies and disciplines suggests that interfirm competition, as opposed to inter-product competition, is essentially concerned with acquisition of

BOX 6.2

COLLABORATING TO COMPETE

- CMC Ltd and HCL-HP are fierce competitors in the systems integration market. However, they collaborated extensively with each other (in terms of information sharing and training skills) when they were putting the stock exchanges on-line. The reason for this was that CMC had already developed the software for the stock exchanges but was finding it difficult to sell it on the costly Tandem machines; HCL-HP, on the other hand, had cheaper computers, but was finding the development and import of software costly. Hence, the alliance was beneficial to both (Srivastava, 1996).

- BPL and Videocon are both contenders for dominance in the consumer electronics market. However, when the colour tubes facility of Uptron was put up for sale, both companies joined hands (along with Toshiba) to take it over and run it.

- Philips India and Videocon are competitors in the market. However, the semiconductor unit of Philips India supplies components to Videocon for its Bazooka model.

- Godrej Foods sells tomato puree; so does Hindustan Lever Ltd (HLL), under the Kissan brand. Both brands of puree, however, are produced at the Godrej factory in Bhopal—using the tomato paste supplied by HLL. HLL, incidentally, supplies paste also to its competitor, Nestle, for making tomato ketchup, which competes with its own Kissan Ketchup.

skills. In this view global competitiveness is largely a function of [the] firm's pace, efficiency, and extent of knowledge accumulation.

Lastly, the emerging business context also questions the conventional focus of the strategy on better returns and increased market share. This focus is valid when well-defined markets exist (and hopefully, will continue to exist). In a shifting, turbulent market, however, a whole range of products and industries can become obsolete overnight. Organisations, therefore, must think not in terms of increasing market share, but in terms of creation of new markets. According to Hamel and Prahalad (1991):

> To realise the potential that core competencies create, a company must also have the imagination to envision markets that do not yet exist and the ability to stake them out ahead of the competition. A company will strive to create new competitive space only if it possesses an opportunity horizon that stretches far beyond the boundaries of the current businesses.

EMERGING ORGANISATIONAL FORMS: HIERARCHY TO NETWORKS

An organisation's structure is merely a tool that puts its purpose and aims into practice. When the nature and purpose of the business starts changing, the structure also needs to change (Exhibit 6.3).

Exhibit 6.3 **The concept of organisation**

Industrial Paradigm	*Learning Paradigm*
* Clear boundaries	* Permeable boundaries
* Pre-designed	* Evolving design
* Minimise skills	* Maximise skills
* Segmented tasks	* Integrated processes
* Functional, hierarchical groupings	* Open, multi functional network

The organisational forms of the industrial paradigm were instruments of control. Since they aimed at stability and predictability, they were built to ensure that jobs could be planned and pre-designed. The total work was divided into smaller, segmented units, with clear boundaries and controls. Clear boundaries also separated the organisation from its environment so as to minimise the influences of environmental fluctuations. These structures, however, were neither designed for learning nor were they meant to evolve and transform themselves in response to new demands.

Learning structures, on the other hand, need to be flexible, and capable of self-monitoring and self-designing (Hedberg, Nystrom and Starbuck, 1976; Mohrman and Cummings, 1989; Morgan and Ramirez, 1983). Instead of following mechanical design principles, these organisations are structured on *holographic design principles* which 'create systems that are able to learn from their own experience, and to modify their structure and design to reflect what they have learned' (Morgan and Ramirez, 1983). Many of the organisations described in Chapter 5 (e.g., Amtrex, PGR, Core) reflect this principle in practice (Box 6.3).

BOX 6.3

'HOLOGRAPHIC' ORGANISATIONS

Amtrex Appliances Ltd

In April 1993, Amtrex started to mould itself into what its CEO described as 'a horizontal-circular structure' (see also Box 5.5). Most of its activities were reorganised around a number of teams: '100% OK Teams', 'Customer Care Teams', 'Teams for Accelerated Innovation', and so on. To ensure customer focus, the company re-engineered itself into a process-based organisation, and redefined each function as a part of the service chain. The company also invested heavily in information technology to network the various parts of its processes, so that relevant information was available all the time to anyone, anywhere in the organisation (Misra, 1996).

Eastman Chemical Co.

In January 1993, Eastman Chemical Co., a division of Eastman Kodak, changed itself into a circular 'Pizza Chart' organisation. Each function, geographic region, or 'core competence' is represented by a pepperoni on the pizza. The white space around the pepperoni is where the actual collaborative work takes place. Hierarchy has been abolished, and functions are not supposed to have separate goals. People work in self-directed work teams; all managers are members of at least one such team (Byrne, 1993).

> ### Federal Express
>
> In 1988, Federal Express organised its 1,000 clerical workers into superteams of five to ten people. These teams were trained and given the authority to make improvements in their work. Without any formal supervision, in just one year, these teams were able to bring down costs due to incorrect billing and lost packages by 13 per cent (Dumaine, 1990).
>
> ### Intel
>
> Chip-maker Intel is organised into several dozen small 'councils', which not only manage the research and product development activities, but are also responsible for the traditional support functions (e.g., purchase policy, operating procedures, employee compensation). The performance of the teams is judged against the targets set by them. According to its CEO, Andy Grove, the aim 'is to remove authority from an artificial place at the top and to place it where the most knowledgeable people are' (Quinn, 1992).

Holographic organisational designs are based on three principles. First, such organisations build in the 'requisite variety' (of skills, knowledge, perspectives, etc.) into their processes and people, instead of in their controlling parts (i.e., departments and functions). Unlike organisations of the industrial era, knowledge-based organisations maximise the availability of skills at the point of operation, instead of minimising them. Thus, the organisation is designed as a set of parallel, interlinked business processes, and not as a collection of separate tasks and functions. The shift is from a functional view of the organisation to a process-based one.

Second, these organisations replace hierarchical controls by building capacities for self-monitoring. The ability of the system to question itself is necessary to translate the 'requisite variety' into learning capacities. According to Morgan and Ramirez (1983):

> Decision-making processes in such an organisation are spread as widely as possible to gain a wide range of information required. ....
> Holographic organisation encourages such substantial rationality by recognising that every member of a system may have something of value to contribute to an understanding of the system, and that

resource should be tapped in as many ways as possible to enhance the learning capacity of the system as a whole.

Lastly, as discussed in Chapter 5, these organisations are designed on the principle of 'minimum critical specifications' (Herbst, 1974; Morgan and Ramirez, 1983). Unlike the over-designed organisations of the industrial era, the design of these organisations specifies only the conditions that enable the system to start functioning. Thus, these organisations might be designed around the teams accountable for a goal, and comprise members who are functionally competent to collectively handle the task. Beyond these specifications, the design (i.e., how members relate to and work with each other) is allowed to evolve; it is neither predetermined nor imposed.

One of the corollaries of viewing an organisation as a hologram is acknowledging it as a network of relationships in which each part is related to the others and influences, and in turn is influenced by, them (Nohria and Eccles, 1992). A network perspective also recognises and legitimises the informal relationships that shape the organisation and its activities. This connectivity is essential for the creation of knowledge as well for its smooth diffusion across organisational boundaries. As Savage (1992) observed: 'Peer-to-peer networking assumes that as we network, we add value based on our thinking, observing, knowledge, and vision... we are knowledge contributors and decision points, or nodes, within the network.'

This shift is evident in the basic principles of organising and coordinating work in most of the contemporary approaches to organisational restructuring, for example, in re-engineering, process-based designs, and network organisations (Hammer and Champy, 1994; Nadler, 1989; Savage, 1992). As Box 6.4 shows, these approaches essentially give concrete shape to the principles governing the structures of knowledge creation.

MEANS OF CONTROL: FORMAL RULES TO INFORMAL CULTURE

Transformations in the definition of the organisation and its strategies are also making the control and coordination methods

> BOX 6.4
>
> ## THE NEW ORGANISING PRINCIPLES
>
> In spite of the differences in terminologies, there is considerable similarity among the blueprints suggested for the new paradigm organisations (Byrne, 1993; Hammer, 1990; Hammer and Champy, 1994; Ross, 1990; Savage, 1992; Stewart, 1992). The following are some of the basic principles:
>
> - Organise work around integrated processes, not around segmented tasks.
> - Create flatter structures, with parallel instead of sequential teams.
> - Make teams (not individuals) accountable for the total task; empower teams to take all relevant decisions pertaining to their work.
> - Make organisational boundaries permeable in order to bring teams in contact with customers, suppliers, and each other.
> - Evaluate the performance of the teams on the basis of customer feedback. Use peer rating to evaluate individual performances.
> - Invest in and reward acquisition of new skills by the individual.

of the industrial era obsolete. New and more appropriate ways of regulating and balancing activities are being developed and used by organisations. These practices are shifting and upturning some of the basic tenets of organisational control (Exhibit 6.4).

Exhibit 6.4 **The nature of controls**

Industrial Paradigm	Learning Paradigm
* Individual focused	* Team focused
* Regulate behaviour	* Enable initiative
* Power of position	* Power of knowledge
* Use information to control	* Use information to empower
* Control through rules and procedures	* Control through vision, culture, and technology

The shift in the control and coordination mechanisms is apparent in several areas. First, there is a change in the focus of control: from individuals to teams. With organisations moving towards team-based designs, individual accountability is being superseded by team accountability. Cohen (1993) noted that in effective team-based designs, controls on the performance of individuals and the team exist side by side; while the team is evaluated and rewarded for its overall achievement, the individual is evaluated by peers for his/her contribution to the team.

Second, there is the shift in the source of control of organisational activities. Conventionally, the superior was the controlling authority, because he had the power of position. However, with organisations becoming flatter and more team based, this power is being replaced by knowledge-based power. As Savage (1992) noted:

Authority of knowledge is fast becoming more important for success in the marketplace. This is not knowledge doled out in tiny bits like currency, but knowledge available to all. As steep hierarchies are replaced by multiple task-focusing teams, the individual's knowledge becomes both more important and more accessible. . . . People quickly learn who has knowledge and who will share it. They are the ones who become key players on task-focusing teams.

Moreover, organisations are realising that the feedback from customers is perhaps the most reliable (objective and real-time) measure of corporate effectiveness. With the increasing focus on customers, the authority of the superior is being usurped by that of the customers (internal or external). A growing number of organisations are experimenting with and implementing new forms of evaluation procedures (e.g., customer feedback, 360° feedback, peer rating), replacing the conventional annual performance review by the boss.

Another shift in the control and coordination mechanisms has been in the role of information. In the hierarchical structures, information was inequitably distributed. It was the principle means of control for the superiors, and was used to evaluate people in order to create reliability and stability. In a knowledge-based organisation, on the other hand, information is the primary fuel of business activities. It has to be widely distributed and easily accessible in order to empower people to solve problems. Greater networking of organisations and the increasing permeability of boundaries is changing the role of information from a controlling mechanism to an enabling resource.

Lastly, there has been a shift in the very nature of organisational control mechanisms. In the hierarchical organisations, activities were controlled by means of rules and procedures. Rules embodied an organisation's wisdom and past learning, and provided continuity and stability to its activities.

In a changing and turbulent environment, however, these rules and systems become constricting and dysfunctional. Most of the contemporary organisations realise the need for mechanisms that align the actions of their members—not with a common past, but —with a shared present and envisioned future. That is why in knowledge-based organisations, corporate vision and culture are the prime means of integrating the efforts of members. Moreover, in these systems controls are built into the work processes and technology, instead of being externally imposed. According to Nonaka and Takeuchi (1995), the 'knowledge-layer' of the organisation (i.e., the lower hierarchical levels where knowledge is created)

> is embedded in corporate vision, organisational culture, and technology. Corporate vision provides the direction in which the company should develop its technology or product, and clarifies the 'field' in which it wants to play. Organisational culture orients the mindset and action of every employee. While corporate vision and organisational culture provide the knowledge base to tap tacit knowledge, technology taps explicit knowledge ...

CONCLUSIONS

So, how does one create a learning organisation? As is apparent from the foregoing discussion, building a learning organisation involves more than just making isolated changes in the organisational structure and systems, or implementing certain practices. Since a knowledge-based strategy aims at creating new operating paradigms or industry standards, an organisation can succeed in doing so only by developing capabilities to continuously transform itself. Only then can it create and participate in the envisioned futures. To create new paradigms outside, the organisation must also create new paradigms for itself.

Such a goal, however, requires radical efforts to change the mind-set and mental model of people about the organisation per se. As discussed in this chapter, the changes in technology and business practices have rendered obsolete a large number of cherished assumptions about organisations. Given the fact that the rate and complexity of change will only go on increasing, the conventional models of organisation (which focused on creating stability) will need review and revision as well.

It is a historical fact that paradigmatic changes in society (e.g., the shift from cottage to mass-manufacturing industries) are not *pushed* and imposed from above; they occur because of the *pull of* emerging practices and technologies. Social systems (whether political structures, families or organisations) invariably resist, or are the last to adapt to, new realities. Thus, the greatest challenge in the future will not be quick adaptation or creation of new practices and technology; the greatest challenge for organisations will be to develop the capabilities to learn new ways of operating and re-creating themselves. Those that will be able to do so, will the emerge as the learning organisations.

References

Abraham, S., 'Globalisation: Window to the world', *Business India*, 9 May 1994, 65–72.

Abreu, R., 'Problems of producing', *India Today*, 31 March 1994, 148–50.

Agarwal, A., 'A galaxy of choices', *India Today*, 28 February 1995, 164–68.

Anderson, J.V., Weirder than fiction: The reality and myth of creativity, *Academy of Management Executive*, 1992, 6(4), 40–47.

Andreu, R. and C. Ciborra, 'Core capabilities and information technology: An organisational learning approach', in B. Moingeon and A. Edmondson (eds)', *Organisational Learning and Competitive Advantage*, London: Sage, 1996.

Arbose, J., 'ABB: 'The new energy powerhouse', *International Management*, June 1988, 24–30.

Argyris, C., 'Double loop learning in organisations', *Harvard Business Review*, September–October 1977, 115–25.

Argyris, C., and D. Schon, Organisational Learning, London: Addison-Wesley, 1978.

Arora, S. *et al.*, 'The new-found cost offensive', *The Strategist*, September 1995, 1–2.

Arvedson, L., 'Coming to grips with learning (in) organisations,' *efmd forum*, 1993, 1, 5–10.

Ashby, R., *Introduction to Cybernetics*, New York: Wiley, 1956.

Badaracco Jr., J.L., *The Knowledge Link: How Firms Compete Through Strategic Alliances*, Boston, Mass.: Harvard Business School Press, 1991.

Banner, D.K., Self-managed work teams: An innovation whose time has come?' *Creativity and Innovation Management*, March 1993, 2(1), 27–36.

Bantel, K.A. and S.E. Jackson, 'Top management and innovations in banking: Does the composition of the top team make a difference?', *Strategic Management Journal*, 1989, 10, 107–24.

Barr, P.S., J.L. Stimpert, and A.S. Huff, 'Cognitive change, strategic action, and organisational renewal', *Strategic Management Journal*, 1992, 13, 15–36.

Barrell, F., 'Changing the skyline', *Management Today*, January 1989, 93–101.

Belusi, F., 'Benetton: Information technology in production and distribution (A case study of innovative potential of traditional sectors)', University of Sussex: SPRU Occasional Paper Series No. 25, 1987.

Bhardwaj, N., 'Unleashing the force within', *Business India*, 9 October 1995, 150–56.

Bhimal, S., 'Labour gains', *India Today*, 30 November 1992, 118–19.

Bist, Raju, 'Media explosion,' *Business India*, 22 May 1995, 54–65.

Bogan, C.E. and M.J. English, *Benchmarking for Best Practices*, New York: McGraw-Hill, 1994.

Bohra, K.A., personal communication, 1996.

Boisot, M.H., 'Convergence revisited: Codification and diffusion of knowledge in a British and a Japanese firm', *Journal of Management Studies*, 1983, 20,159–90.

_____; *Information and Organisation: The Manager as Anthropologist*, London: Collins, 1987.

_____, 'Schumpeterian learning versus neoclassical learning: Development options for post communist societies', Esade Working Paper No. 64, Barcelona: ESADE, October 1991.

_____, 'Is your firm a creative destroyer?', Esade Working Paper No. 81, Barcelona: ESADE, March 1992.

_____, 'Learning as creative destruction: The challenge for Eastern Europe, Esade Working Paper No. 107, Barcelona: ESADE, July 1993.

Bose, M. and S. Ghosh, 'A turn for better?', *Business India*, 4 February 1991, 43.

Boulding, Kenneth, 'The economics of knowledge and the knowledge of economics', *American Economic Review*, May 1966, 1–13.

Boyer, E., 'Citicorp: What the new boss is up to', *Fortune*, 17 February 1986, 32–35.

Brown, J.S., 'Research that reinvents the corporation', *Harvard Business Review*, January–February, 1991 102–11.

Brown, J.S., and P.Duguid, 'Organisational learning and communities-of-practice: Toward a unified view of working, learning, and innovation', in M.D. Cohen and L.S. Sproull (eds). *Organisational Learning*, London: Sage, 1996.

Bruce, L., 'The bright new worlds of Benetton', *International Management*, November 1987, 24–35.

Business India, 'Trucking with India for Mercedes Benz', 18 July 1994(a), 15.

————, 'Business India Super100: Oh! what a lovely year', 7 November 1994(b), 52–136.

Business Today, 'How to privatise—II, 7 July 1995, 100–7.

Business Week, 'From "bloody awful" to bloody awesome,' 9 October 1989, 74–76.

————, 'Air raid: British Air's bold global push', 24 August 1992, 38–43.

Butler, S., 'Cutting down and reshaping the core', *Financial Times* (London), 20 March 1990.

Byrne, J.A., 'The horizontal corporation', *Business Week*, 20 December 1993, 44–49.

Cameron, K.S., and R.F. Zammuto, 'Matching managerial strategies to conditions of decline, in K.S. Cameron, R.I. Sutton and D.A. Whetten (eds), *Readings in Organisational Decline: Frameworks, Research and Prescriptions*, Cambridge, Mass.: Ballinger, 1988.

Cameron, K.S., R.I. Sutton, and D.A. Whetten (eds), *Readings in Organisational Decline: Frameworks, Research and Prescriptions*, Cambridge, Mass.: Ballinger, 1988.

Cangelosi, V. and W.R. Dill, 'Organisational learning: Observations toward a theory', *Administrative Science Quarterly*, 1965, 10, 175–203.

Carvalho, Chhaya, 'The flavour of success', *Business Today*, 7–21 August 1994, 82–85.

Chakravarti, S., 'Readying for a boost', *India Today*, 15 July 1994, 138–51.

Chapman, P., 'Changing corporate culture at Rank Xerox', *Long Range Planning*, 1988, 21(2), 23–28.

Chatterjee, A., 'Pace', *Business Today*, 7–21 November 1994, 78–89.

————, 'Quality as marketing', *Business Today*, 7 January 1995(a), 224–31.

————, 'Morph Marketing', *Business Today*, 22 April, 1995(b), 70–77.

Chhachhi, V., 'Rebuilding Mahindra & Mahindra', *Business Today*, 22 November 1995, 72–81.

————, 'How to build teams', *Business Today*, 7 January 1996(a), 138–43.

————, 'The job designing technique', *Business Today*, 7 January 1996(b), 172–75.

Chhaya, 'How to measure productivity', *Business Today*, 7 January 1996, 240–43.

Clement, A., 'Computing at work: Empowering action by "low-level users"', *Communications of the ACM*, 1994, 37(1), 53–63.

CMIE, *Basic Statistics Relating to Indian Economy*, Bombay: CMIE, August 1994(a).

_____, *World Economy and India's Place in it*, Bombay: CMIE, October 1994 (b).

_____, *CMIE Monthly Review*, Bombay: CMIE, March 1995(a).

_____, *CMIE Monthly Review*, Bombay: CMIE, April 1995(b).

_____, *Foreign Trade Statistics of India*, Bombay: CMIE, May 1996(a).

_____, *CMIE Monthly Review*, Bombay: CMIE, July 1996(a).

Cobb, T., P.J. Eliopoulos, M. Oxelius, and Rovirosa, *Citibank and Citibanking in Citibank Espanya*, Project report submitted to course in Strategic Management of Technology, ESADE (Barcelona), December 1992.

Cohen, S.G., 'New approaches to teams and teamwork', in J.R. Galbraith and E.E. Lawler, III (eds), *Organising for the Future: The New Logic for Managing Complex Organisations*, San Francisco: Jossey-Bass, 1993.

Dass, B., and R. Jayakar, 'Snorting before the bull run', *Business Today*, 22 August 1993, 47–49.

Davidow, W.H., and M.S. Malone, *The Virtual Corporation*, New York: Edward Buringame/Harper Business, 1992.

De Geus, A.P., 'Planning as learning,' *Harvard Business Review*, March–April 1988, 70–74.

Denton, D.K., and B.I. Wisdom, 'The learning organisation involves entire workforce', *Quality Progress*, December 1991, 69–72.

Dhawan Radhika, 'Quality as infrastructure', *Business Today*, 7 January 1995, 156–65.

_____, 'Benchmarking', *Business Today*, 7 July 1996, 92–103.

DiBella, A.J., E.C. Nevis, and J.M. Gould, 'Organisational learning style as a core capability', in B. Moingeon and A. Edmondson (eds), *Organisational Learning and Competitive Advantage*, London: Sage, 1996.

Dodgson, M., *The Management of Technological Learning*, Berlin: De Gruyter, 1991.

_____, 'Organisational learning: A review of some literature, *Organisational Studies*, 1993, 14 (3), 375–94.

Downham, T.A., J. Noel, and A.E. Prendergast, 'Executive development, *Human Resource Management*, 1992, 31(1&2), 95–107.

Drucker, P., 'The coming of the new organisation', *Harvard Business Review*, January–February 1988, 45–53.

Dumaine, B., 'Corporate spies snoop to conquer', *Fortune*, 7 November 1988, 66–70.

_____, 'How managers can succeed through speed', *Fortune*, 13 February 1989, 30–35.

_____, 'Who needs a boss?', *Fortune*, 7 May 1990, 40–47.

_____, 'The bureaucracy busters', *Fortune*, 17 June 1991, 26–36.

_____, 'Unleash workers and cut costs', *Fortune*, 18 May 1992, 62.

————, 'Times are good? Create a crisis,' *Fortune*, 28 June 1993, 80–83.

Emery, F.E., and E. Trist, 'Causal texture of organisational environments,' *Human Relations*, 1965, 18, 21–32.

English, H.B., and A.C. English, *A comprehensive Dictionary of Psychological and Psychoanalytical Terms*, New York: Longman Green, 1958.

Filipowski, Diane, 'The Tao of Tandem', *Personnel Journal*, October 1991, 72–78.

Finney, M., D.E. Bowen, C.M. Pearson, and C. Siehl, Designing blueprints for organisation-wide transformation', in R.H. Kilmann, T.J. Covin, and associates (eds), *Corporate Transformation: Revitalising Organisations for a Competitive World*, San Francisco: Jossey Bass, 1988.

Fiol, C.M., and M.A. Lyles, 'Organisational learning', *Academy of Management Review*, 1985, 10(4), 803–13.

Fombrun, C.I., *Turning Points: Creating Strategic Change in Corporations*, New York: McGraw-Hill, 1992.

Ford, D., and C. Ryan, 'Taking technology to market', *Harvard Business Review*, March–April 1981, 117–26.

Fortune, 'Quality 93: Empowering people with technology, 20 September 1993.

Galbraith, J.R., *Designing Complex Organisations*, Reading, Mass.: Addison-Wesley, 1973.

Galbraith, J.R., and E.E. Lawler, III (eds), *Organising for the Future: The New Logic for Managing Complex Organisations*, San Francisco: Jossey-Bass, 1993.

Ganguly, D, 'The second draught', *The Economic Times Corporate Dossier*, 12 July 1996, 2.

Garratt, B., *The Learning Organisation*, London: Fontana, 1987.

————, *Creating a Learning Organisation*, Cambridge: Director Books, 1990.

Garrison, W., *Why didn't I think of that?*, New York: Random House', 1977.

Garvin, D.A., 'Building a learning organisation', *Harvard Business Review*, July–August 1993, 48–49.

Garza, C.E., 'Studying natives on the shopfloor', *Business Week*, 30 September 1991, 48–49

Gemmill, G., and C. Smith, 'A dissipative structure model of organisation transformation', *Human Relations*, 1985, 38(8), 751–66.

Gerstein, M.S., 'From Machine Bureaucracies to networked organisations: An architectural journey', in D.A. Nadler, M.S. Gerstein, and

R.B. Shaw (eds), *Organisational Architecture: Designs for Changing Organisations*, San Francisco: Jossey-Bass, 1992.

Ghosh, S., 'Gas, the burning question', *Business Today*, 7 September 1992, 14.

Gopinath, C., 'Recognising decline and initiating intervention', *Long Range Planning*, 1991, 24(6), 96–101.

Goss, T., R. Pascale, and A. Athos, 'The reinvention roller, coaster: Risking the present for a powerful future, *Harvard Business Review*, 1993 November–December, 97–108.

Government of India, *India 1992: A Reference Annual*, New Delhi: Ministry of Information and Broadcasting, Government of India, 1993.

Grof, S., *Beyond the Brain*, New York: State University of New York Press, 1985.

Gupta, I., 'The stretch principle', *The Strategist*, 7 March 1995(a), 1.

————, 'The domino effect', *The Strategist*, 30 May 1995 (b), 1–2.

Gupta, I., and A. Bakaya, 'Untying the media tangle', *The Strategist*, 6 December 1994, 1–2.

Gupta, I., Srivastava, and Nanda Majumdar, 'The inforcorp', *The Strategist*, 31 January 1995, 1, 5.

Gupta, I., and N. Majumdar, The price of success, *The Strategist*, 28 February 1995, 1–2.

Gupta, I., and N. Bhatt, 'Tackling the information maze', *The Strategist*, 11 April 1995, 1–3.

Gupta, P.P., personal communication, 1995.

Hambrick, D.C. and R.A. D' Aveni, 'Large corporate failures and downward spirals', *Administrative Science Quarterly*, 1988, 33, 1–23.

Hamel, G., 'Competition for competence and inter-partner learning within international strategic alliances', *Strategic Management Journal*, 1991, 12, 83–103.

Hamel, G., Y.L. Doz, and C.K. Prahalad, 'Collaborate with your competitor and win', *Harvard Business Review*, January–February 1989, 133–39.

Hamel, G., and C.K. Prahalad, 'Corporate imagination and expeditionary marketing', *Harvard Business Review*, July–August, 81–92.

Hammer, M., 'Reengineering work: Don't automate, obliterate', *Harvard Business Review*, July–August 1990, 104–12.

Hammer, M., and J.Champy, *Reengineering the Corporation*, London: Nicholas Brealey, 1994.

Handy, C., *The Age of Unreason*, London: Arrow Books, 1990.

————, 'Managing the dream', in S. Chawla and J. Renesch (eds), *Learning Organisations: Developing Cultures for Tomorrow's Workplace*, Portland, Oregon: Productivity Press, 1996.

Hanley, J., 'AT&T's speedier product cycles', *World Link*, March–April 1990, 106–7.

Hayes, R.H., S.C. Wheelwright, and K.B. Clark,. *Dynamic Manufacturing: Creating Learning Organisation*, New York: Free Press, 1988.

Hector, G., 'Atari's new game plan', *Fortune*, 8 August 1983, 46–52.

Hedberg, B.L.T., 'How organisations learn and unlearn', in P. Nystrom and W. Starbuck (eds), *Handbook of Organisational Design*, New York: Oxford University Press, 1981.

Hedberg, B.L.T., P.C. Nystrom, and W.H. Starbuck, 'Camping on see-saws: Prescriptions for self-designing organisations', *Administrative Science Quarterly*, 1976, 21, 41–65.

Heller, R., 'How BA engineered its turnaround', *Management Today*, September 1992, 50–55.

Herbst, P.G., *SocioTechnical Design*, London: Tavistock, 1974.

Heskett, J.L., and S. Signorelli, 'Benetton (B)', in W.H. and Davidson, Jose de al Torre, *Managing the Global Corporation: Case Studies in Strategy and management*, New York: McGraw-Hill, 1989.

Hodgetts, R.M., F Luthan, and S.M. Lee, 'New Paradigm Organisations: From Total Quality to Learning to World-Class', *Organisational Dynamics* Winter 1994, 5–19.

Holstein, W.J., 'The stateless corporation', *Business Week*, 14 May 1990, 52–59.

Horovitz, J., and M.J. Panak, *Total Customer Satisfaction*, London: Pitman, 1992.

Howard, R., 'The CEO as organisational architect: An interview with Xerox's Paul Allaire', *Harvard Business Review,* September–October 1992, 107–21

Huey, J., 'Nothing is impossible', *Fortune*, 13 September 1991, 90–96.

Ichbiah, D., and S.L. Knepper, *The Making of Microsoft*, New Delhi: BPB Publications, 1992.

International Management, Global Hero, September 1992, 82–89.

Itami, H., *Mobilizing Invisible Resources*, Cambridge, Mass.: Harvard University Press, 1987.

Jacob, V.M., 'The Core group: The global vision', *Business Today*, 7 January 1994, 140–45.

Jaikumar, R., 'Postindustrial manufacturing', *Harvard Business Review*, November–December 1986, 69–76.

Jain, S., 'More for less', *India Today*, 30 September 1992, 110–11.

————, 'The human face', *India Today*, 15 August 1996, 74–75.

Janson, F.W., *History of Art*, New York: Abrams, 1991.

Jayakar, R., 'The flood that never came', *Business Today*, 22 May 1993, 16.

Jayakar, R., 'The badla bogey', *Business Today*, 7 June 1994, 20.

Jinshu, L. and S. Narayan, 'Stepping out', *Business World*, 3 May 1995, 44–51.

Joglekar, S., 'In time initiative', *Business India*, 5 December 1994, 157–60.

Joseph, T., 'Remaking the factory', *The Strategist Quarterly*, July–September 1995, 7–13.

Kanavi, Shivanand, 'Where research is red hot', *Business India*, 17-39 January 1994(a), 159–61.

————, 'Remotely sensing profits', *Business India*, 28 February–13 March 1994(b) 131–32.

Kanter, R.M., *When Giants Learn to Dance*, New York: Simon and Schuster, 1989.

Kantrow, A.M., 'Wide-open management at Chaparral Steel', *Harvard Business Review*, May–June 1986, 96–102.

Kapstein, J. and S. Reed, Preaching the Euro-gospel', *Business Week*, 23 July 1990, 34–38.

Karnani, R., 'On the fast track', *Business India*, 18 January 1983, 113–14.

Katiyar, A, 'Wiring into the world', *India Today*, 3 July 1994, 58–71.

Kaul, V., 'Aliens at work', *The Strategist*, 5 November 1996, 1–2.

Kawatra, Pareena, 'Crowded skies', *Business Today*, 7–21 November 1994, 20–21.

Kearns, D.I., 'Changing a corporate culture: Leadership through quality', in R.L. Kuhn (ed.), *Handbook for Creative and Innovative Managers*, New York: McGraw-Hill, 1988.

Kelkar, V.Y., 'Innovating on the shopfloor', *The Strategist*, 10 August 1993, 1, 3.

————, 'Learning to serve', *The Strategist*, 8 March 1994(a), 1, 4.

————, 'Sticking to basics', *The Strategist*, 7 June 1994 (b), 1–2.

————, 'Offence as defence', *The Strategist*, 28 June 1994(c), 4.

Keller, D.A., and J.F. Campbell, 'Building human resource capability', *Human Resource Management*, 1993, 31 (1&2), 109–26.

Kennedy, C., 'ABB: Model merger for the New Europe', *Long Range Planning*, 1992, 25(3), 10–17.

Ketelhohn, W., 'What do we mean by cooperative advantage', *European Management Journal*, 1993 (a), 11(1), 30–37.

————, 'An interview with Aldo Palmeri of Benetton', *European Management Journal*, 1993 (b), 11(3), 321–31.

Kets de Vries, M.F.R., and D. Miller, *Unstable at the Top*. New York: Mentor Books, 1989.

Khanna, S., 'The infotech edge', *Business Today*, 7 August 1992, 32–41.

Kiesler, S., and L. Sproull, 'Managerial response to changing environments: Perspectives on problem sensing from social cognition', *Administrative Science Quarterly*, 1982, 27, 48–70.

Kilmann, R.H., T.J. Covin, and associates (eds), *Corporate Transformation: Revitalizing Organisations for a Competitive World*, San Francisco: Jossey-Bass, 1988.

Kindler, H.S., 'The planning strategies: Incremental change and transformational change', *Group and Organisation Studies*, 1979, 4, 476–84.

Kodama, F., 'Technology and the new R&D', *Harvard Business Review*, July–August 1992, 70–78.

Kotter, J.P., 'What leaders really do?', *Harvard Business Review*, May–June 1990, 103–11.

Kotter, J.P., and J.L. Heskett, *Corporate Culture and Performance*, New York: Free Press, 1992.

Krishnamurthy, Vasu, personal communication, 1995.

Kuhn, T., *The Structure of Scientific Revolution*. Chicago: The University of Chicago Press, 1962.

Labick, K., 'The big comeback as British Airways,' *Fortune*, 5 December 1988, 103–8.

———, 'The innovators', *Fortune*, 6 June 1989, 27–32.

Lahiri, J., and P Datta., 'The system manager', *The Strategist Recollected*, 1993–94, 37–43.

Lahiri, J., 'The trouble with success', *The Strategist*, 6 July 1993(a), 1–2.

———, 'Learning to serve better', *The Strategist*, 20 July 1993(b), 4.

———, 'When safe is dangerous', *The Strategist*, 29 August 1993(c), 4.

Lakshman, N., 'Making quality work', *The Strategist*, October 1993, 1–2.

Lalbhai, S., 'Government policy and corporate strategy: Arvind's experience', *Indian Management*, September 1993, 16–23.

Lant, T.K., F.J. Milliken, and B. Batra, 'The role of managerial learning and interpretation in strategic persistence and reorientation: An empirical exploration, *Strategic Management Journal*, 1992, 13, 585–608.

Lauermann, E., 'British Airways in Europe: A human resources viewpoint of development, *European Management Journal*, March 1992, 10(1), 85–86.

Leonardo-Barton, Dorothy, 'The factory as a learning laboratory', *Sloan Management Review*, Fall 1992, 23–38.

Levering, R., M. Moskowitz, and M. Katz, *The 100 Best Companies to Work in America*, Reading, Mass.: Addison-Wesley, 1984.

Levitt, B., and J.G. March, 'Organisational learning', *Annual Review of Sociology*, 1988, 14, 319–40.

Lewin, K., 'Frontiers of group dynamics', *Human Relations*, 1947, 1, 5–41.

Lipnack, J. and J. Stamps, *The TeamNet Factor*, Essex Junction, VT: Oliver Wright, 1993.

Lynn, M, 'Battle of the Atlantic', *Management Today*, November 1991, 48–52.

McGill, M.E., J.W. Slocum, Jr., and D. Lei, 'Management practices in learning organisations', *Organisational Dynamics*, Summer 1992, 5–17.

Main J., 'How to steal the best ideas around', *Fortune*, 19 October 1992, 86–89.

Majumdar, N., 'Managing growth', *The Strategist*, 17 January 1995(a), 4.

——————, 'Developing staying power', *The Strategist*, 28 November 1995(b), 1, 5.

Makridakis, S., 'What can we learn from organisational failures?', *Long Range Planning*, 1991, 24(4), 115–26.

Mansfield, E., 'R&D and innovation', in Zvi Grilches (ed.), *R&D, Patents and Productivity*, Chicago: University of Chicago Press, 1984.

March, J.G., and J.P. Olsen, 'The uncertainty of the past: Organisational learning under ambiguity', *European Journal of Political Research*, 1975, 3, 147–71.

Moremont M., 'How British Airways butters up the passenger', *Business Week*, 12 March 1990, 56.

Marshall, L.J., S. Mobley, and G. Calvert, 'Why smart organisations don't learn', in S. Chawla and J. Renesch (eds), *Learning Organisations: Developing Cultures for Tomorrow's Workplace*, Portland, Oregon: Productivity Press, 1996.

Meehan, J., 'All that is plastic is still fantastic for Citibank', *Business Week*, 18 May 1990, 52–54.

Merrifield, D.B. 'Forces of change affecting high technology industries', *National Journal*, 29 January 1983, 255.

Miller, D., *The Icarus Paradox*, New York: Harper Collins, 1990.

——————, 'The Icarus Paradox: How exceptional companies bring about their own downfall', *Business Horizon*, 1992, 35 (1), 24–35.

Miller, D., and P. Friesen, 'Successful and unsuccessful phases of corporate life cycle, *Organisational Studies*, 1983, 4, 339–56.

Misra, Rajesh, personal communications, 1996.

Mitchell, R., 'Masters of Innovation', *Business Week*, 10 April 1989, 34–39

Mohrman, S.A., and T.G. Cummings, *Self-Designing Organisations*, Reading, Mass.: Addison–Wesley, 1989.

Mohrman, S.A., and A.M. Mohrman, Jr., 'Organisational change and learning, in J.R. Galbraith, EE Lawler III, and associates (eds),

Organising for the Future: The New Logic for Managing Complex Organisations, San Francisco: Jossey-Bass, 1993.

Morgan, G., and R. Ramirez, 'Action learning: A holographic metaphor for guiding social change', *Human Relations,* 1983, 37(1), 1–28.

Murthy, K.R.S., 'Managing diversifications', *Business Today,* 7 August 1994, 77.

Nadler D.A., 'Organisational frame bending: Types of change in complex organisation', in R.H. Kilmann, T.J. Covin, and associates (eds.), *Corporate Transformation: Revitalizing Organisations for a Competitive World,* San Francisco: Jossey-Bass, 1988.

————, 'Organisational architecture for the corporation of the future', *Benchmark,* Fall 1989, 12–13.

————, 'Organisational architecture: A metaphorfor for change', in D.A. Nadler, M.S. Gerstein, and R.B. Shaw (eds.), *Organisational Achitecture: Designs for Changing Organisations,* San Francisco: Jossey-Bass, 1992.

Nadler, D.A., M.S. Gerstein, and R.B. Shaw (eds.), *Organisational Architecture: Designs for Changing Organisations,* San Francisco: Jossey-Bass, 1992.

Nair, A., personal communications, 1994.

Nevis, E.C., A.J. DiBella, and J.M. Gould, 'Understanding organisations as learning systems', *Harvard Business Review,* Winter 1995, 73–83.

Ninan, T.N., and C.V. Singh, 'The consumer boom', *The Best of India Today,* 1975–1990, New Delhi: Living Media Ltd., 1990, 205–06.

Noel, J. and Ram Charan, 'Leadership development at GE's Crotonville', *Human Resources Management,* 1988, 27(4), 433–47.

Neol, J., and Ram Charan, 'GE brings global thinking to light', *Training and Development,* 1992, 46(7), 29–33.

Neol, J., D. Ulrich, and S.R. Mercer, 'Customer education: A new frontier for human resource development', *Human Resource Management,* 1990, 29(4), 411–34.

Nohria, N., and R.G. Eccles (eds), *Networks and Organisations,* Boston, Mass.: Harvard Business School Press, 1992.

Nonaka, I., 'Creating organisational order out of chaos: Self renewal in Japanese firms', *California Management Review,* 1988, 30(3), 57–73.

————, 'Managing globalization as a self-renewal process: Experiences of Japanese MNCs', In C.A. Bartlett, Y. Doz, and G. Hedlund (Eds), *Managing the Global Firm,* London: Rootledge, 1990,

————, 'The knowledge-creating company,' *Harvard Business Review,* November–December 1991, 96–104.

Nonaka, I., and H. Takeuchi, *The Knowledge-creating Company,* New York: Oxford University Press, 1995.

Norman., J.R. 'Xerox rethinks itself—and this could be the last time', *Business Week*, 13 February 1989, 48–51.

Norman, R., and R. Ramirez, 'From value chain to value constellation', *Harvard Business Review*, July–August 1993, 65–77.

Norton , R.E., 'Citibank wows the consumers', *Fortune*, 8 June 1987, 38–43.

Ohno, T., *Toyota Production System: Beyond Large-scale production*. Madras: Productivity Press, 1992.

Owens, H., 'The business of business is learning', *Newsletter of Mithya*, Summer 1990.

Pantling, S., 'Directing improvements', *The TQM Magazine*, June, 1993 23–26.

Parekh, M., 'Arvind's success blueprint', *Business World*, 17 July 1991, 8–9.

Parikh, D, 'Indian multinationals: On the wings of hope', *India Today*, 15 September 1994, 106–12.

Parker, M.J., and R. Krishnamoorthy, 'Employee surveys: Giving workers a voice', *Business India*, 6 December 1993, 211.

Pascale, R.T., *Managing on the Edge*, New York: Touchstone, 1990.

Pavitt, K., 'Key characteristics of large innovative firms', *British Journal of Management*, 1991, 2, 41–50.

Pearson, A.L., 'Institutionalising innovation: Key activities for market leadership', *European Management Journal*, 1989, 7(4), 403–12.

Pedler, M., T. Boydell, and J. Burgoyne, 'Towards the learning company', *Management Education and Development*, 1989, 20(1), 1–8.

Peters, T., *Thriving on Chaos*, New Delhi: Tata McGraw-Hill, 1989.

————, *Liberation Management*, London: Pan Books, 1992.

————, *The Tom Peters Seminar*, London: Pan Books, 1994.

Peters, T., and R.H. Waterman, Jr., *In Search of Excellence*, New York: Harper & Row, 1982.

Petre, P., 'Jack Welch: The man who brought GE to life', *Fortune*, 5 January 1987, 76–77.

Prahalad, C., and G. Hamel, 'The core competence of the corporation, *Harvard Business Review*, May–June 1990, 79–91.

Prusak, L. and J. Matarrazo, 'Information management and Japanese Success', Ernst & Young Center for Information Technology & Strategy, Special Libraries Assocaition, 1700 Eighteenth St NW, Washington, D.C., 1992.

Pucik, V., 'Strategic alliances, organisational learning and competitive advantage', *Human Resources Management*, 1988, 27(1), 77–93.

Quinn, J.B., 'Xerox Corporation (A & B)', in L.L. Byars (ed.), *Strategic Management: Planning and Implementation*, New York: Harper & Row, 1984.

————, 'Pilkington Brothers PLC', in James B. Quinn, Henry Mintzberg, and Robert M. James (eds), *The Strategy Process*, Englewood Cliffs, New Jersey: Prentice-Hall International, 1988.

————, *Intelligent Enterprise*, New York: Free Press, 1992.

Rai, A., 'The creative imitator', *The Strategist*, 29 June 1993, 4.

Raman, A.T., 'Making waves', *Business India*, 8–21 November 1993, 23.

Rao, S.L., 'Our consumer is no yuppie', *Business India 15th Anniversary Issue*, 1993, 117–18.

Rapoport, C., 'Nestle's brand building machine', *Business Today*, 7 November 1994, 156–61.

Rawla, Bharti, 'The battle of the Times, *The Economic Times Brand Equity*, 11 September 1996, 6.

Reich, R.B., 'Entrepreneurship reconsidered: The team as a hero', *Harvard Business Review*, May–June, 1987, 77–83.

Rekhi, S., 'The big fight for the big pie,' *India Today*, 15 August 1994, 106–15.

Rice, F., 'How copycats steal billions', *Fortune*, 22 April 1991, 85–88.

Rolls, J., The transformational leader: The wellspring of learning organisation', in S. Chawla and J. Renesch (eds), *Learning Organisations: Developing Cultures for Tomorrow's Workplace*, Portland, Oregon: Productivity Press, 1996.

Rosenberg, N., and C. Frischtak, *International Technology Transfer: Concepts, Measures and Comparisons*, New York, Praeger, 1985.

Ross, G.B.H., 'Revolution in management accounting', *Management Accounting*, November 1990, 23–27.

Roy, C., 'Betting on core competencies,' *ET Esquire*, 27 January 1995, 1.

Roy, Mahasweta Ghosh, 'Man of the Times', *Business World*, 22 February 1995, 42–51.

Roy, M.S., and B.D. Augustine, 'Outsourcing has come of age,' *Business World*, 9–22 August 1995, 84–86.

Roy, S., 'New drive', *Business World*, 15 January 1992, 66–73.

Sakai, K., 'The fedual world of Japanese manufacturing', *Harvard Business Review*, November–December 1990, 38–49.

Saran, R, 'Falling relevance', *Business Today*, 7–21 June 1994, 15.

Sarangdhar, V.V., M. Pednekar, and P. Rajappan, 'Mahindra & Mahindra Ltd', 'In All India Management Association (ed.), *Restructuring for Change*, New Delhi: AIMA Excel Books, 1995.

Sarin, S., 'Multinational corporations: Compilation of some facts and views', International Management Centre, XLRI (Jamshedpur): February, 1995.

Savage, C.M. *5th Generation Management,* New Delhi: Prentice-Hall of India, 1992.

Schares, G.E., 'Percy Barnevik's global crusade', *Business Week,* 6 December 1993, 56–59.

Schlender, B.R., 'How Sony keeps the magic going', *Fortune,* 24 February 1992, 22–27.

Schwartz, E.I., 'Smart programs go to work', *Business Week,* 2 march 1992 47–51.

Schweizer, Peter, 'Gold war: The business of spying in the '90s', *The Asian Age,* 15 January 1996, 12.

Semler, R., *Maverick!,* London: Arrow Books, 1994.

Sen, G., 'Car wars', *Business India,* 20 June 1994 54–65.

Senge, P.M., *The Fifth Discipline: The Art and Practice of Organisational Learning,* New York: Doubleday, 1990.

Sethi, Neera, 'Profiting by quality', *Business India,* 27 April 1992, 125–26.

Sharma, Ajay, 'Designing the difference', *The Strategist,* 14 December 1993, 1–2.

_____, 'In search of a focus', *The Strategist,* 18 January 1994, 1.

Sharma, Ajay, and Indrajit Gupta, 'Managing for ideas', *The Strategist,* 1 March 1994, 1–2.

Shaw, R.B., and D.N.T. Perkins, 'Teaching organisations to learn: The power of productive failures', in D.A. Nadler, M.S. Gerstein, and RB Shaw (eds), *Organisational Architecture: Designs for Changing Organisations,* San Francisco: Jossey-Bass, 1992.

Sheikh, M, 'Tuned to success', *Business Today,* 28 September 1992, 129–31.

Shekhar, S., and S. Vijay, 'Music Mughal, *Business World,* 7 November 1990, 62–69.

Sheldon, A., 'Organisational paradigms: A theory of organisational change', *Organisational Dynamics,* 1980, 8, 61–80.

Sherman, S.P., 'Inside the mind of Jack Welch', *Fortune,* 27 March 1989, 36–44.

Shrikhande, F., 'A new culture takes shape at Richardson Hindustan', *Business India,* 25 March 1985, 100–12.

Shukla, M., 'Corporate failures: Why organisations fail to learn', *Productivity,* 1994(a), 34(4), 629–39.

_____, 'Building corporate culture for transformation', *Productivity,* 1994(b), 35(3), 418–28 (b).

Shukla M., 'Corporate learning as a competitive strategy', *Indian Mana gement*, January 1995(a), 11–28.

———, 'The learning edge: Building capabilities for competitive advantage', in K.B. Akhilesh, L. Prasad, and P. Singh (eds), *Evolving Performing Organisations through People*, New Delhi: New Age International 1995 (b).

Signorelli, S., and J.L. Heskett, 'Benetton (A)', in W.H. Davidson and Jose de al Torre, *Managing the Global Corporation: Case Studies in Strategy and Management*, New York: McGraw-Hill, 1989.

Simmon, J., and G. Blitzman, 'Training for self-managed work teams,' *The Quality Circle Journal*, 1986, 9(4), 9.

Singh, P., and A. Bhandarkar, *Corporate Success and Transformational Leadership*, New Delhi: Wiley, 1990.

Sinkula, J.M., 'Market information processing and organisational learning', *Journal of Marketing*, 1994, 58(1), 35–42.

Slywotzky, A.J., *Value Migration*, Boston, Mass.: Harvard Business School Press, 1996.

Smart, T., 'Can Xerox duplicate its glory days', *Business Week*, 4 October 1993, 56–57.

Smirchich, L., and G. Morgan, 'Leadership: The management of meaning', *Journal of Applied Behavioural Science*, 1982, 18(3), 257–73.

Smith, G., 'GE's brave new world', *Business Week*, 8 November 1993, 42–48.

Solo, S., 'How to listen to consumers', *Fortune*, 11 January 1991, 53–54.

Sonnenberg, F.K., 'The age of intangibles', *Management Review*, January 1994, 48–53.

Spender, J.C., 'Limits to learning from the West: How Western Management advice may prove limited in Eastern Europe', *International Executive*, September–October 1992, 34(5), 389–410.

———, 'Competitive advantage from tacit knowledge? Unpacking the concept and its strategic implications', in B. Moingeon and A. Edmondson (eds), *Organisational Learning and Competitive Advantage*, London: Sage, 1996.

Srinivas, A., and P. Sharma, 'Number of problems', *India Today*, 15 June 1994, 107–8.

Srivastava, N., 'Thriving on chaos', *The Strategist Quarterly*, September–November 1996, 7–12.

Srivastava, N., and I. Gupta, 'Winning in the nineties', *The Strategist*, 2 January 1996, 1–2.

Stalk, G., 'Time—The next source of competitive advantage', *Harvard Business Review*, July–August 1988, 41–51.

Stalk, G., and T.M. Hout, *Competing against Time: How Time-based competition is Reshaping Global Markets*, New York: Free Press, 1990.

Starbuck W.H., A. Greve, and B.L.T. Hedberg, 'Responding to crisis', *Journal of Business Administration*, 1978, 9, 111–37.

Stewart, T.A., 'Lessons from US business blunders', *Fortune*, 23 April 1990,(a) 84–88.

_____, 'Do you push your people too hard?', *Fortune*, 22 October 1990(b), 87–89.

_____, 'GE keeps those ideas coming', *Fortune*, 12 August 1991, 41–49.

_____, 'In search of tomorrow's organisation', *Fortune*, 18 May 1992, 67–72.

_____, 'The information age in charts', *Fortune*, 4 April 1994, 55–59.

Subramaniam, J., 'Bottled magic', *Business India*, 1 August 1994, 70–72.

Sundaram, I.S., 'Machine tool industry: Welcome turnaround', *Facts for You*, August 1995, 23–26

_____, 'Airconditioning and refrigerating', *Facts for You*, March 1996, 27–29.

Taylor, W., 'The logic of global business: An interview with ABB's Percy Barnevik', *Harvard Business Review*, March–April 1991, 91–105.

Teitelbaum, R.S., 'The new race for intelligence', *Fortune*, 2 November 1992, 66–68.

The Telegraph Business, 'Cos mastering the merger art', 20 November 1994, 19.

The Wall Street Journal, 'A Citibank consistently under change', 18 March 1992, A-11.

Tichy, N., 'GE's Crotonville: A staging ground for corporate revolution', *Academy of Management Executive*, 1989, 3(2), 99–106

Tichy, N., and M.A. Devanna, *The Transformational Leader*, New York: John Wiley & Sons, 1986.

Tichy, N., and R. Charan, 'Speed, simplicity, self-confidence: An interview with Jack Welch', *Harvard Business Review*, September–October 1989, 112–20.

Tichy, N., 'Citicorp faces the world: An interview with John Reed', *Harvard Business Review*, November–December 1990, 135–44.

Toffler, A., *Power Shift*, New York: Bantam Books, 1990.

Tully, S., 'The modular corporation', *Fortune*, 8 February 1993, 52–56.

Tushman, M.L., W.H. Newman, and D.A. Nadler, 'Executive leadership and organisational evolution: Managing incremental and discontinuous change', in R.H. Kilmann, T.J. Covin, and associates (eds), *Corporate Transformation: Revitalising Organisations for a Competitive World*, San Francisco: Jossey-Bass, 1988.

Upadhyay, Ashok 'Rash of sickness', *Business India*, 24 October 1994, 52.

Upadhye, N., 'Intrapreneur Inc.', *Business Today*, 22 May 1995, 72–79.

Urban, G.L. and S.H. Stars, *Advanced Marketing Strategy*, Prentice-Hall International Editions, 1991.

Urs, S.Y., 'Titan takes aim at the whole world', *Business World*, 12 July 1995, 72–73.

Uttal, B., 'The lab that ran away from Xerox', *Fortune*, 5 September 1983, 97–102.

Virany, B., M.L. Tushman, and R. Romanelli, 'Executive succession and organisational outcomes in turbulent environment: An organisational learning approach', in M.D. Cohen and L.S. Sproull (eds), *Organisational Learning*, London: Sage, 1996.

Viswanathan, A., 'Caring for customers', *Business Today*, 7 October 1994, 70–81.

Vora, Sona, 'Battle of the bulge', *Business India*, 10 October 1994, 166–73.

Walker, R 'Rank Xerox—management revolution', *Long Range Planning*, 1992, 25(1), 9-21.

Watkins, K.E., and V.J. Marsick, *Sculpting the Learning Organisation*, San Francisco: Jossey-Bass, 1993.

Welch, J., 'Jack Welch's lessons for success', *Fortune*, 25 January 1993, 68–72.

Williamson, O., *The Economic Institutions of Capitalism*, New York: Free Press, 1985.

Young, M., and J.E. Post, 'Managing to communicate, communicating to manage: How leading companies communicate with employees', *Organisational Dynamics*, Summer 1993, 31–43.

Zuboff, S., 'Automate/Informate: The two faces of intelligent technology', *Organisational Dynamics*, Autumn 1985, 4–18.

————, *In the Age of the Smart Machine*, New York: Basic Books, 1988.

Author Index

Abraham, S., 40, 54, 308
Abreu, R., 117, 308
Agarwal, A., 54, 308
Anderson, J.V., 109, 308
Andreu, R., 284, 308
Arbose, J., 151, 308
Argyris, C., 19, 77, 83, 215, 308
Arora, S., 289, 308
Arvedson, L., 22, 308
Ashby, R., 280, 308
Athos, A., 84, 313
Augustine, B.D., 293, 320

Badaracco Jr, J.L., 25, 64, 115, 116, 283, 308
Bakaya, A., 54, 313
Banner, D.K., 278, 308
Bantel, K.A., 265, 309
Barr, P.S., 21, 63, 309
Barrell, F., 165, 309
Batra, B., 251, 316
Belusi, F., 125, 309
Bhandarkar, A., 250, 322
Bhardwaj, N., 289, 309
Bhatt, N., 286, 313
Bhimal, S., 70, 309
Bist, Raju, 54, 309
Blitzman, G., 32
Bogan, C.E., 108, 267, 309
Bohra, K.A., 277, 280, 309
Boisot, M.H., 111, 125, 309
Bose, M., 80, 309
Boulding, Kenneth, 110, 309
Bowen, D.E., 72, 312
Boydell, T., 12, 18, 319
Boyer, E., 202, 309

Brown, J.S., 237, 243, 269, 273, 309
Bruce, L., 125, 310
Burgoyne, J., 12, 18, 319
Butler, S., 73, 310
Byrne, J.A., 92, 292, 301, 304, 310

Calvert, G., 78, 317
Cameron, K.S., 61, 259, 310
Campbell, J.F., 222, 315
Cangelosi, V., 19, 310
Carvalho, C., 286, 310
Chakravarti, S., 54, 310
Champy, J., 92, 283, 303, 304, 313
Chapman, P., 243, 310
Charan, R., 202, 221, 222, 318, 323
Chatterjee, A., 36, 66, 71, 310
Chhachhi, V., 279, 280, 289, 310
Chhaya, 279, 311
Ciborra, C., 284, 308
Clark, K.B., 20, 21, 25, 181, 314
Clement, A., 284, 311
Cobb, T., 202, 311
Cohen, S.G., 305, 311
Covin, T.J., 72, 316
Cummings, T.G., 301, 317

D'Aveni, R.A., 61, 313
Dass, B., 54, 311
Datta, P., 99, 316
Davidow, W.H., 12, 292, 311
De Geus, A P., 19, 21, 69, 274, 311
Denton, D.K., 276, 311
Devanna, M.A., 250, 323
Dhawan, Radhika, 89, 92, 311

DiBella, A.J., 85, 248, 275, 297, 311, 318
Dill, W.R., 19, 310
Dodgson, M., 18, 21, 64, 77, 83, 311
Downham, T.A., 221, 311
Doz, Y.L., 21, 268, 313
Drucker, P., 12, 215, 311
Duguid, P., 243, 273, 283, 309
Dumaine, B., 87, 181, 222, 243, 259, 302, 312

Eccles, R.G., 292, 303, 318
Eliopoulos, P.J., 202, 311
Emery, F.E., 52, 312
English, A.C., 152, 312
English, H.B. 152, 312
English, M.J., 108, 267, 309

Filipowski, Diane, 89, 312
Finney, M., 72, 312
Fiol, C.M., 77, 83, 312
Fombrun, C.J., 66, 312
Ford, D., 118, 312
Friesen, P., 64, 317
Frischtak, C., 124, 320

Galbraith, J.R., 52, 289, 312
Ganguly, D., 267, 312
Garratt, B., 12, 20, 21, 56, 312
Garrison, W., 107, 108, 312
Garvin, D.A., 22, 243, 281, 312
Garza, C.E., 243, 313
Gerstein, M.S., 248, 313, 318
Ghosh, S., 41, 80, 309, 313
Gopinath, C., 63, 251, 313
Goss, T., 84, 313
Gould, J.M., 85, 248, 277, 297, 311, 318
Greve, A., 77, 86, 323
Grof, S., 293, 313
Gupta, I., 48, 49, 50, 54, 89, 277, 286, 289, 313, 321, 322
Gupta, P.P., 293, 313

Hambrick, D.C., 61, 313
Hamel, G., 21, 36, 116, 268, 269, 297, 298, 300, 313, 319
Hammer, M., 92, 283, 303, 304, 313

Handy, C., 12, 22, 58, 314
Hanley, J., 267, 314
Hayes, R.H., 20, 21, 25, 181, 314
Hector, G., 62, 314
Hedberg, B.L.T., 64, 77, 81, 86, 281, 300, 314, 323
Heller, R., 165, 314
Herbst, P.G., 278, 302, 314
Heskett, J.L., 78, 80, 125, 314, 316, 322
Hodgetts, R.M., 293, 314
Holstein W.J., 46, 314
Horovitz, J., 151, 165, 202, 314
Hout, T.M., 202, 322
Howard, R., 243, 314
Huey, J., 119, 314
Huff, A.S., 21, 63, 309

Ichbiah, D., 121, 314
Itami, H., 17, 64, 297, 314

Jackson, S.E., 265, 309
Jacob, V.M., 289, 314
Jaikumar, R., 17, 314
Jain, S., 71, 279, 289, 315
Janson, F.W., 248, 315
Jayakar, R., 54, 311, 315
Jinshu, L., 54, 315
Joglekar, S., 289, 315
Joseph, T., 289, 315

Kanavi, Shivanand, 68, 87, 315
Kanter, R.M., 53, 315
Kantrow, A.M., 181, 315
Kapstein, J., 151, 315
Karnani, R., 270, 315
Katiyar, A., 285, 315
Kaul, V., 289, 315
Kawatra, Pareena, 54, 315
Kearns, D.T., 227, 243, 315
Kelkar, V.Y., 87, 93, 118, 285, 289, 315
Keller, D.A., 221, 315
Kennedy, C., 151, 315
Ketelhohn, W., 125, 315
Kets de Vries, M.F.R., 63, 316
Khanna, S., 91, 285, 316
Kiesler, S., 61, 316

Kilmann, R.H., 72, 316
Kindler, H.S., 72, 288, 316
Knepper, S.L., 121, 314
Kodama, F., 296, 316
Kotter, J.P., 78, 80, 250, 316
Krishnamoorthy, R., 87, 319
Krishnamurthy, Vasu, 79, 316
Kuhn, T., 293, 294, 316

Labick, K., 101, 165, 222, 316
Lahiri, J., 74, 79, 91, 99, 316
Lakshman, N., 289, 316
Lalbhai, S., 289, 316
Lant, T.K., 251, 316
Lauermann, E., 164, 165, 316
Lawler III, E.E., 53, 312
Lee, S.M., 293, 314
Lei, D., 22, 317
Leonardo-Barton, Dorothy, 181, 260, 316
Levering, R., 202, 316
Levitt, B., 90, 317
Lewin, K., 253, 317
Lipnack, J., 47, 151, 317
Luthan, F., 293, 314
Lyles, M.A., 77, 83, 312
Lynn, M., 165, 317

McGill, M.E., 22, 317
Main J., 87, 243, 317
Majumdar, N., 50, 270, 277, 285, 289, 313, 317
Makridakis, S., 60, 317
Malone, M.S., 12, 292, 311
Mansfield, E., 69, 317
March, J.G., 19, 90, 317
Maremont, M., 165, 317
Marshall, L.J., 78, 317
Marsick, V.J., 21, 324
Matarrazo, J., 266, 319
Meehan, J., 202, 317
Mercer, S.R., 222, 318
Merrifield, D.B., 25, 317
Miller, D., 63, 64, 78, 316, 317
Milliken, F.J., 251, 316
Misra, Rajesh, 301, 317
Mitchell, R., 94, 317
Mobley, S., 78, 317

Mohrman Jr, A.M., 67, 318
Mohrman, S.A., 67, 301, 317, 318
Morgan, G., 252, 278, 200, 302, 318, 322
Murthy, K.R.S., 37, 318

Nadler, D.A., 248, 249, 251, 260, 303, 318, 323
Nair, A., 279, 318
Narayan, S., 54, 315
Nevis, E.C., 85, 248, 275, 297, 311, 318
Newman, W.H., 251, 323
Ninan, T.N., 43, 54, 318
Noel, J., 207, 219, 221, 222, 311, 318
Nohria, N., 292, 303, 318
Nonaka, I., 12, 90, 94, 108, 125, 252, 253, 259, 281, 282, 283, 289, 292, 306, 318, 319
Norman, J.R., 243, 319
Normann, R., 116, 319
Norton, R.E., 202, 319
Nystrom, P.C., 281, 301, 314

Ohno, T., 107, 319
Olsen, J.P., 19, 317
Owens, H., 11, 319
Oxelius, M., 202, 311

Panak, M.J., 151, 165, 202, 314
Pantling, S., 243, 319
Parekh, M., 289, 319
Parikh, D., 40, 54, 319
Parker, M.J., 87, 319
Pascale, R., 84, 202, 221, 264, 313, 319
Pavitt, K., 65, 319
Pearson, A.L., 100, 319
Pearson, C.M., 72, 312
Pedler, M., 12, 18, 319
Pednekar, M., 289, 320
Perkins, D.N.T., 272, 276, 321
Peters, T., 47, 60, 62, 63, 122, 151, 292, 319
Petre, P., 222, 319
Post, J.E., 282, 324
Prahalad, C.K., 21, 36, 116, 268, 269, 297, 300, 319
Prendergast, A.E., 221, 311

Prusak, L., 266, 319
Pucik, V., 21, 319

Quinn, J.B., 12, 17, 98, 102, 243, 292, 297, 302, 320

Rai, A., 111, 320
Rajappan, P., 289, 320
Raman, A.T., 54, 320
Ramirez, R., 116, 278, 300, 301, 302, 319
Rao, S.L., 40, 320
Rapoport, C., 46, 320
Rawla, Bharti, 289, 320
Reed, S., 151, 315
Reich, R.B., 69, 320
Rekhi, S., 34, 320
Rice, F., 17, 320
Rolls, J., 251, 320
Romanelli, R., 251, 265, 324
Rosenberg, N., 124, 320
Ross, G.B.H., 92, 304, 320
Rovirosa, 202, 311
Roy, C., 289, 320.
Roy, Mahasweta Ghosh, 289
Roy, M.S., 293, 320
Roy, S., 67, 320
Ryan, C., 118, 312

Sakai, 112, 320
Saran, R., 44, 320
Sarangdhar, V.V., 289, 320
Sarin, S., 45, 321
Savage, C.M., 284, 303, 304, 305, 321
Schares, G.E., 151, 321
Schlender, B.R., 122, 321
Schon, D., 19, 77, 83, 308
Schwartz, E.I., 17, 321
Schweizer, Peter, 118, 119, 321
Semler, R., 290, 321
Sen, G., 43, 321
Senge, P.M., 12, 18, 20, 21, 77, 83, 88, 274, 321
Sethi, Neera, 289, 321
Sharma, P., 99, 322
Sharma, Ajay, 61, 68, 79, 89, 321
Shaw, R.B., 248, 272, 276, 318, 321
Sheikh, M., 122, 321

Shekhar, S., 122, 321
Sheldon, A., 88, 252, 321
Sherman, S.P., 222, 321
Shrikhande, F., 81, 321
Shukla, M., 16, 60, 78, 85, 259, 321, 322
Siehl, C., 72, 312
Signorelli, S., 125, 314, 322
Simmon, J., 280, 322
Singh, C.V., 43, 54, 318
Singh, P. 250, 322
Sinkula, J.M., 269, 322
Slocum Jr, J.W., 22, 317
Slywotzky, A.J., 266, 297, 322
Smart, T., 243, 322
Smircich, L., 252, 322
Smith, G., 221, 322
Solo, S., 101, 322
Sonnenberg, F.K., 11, 322
Spender, J.C., 124, 283, 289, 322
Sproull, L., 61, 316
Srinivas, A., 99, 322
Srivastava, N., 285, 289, 299, 313, 322
Stalk, G., 25, 124, 202, 322, 323
Stamps, J., 47, 151, 317
Star, S.H., 202, 324
Starbuck, W.H., 77, 86, 281, 301, 314, 323
Stewart, T.A., 92, 165, 222, 243, 283, 296, 304, 323
Stimpert, J.L., 21, 63, 309
Subramaniam, J., 289, 323
Sundaram, I.S., 42, 43, 323
Sutton, R.I., 61, 310

Takeuchi, H., 12, 125, 253, 283, 292, 306, 319
Taylor, W., 151, 260, 323
Teitelbaum, R.S., 100, 323
Tichy, N., 202, 221, 250, 323
Toffler, A., 15, 47, 323
Trist, E., 52, 312
Tully, S., 100, 292, 323
Tushman, M.L., 251, 265, 323, 324

Ulrich, D., 222, 318
Upadhyay, Ashok, 59, 324

Upadhye, N., 93, 324
Urban, G.L., 202, 324
Urs, S.Y., 116, 324
Uttal, B., 112, 243, 324

Vijay, S., 122, 321
Virany, B., 251, 265, 324
Viswanathan, A., 91, 289, 324
Vora, Sona, 34, 324

Walker, R., 243, 324
Waterman Jr, R.H., 60, 319

Watkins, K.E., 21, 324
Welch, J., 222, 324
Wheelwright, S.C., 20, 21, 25, 181, 314
Whetten, D.A., 61, 310
Williamson, O., 109, 324
Wisdom, B.L., 276, 311

Young, M., 282, 324

Zammuto, R.F., 61, 259, 310
Zuboff, S., 108, 284, 324

Subject Index

Action learning, 19, 192–94, 207, 216

Adaptive learning, 66, 77

American textile industry, 109–10

Assembly line technology, 108

Band-Aid, 107

Bar codes, 15–16

Benchmarking, 14, 86, 87, 91–92, 112–13, 150, 176–77, 216–18, 226, 227, 235, 236, 256, 258, 267–68

Business environment, changes in, 11–12, 29–50, 56–58, 297

Business failures, 58–61, 76, 78–81, 297

Codified knowledge, 17, 77, 105, 109–11, 116–17

Competition,
    capability-based, 297–300
    changing rules of, 50–53, 57
    cross-industry, 48–50, 297
    from MNCs, 34–35,
    knowledge-based, 58, 64–65, 68–69, 70, 98–99, 101, 105 116–18, 120–25, 249
    product-based, 111, 297–300
    time-based, 13, 35–36, 122

Core competence, 12, 21, 36–37, 116, 297, 298, 300

Culture, organisational, 17, 77, 81, 84, 95, 303–6

Customer orientation, 99, 156–58, 180, 194–99, 218–21, 227, 236, 305; and learning, 67, 71, 86, 87, 91, 101, 161, 177, 219–20, 268–72

Discovered knowledge, 105, 106–9

Disequilibrium, as source of change, 89, 141, 145, 253, 259–60, 264–66

Dissemination of knowledge, 84–85, 86, 90–92, 281–82

Diversity of employee profile (See Internal variety.)

Embedded knowledge, 61, 64, 113–15, 116, 124, 249, 283–84, 289, 306

Empowerment, 94, 142–44, 172–73, 191, 210–15, 237, 242, 252, 276–80, 305

Environmental scanning capabilities, 64, 85, 86–88

Experimentation, 86, 92–94, 252, 276, 297

Explicit knowledge, 105, 109–10, 281, 284, 289

Float glass technology, 102–5, 113

Globalisation of Indian economy, 30–36, 43

HP LaserJet, 119–20

IBM PC, 74, 75, 115, 120

Icarus complex, 78, 226

Imitation (See Intellectual piracy)
Incremental change, 66, 77, 288
Indian economy, liberalisation of,
36–39,
growth of, 39–44,
Industry standards, 15, 68, 69, 106,
115, 119–24, 306
Information. (See knowledge.
Information technology, 11, 199–200,
284–87
Innovation, 66–69, 112, 269
Intellectual piracy, 17, 69, 112, 117,
Intellectual property, 12, 17, 68–69,
110, 111, 117, 118, 119
Internal variety, 90, 145–48, 150,
162–63, 187–90, 236, 264–66
Invisible assets, 17, 64, 297
Invisible knowledge, 84, 106,
113–16, 120–25, 249
Japanese companies, learning practices
of, 13–14, 112, 266, 268, 296
Just-in-time system, 107

Knowledge,
characteristics of, 64, 102,
108–9
competitive value of, 12, 16–18,
64, 68, 98–101, 105,
116–18, 120–25, 297–300
stages of maturation of,
105–16
Knowledge connectivity, 91–92,
178–80, 199–201, 281–86,
300–3

Learning from competitors (See also
Benchmarking), 268
Learning intent, 249, 250–60
Learning organisation (See also organi
sational learning), 18–19, 73,
84–85, 94–95, 129, 287–89,
306–07

Mental models, 20, 61–64, 71, 72, 80,
88, 237
Migratory knowledge, 102, 106,
111–13, 116, 119, 266

Minimum critical specification,
principle of, 278, 302–3
MS-DOS, 121
Multi-National Corporations (MNCs),
33–35, 45–47
Multi-skilling 179–80, 258, 281

Networking (See knowledge
connectivity)

Organisation as a hologram, 168,
301–3
Organisations, new forms of,
291–93, 304
Organisational architecture, 21, 124,
247–49, 267–68
Organisational change 19, 20, 62–63
Organisational learning, and continuous improvement, 69–71
and organisational effectiveness,
18, 21–22, 53, 56–58, 64–65
and environmental change, 50-
54, 56–58, 64–65, 66, 88
and strategic reorientation,
19–20, 72–73, 84, 265
barriers to 62–64, 78–81, 86–88,
90, 92, 94
double loop, 83–84
history of the concept, 19–21
outcomes of, 64–73
single loop, 76–77
Organisations as knowledge-based
systems, 18–19, 64, 295–97

Paradigm, definition of 293–94
Paradigm shift, 11, 252, 294–95,
304, 307
Patents (See Intellectual property)
Personal mastery, 20
Problem-solving capabilities, 85,
88–90, 158, 160, 162, 242
Proprietary knowledge, 68, 105,
116–18

Recruitment in learning organisations,
90, 115–156, 160, 168–69,
184–85, 187, 236, 256, 264–66

Re-engineering, 21, 92, 258–59, 283, 301, 303

'Requisite variety', principle of, 280–81, 302

Research in learning organisations, 68, 175, 232–33, 237–39, 255, 256, 269, 271–72

Self-designing, 281–82, 300–1

Self–managed teams, 119–20, 242, 278, 279–80, 283, 301–2

Self-reflection, 70, 83–84, 85, 88–90, 253, 301

Scanning capability, 64, 85, 86–88

Shared knowledge, 90–92

Strategic alliances, 21, 33, 47, 268, 298, 299

Stretch goals, 253, 254–59

Success trap, 78–81

Systems thinking, 20

Tacit knowledge, 86, 105, 106–09, 281, 283–84, 289, 306

Taurus, 113

Team learning, 20, 124, 168–70, 216, 239, 240–43, 273, 274, 284

Top management, 19, 20, 265

Training in learning organisation, 93, 158–60, 164, 169–70, 179, 188, 199–00, 219–21, 227–28, 242, 256, 258, 273–74, 277

Transformational change (See Transformational learning)

Transformational leadership 250–52, 260

Transformational learning, 71–73, 83–84, 115, 250–52, 289

Traveller's cheques, 108

Value chain, 295–97

Vision, 20, 94, 251–53, 259, 306

Walkman, 121–22

Work, as learning, 267, 273, 275–76, 277, 281–82, 297

Work-outs, 212–15, 218, 219–20, 252, 278

Company Index

ABB (Asea Brown Boveri), 18, 33, 35, 47, 131, 135–51, 278, 283, 284

Aditya Birla Group, 31, 43

American Express, 33, 108

Amtrex Appliances Ltd, 52, 267, 279, 301

Apple Computers, 47, 62, 75, 112, 115, 232

Arvind Mills, 43, 254–66

Asian Paints, 31, 91, 285

Atari, 62, 228

AT&T, 33, 47, 100, 267

Bajaj Auto, 43

Benetton, 96–98, 298

Bennett Coleman & Co., 261–63

BPL, 38, 299

British Airways, 68, 131–32, 152–65, 251, 265, 268, 269, 273, 274, 278, 283, 284

Chaparral Steel, 124–25, 132, 166–81, 217, 252, 253, 260, 265, 267, 269, 273, 276, 278, 284.

Cipla Laboratories, 277

Citibank (See Citicorp)

Citibank India, 93

Citicorp, 68, 132–33, 181–202, 252, 265, 268, 269, 276, 278, 281, 283, 284

CMC Ltd, 299

Colgate-Palmolive, 285–86

Comnet Systems and Services, 93, 301

Core Healthcare Ltd (Core Parenterals Ltd), 255–57, 301

Corning, 46–47, 298

Daimler Benz, 46

DCM Data Products, 74–76

Dell Computers, 292

Digital Equipment Corporation (DEC), 47, 62, 63

Eastman Chemical Co., 301

Eicher Tractor, 70

Elbee Courier, 49, 87

Federal Express, 301–2

Ford, 108, 113

General Electric (GE), 33, 118, 133, 203–22, 251, 252, 253, 267, 269, 273, 274, 276, 278, 281

Godrej, 38, 299

HCL Corporation, 93

HCL-HP Ltd, 91, 299

Hero Cycles, 31, 43

Hewlett-Packard, 119–20

Hindustan Lever Ltd (HLL), 34, 36, 66, 77, 299

Hindustan Motors, 18, 38

Hitachi, 118

HMT, 79

HMV, 122

Honda, 116, 124

IBM, 15, 47, 62, 74, 75, 115, 118

Intel, 98, 115, 302

Intercraft, 79

ITC Ltd, 31, 37, 87

Johnson & Johnson, 107
Jolly Boards, 89

KEC International, 43
Kellogg's, 34

Lipton India, 111
Lupin Laboratories, 31, 43

Mahindra & Mahindra Ltd, 37, 47, 67, 91, 257–59
Maruti, 31, 38, 68
Microsoft, 47, 112, 119, 121
Milton Plastics, 68
Modi Xerox, 70–71, 87, 267
Mukund Iron & Steel Ltd, 39, 68, 89,

Nelco, 61, 79
Nestle, 46, 299
NIIT, 93
Nike, 100, 298
Nirma, 43

Oticon, 292
Otis India Ltd, 279

Parle Agro, 285
Pepsico, 100
Philips India, 35–36, 299
PGR Corporation, 277, 279–80
Praj Industries, 270–72, 277
Precision Fasteners Ltd, 286–87
Procter & Gamble, 16, 34, 77, 81–82, 101

Raymond Mills, 43
Reckitt & Coleman, 66

Reebok, 100
Reebok India, 292–93
Remington Rand of India, 58, 80, 297
Richardson Hindustan Ltd (See Procter & Gamble)
RPG Enterprise, 37, 43, 91–92

Semco, 290–91
SIEL Ltd, 52
Singer, 63
Sony, 47, 120–22
Steel Authority of India (SAIL), 39
Super Cassettes Industries (T-Series), 122–23
Tandem Computers, 89
Tata Consultancy Services (TCS), 19, 200
Tata Iron and Steel Company (TISCO), 35, 39
3M Company, 93–94
Titan, 79, 116
Toyota, 107, 272

UBEST, 293

Videocon, 34, 38, 71, 299
VIP Industries, 117–18

Warner Brothers, 63
Whirlpool, 101

Xerox Corporations, 87, 112, 133–34, 223–43, 252, 253, 265, 267, 269, 273, 274, 276, 278, 281, 291

Yamaha, 124